IMAGES
of America

Grafton, Berlin, and Petersburgh

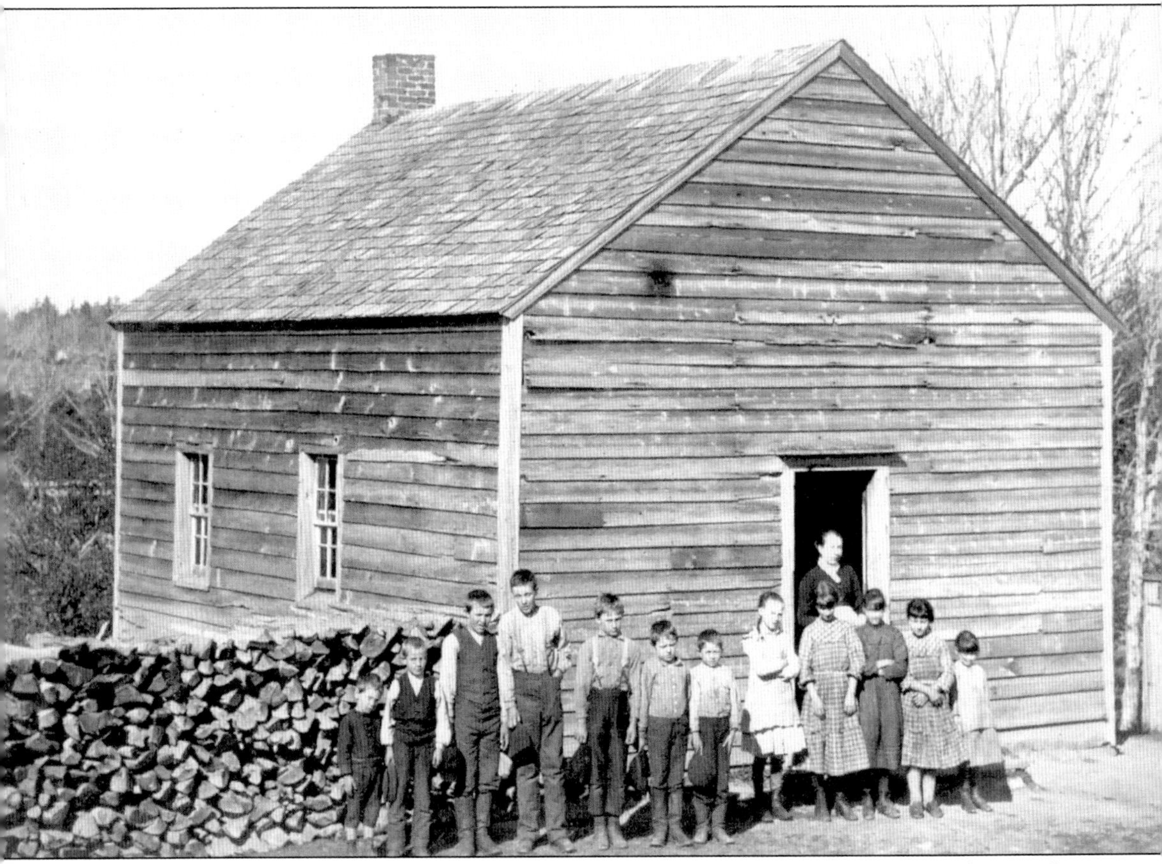

The Foster School was located in School District No. 8 on the south side of Old Road in Grafton.

On the cover: Members of a Grafton Baptist Church Bible study class pose for a group photograph on a hot summer's day. (Courtesy of the New York State Library.)

IMAGES
of America

GRAFTON, BERLIN, AND PETERSBURGH

Warren F. Broderick
with Photographs by James E. West

ARCADIA
PUBLISHING

ISBN 978-0-7385-4523-3

Published by Arcadia Publishing
Charleston, South Carolina

Printed in the United States of America

Library of Congress Control Number: 2006922355

For all general information, please contact Arcadia Publishing:
Telephone 843-853-2070
Fax 843-853-0044
E-mail sales@arcadiapublishing.com
For customer service and orders:
Toll-Free 1-888-313-2665

Visit us on the Internet at www.arcadiapublishing.com

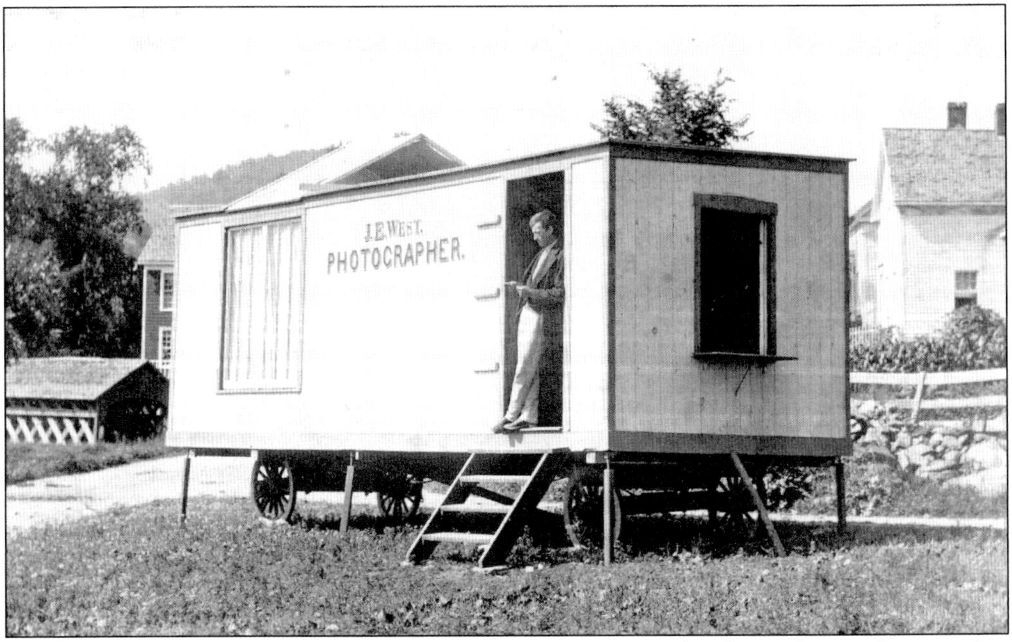

James E. West traveled around eastern Rensselaer County in his horse-drawn photographic wagon, fully equipped with a studio and darkroom. This photograph was taken in downtown Petersburgh in the 1880s.

Contents

ACKNOWLEDGMENTS

The compilation of this book would not have been possible without the assistance and enthusiastic interest of the staff of the Manuscripts and Special Collections, New York State Library, in Albany, with whose permission these photographs are reproduced in this volume. Anyone wishing to study these images should contact the Special Collections Reference Desk at 11th floor, Cultural Education Center, Albany, New York 12230, by telephone (518) 474-6282, or by e-mail MSCOLLS@mail.nysed.gov. In addition, the assistance of the following is also greatly appreciated: Sharon Klein, Berlin Town Historian; Peter Schaaphok, Petersburgh Town Historian; Margery Wager; Doree Cox; William T. Reynolds; Anne Kiely; Gordon Gundrum; Robert and Hilda Goyer; Helen Ellett; the Taconic Valley Historical Society; and the Grafton Historical Society. Unless otherwise indicated all photographs reproduced in this book are owned by the New York State Library.

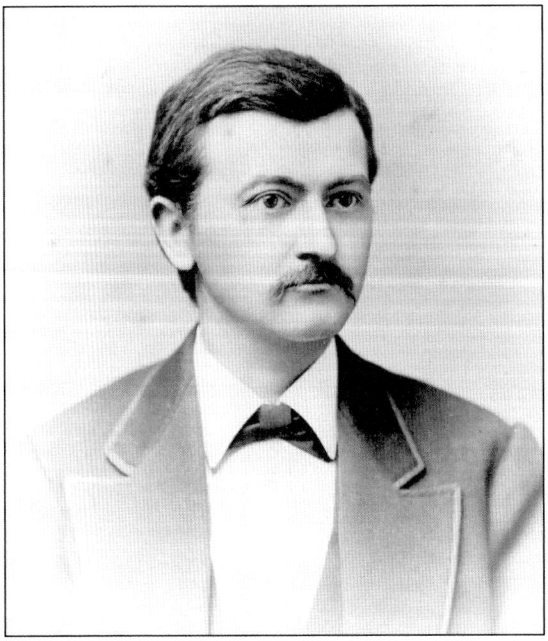

James Emmett West (1852–1937) was one of Rensselaer County's most accomplished photographers.

INTRODUCTION

James Emmett West was born in Grafton, Rensselaer County, New York, on March 30, 1852. His father, Reynolds Palmer West (1819–1897), and his mother, Hannah (Tilley) West (1829–1910), operated a general store in Grafton. The photographer's grandparents were Francis West (1794–1836) and Olive (Reynolds) West (1801–1870). His great-grandfather was Nathan West Sr. (1777–1858), a prominent early settler who served as the town's first justice when it was established in 1807. Nathan West, whose wife was Sarah Scriven (1779–1851), emigrated to Grafton from Hopkinton, Rhode Island, in the late 1700s with his parents, Francis West (1735–1803) and his wife Mary (Lawton) West (1738–1812). In 1793, the elder couple obtained a lease from the patroon, Stephen Van Rensselaer, for 113 acres of land and constructed a substantial wooden dwelling still standing on Shaver Pond or Agan Road. The old West homestead later became the home of noted scholar and literary critic Granville Hicks for many years.

James E. West probably worked in his father's general store as a boy, but how and why he first became interested in photography remains a mystery. His earliest work seems to date from the mid-1870s. He set up a "photographic business" in Berlin in 1878 and began working in earnest not only in that town and in neighboring Petersburgh, but in New Lebanon, a few miles to the south, where both a well-known Shaker community and mineral springs were located. He appears to have supplemented his income in the early years of his career with "haying" and other outdoor tasks.

In a June 8, 1878, diary entry, James wrote that he "went to Lebanon Springs to see Miss Bristol. I think we have an affinity for each other." On March 18 of the following year, James married Kate Bristol (1855–1923) at Lebanon Springs, Columbia County; she was a daughter of Alvin Bristol and Eliza (Olds) Bristol of New Lebanon. While James maintained a permanent residence in Grafton, he lived for short periods of time in Berlin, Petersburgh, and New Lebanon, and traveled between these places with his horse-drawn photographic wagon, fully equipped with a studio and darkroom.

The West family resided in nearby Hoosick Falls in the early 1900s and for a short time in Whitehall, Washington County, about 65 miles to the north by road. Their only child, Maude Marinda, born in Grafton in 1880, married Leon Closson in 1922, outlived her husband by 24 years, and preserved her father's photograph collection at the family home in Grafton. Maude and Leon Closson raised four children: Sylvia Maria, Katherine, John Leon, and James Harrison Closson.

James E. West worked as a professional photographer until his death in Grafton in 1937. Most of his income derived from his very skilled studio portraits, and he also produced and sold photographic postcards. Most of his work was done locally in rural eastern Rensselaer County. West was officially commissioned by the Mount Lebanon Shaker community to produce a series of remarkable views of the community and its buildings, as well as group and individual portraits. These photographs, which have since been reproduced in a number of books on the Shakers, were sold as cabinet photographs and postcards by the Shakers in their village store. The James E. West photograph collection was acquired by the author following the death of Maude (West) Closson and was subsequently acquired by the New York State Library in 1983. The collection (no. SC 17900) consists of nearly 1,000 images, including photographic postcards, stereoscopic photographs, and a few glass plate negatives and lantern slides. Fortunately, the images include not only family and group portraits (many of his family and relatives) but likewise images of residents at work and play. The collection also includes panoramic views, village and street scenes, schools, residences, lakes, and other scenic attractions. Most of these outdoor scenes can be identified today (some were labeled by James or by his daughter or his granddaughter) but the collection contains copies of a number of unidentified studio portraits.

A few notebooks of James E. West survive in the photograph collection. While most of the entries reflect the production of studio portraits, one brief listing documents some scenic views apparently taken merely for his own interest. These are entitled "Ward's Hollow," "Cal Agan's," "Maple Tree," "Grave yard," "Woods Between Agan's and Dunhams," "Group on Cal's stoop," "Dunham's grave," "Second Pond," "J. B. Ford's house," "home," "Stillman Village," and "Grafton Centre." Most of these photographs he lists can be identified today, but another listing dated 1897 indicates he took shots of scenic areas in northern Berkshire County, Massachusetts, that did not survive in this collection. His notebooks also document the purchase of "tin plates" and other photographic supplies and contain detailed formulas he carefully recorded for emulsions and developing solutions.

Photographs taken by James E. West are also found in the collections of other repositories, such as the Grafton Historical Society, Taconic Valley Historical Society, Hoosick Township Historical Society, and Whitehall Historical Society. Major collections of Shaker materials hold copies of various photographs taken by James at the Mount Lebanon Shaker community. Private collections doubtless contain James E. West photographs, probably mainly individual and family group portraits.

One

Village Scenes

The Town of Petersburgh was established in 1788, three years prior to the creation of Rensselaer County. The towns of Berlin and Grafton were established in 1806 and 1807 respectively. All three towns were first settled in earnest beginning in the years immediately following the American Revolution by emigrants from New England, who leased large lots of land from the Van Rensselaer family for annual "ground rent." The first settlers (Dutch, Germans, and New England Yankees) appeared in Berlin and Petersburgh as early as the 1740s and 1750s. Because of the mountainous terrain that covers the entire town, Grafton was the last of the three towns to be developed, mostly in the 1780s and 1790s.

Each of the three towns, Grafton, Berlin, and Petersburgh, features a small unincorporated village center of the same name. The plan of Grafton remains closest to its original layout because of 20th-century highway realignments that altered the appearance of Berlin and Petersburgh. The most noticeable change today from the era these photographs were taken is the loss of stores, inns and taverns, small mills and factories, and other businesses. In the era preceding World War I, these communities were thriving and James E. West often captured the modest yet neat houses and business that lined their unpaved streets.

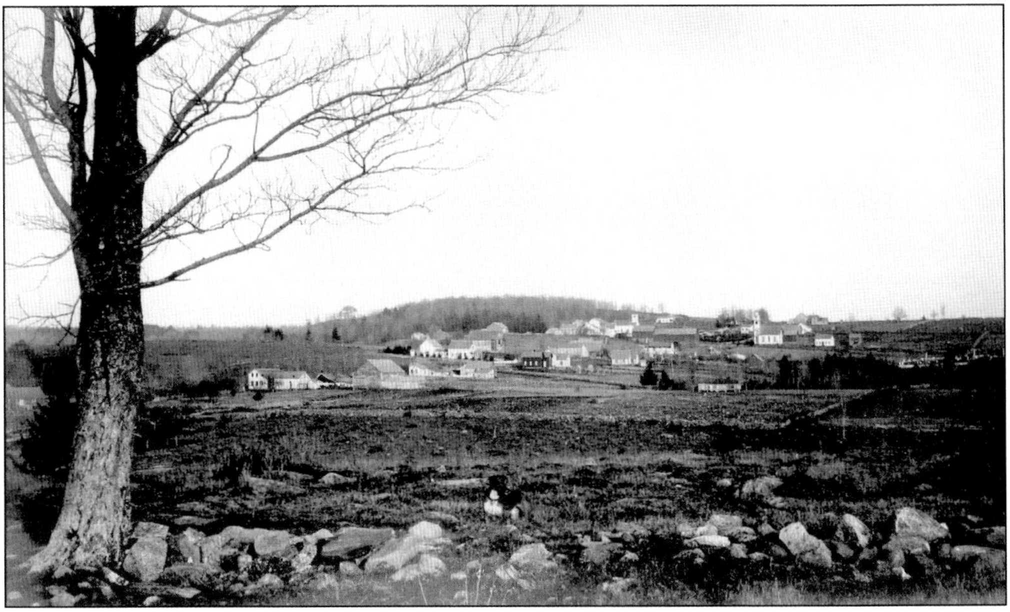

A treeless landscape in the image above presents an unobstructed view of Grafton Center from the Barnhart farm to the west, near the current entrance road to Grafton Lakes State Park. The view below looks west in the 1880s down Main Street from the site of the current Grafton Town Hall.

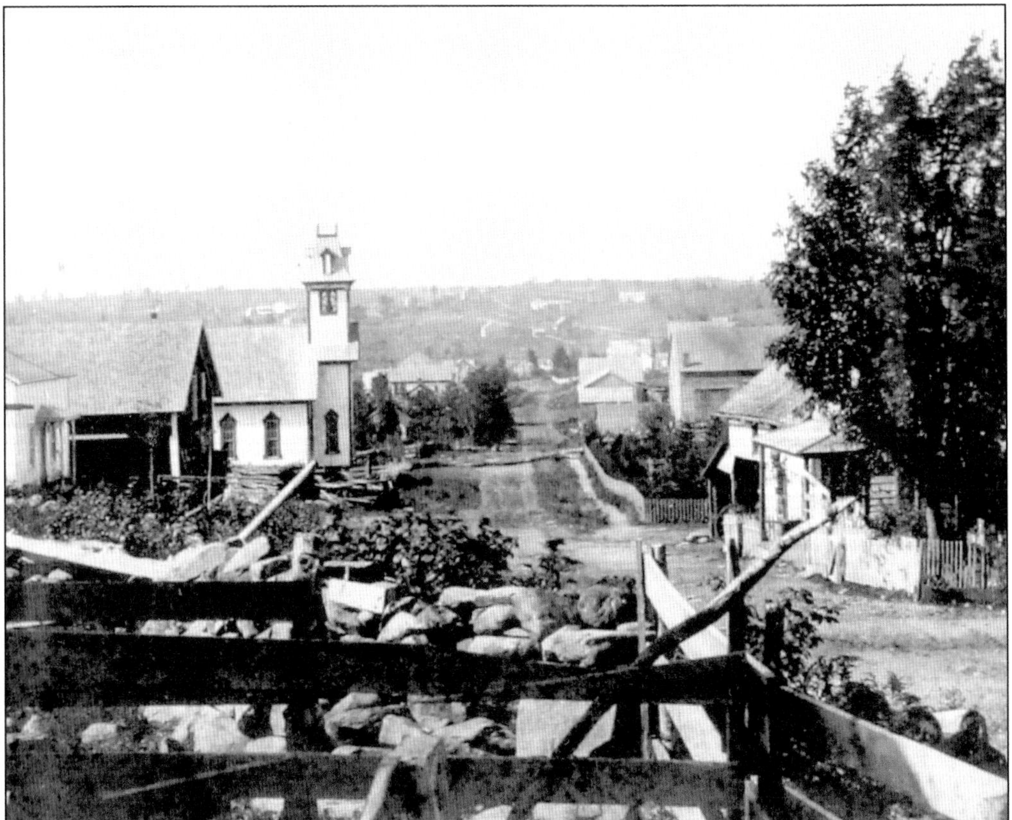

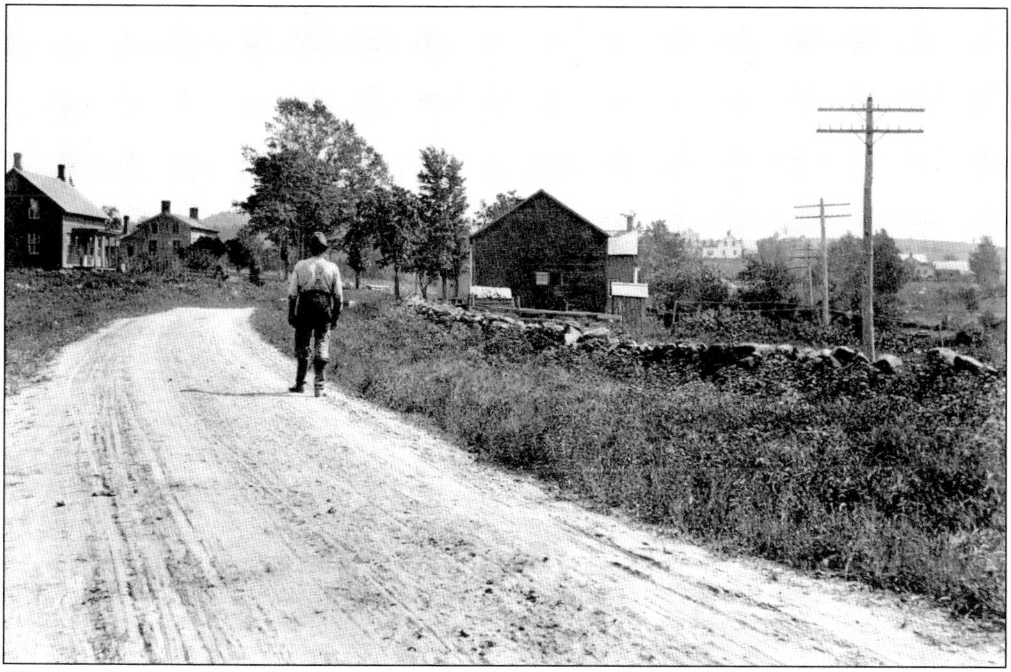

The present Dumbleton Road was part of the main east-west running highway until bypassed by State Route 2 in the 20th century. The view above looks east shortly after electricity was introduced, while the view below looks in the opposite direction.

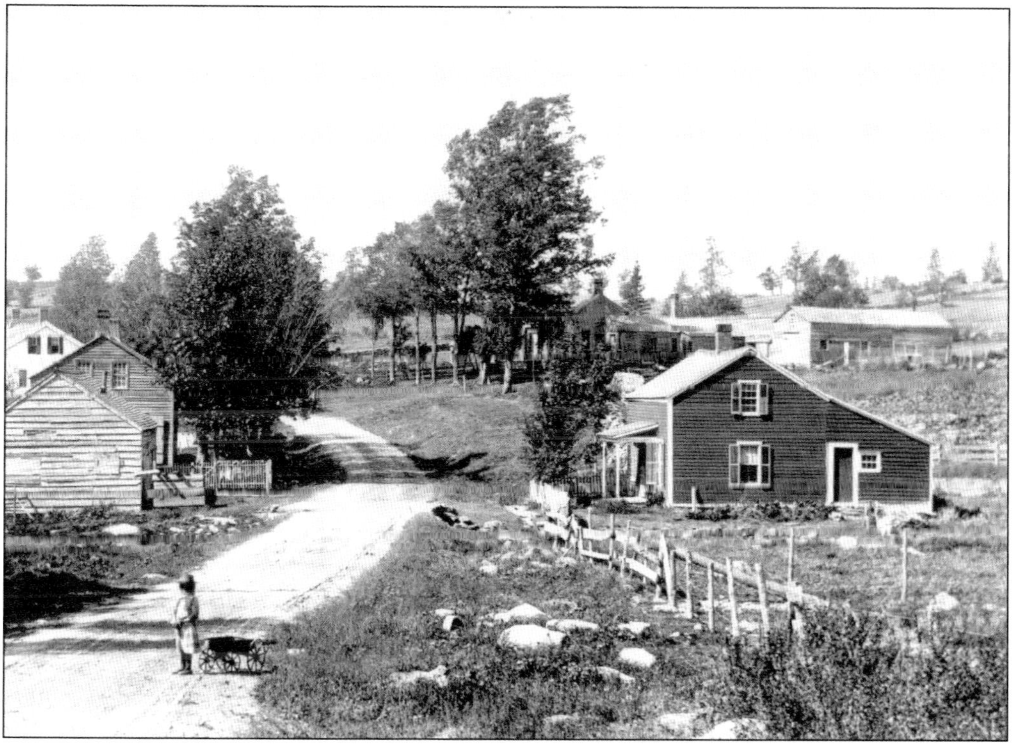

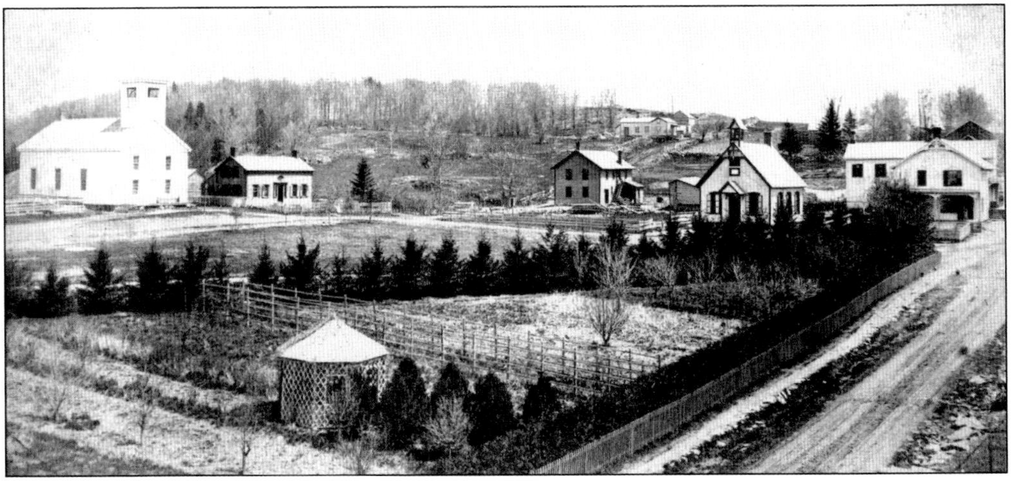

The "village green" in Grafton Center reflects the New England origins of the town's early settlers. The Norway spruce trees so impressive today are still young in these photographs taken in the 1890s. The view above looks east toward the Baptist church and the newly constructed School No. 5, now the post office, while the view below looks northwest to the old Grafton House hotel and the John Dunham residence.

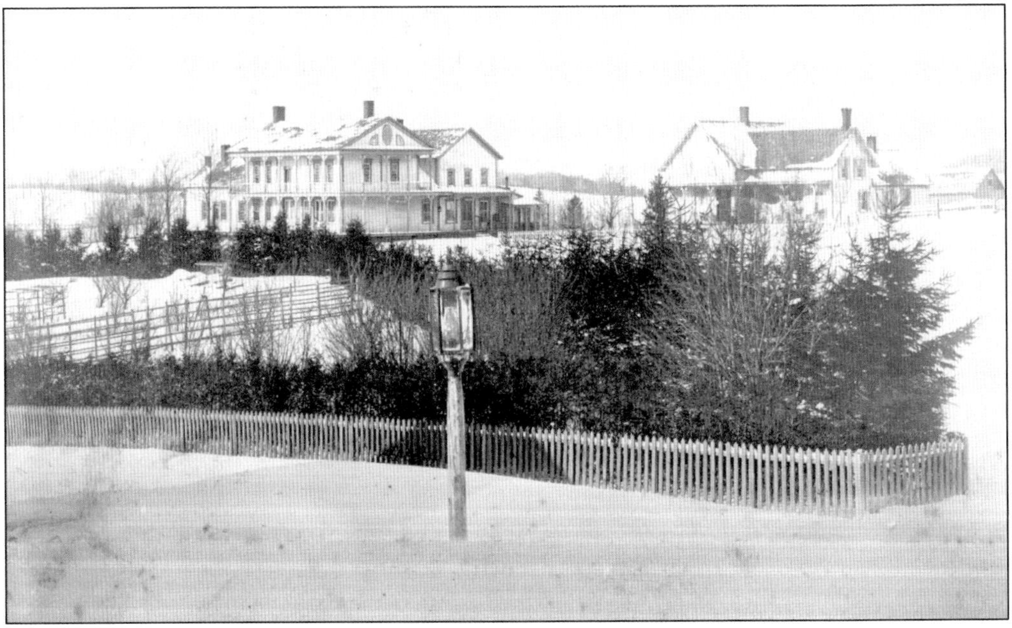

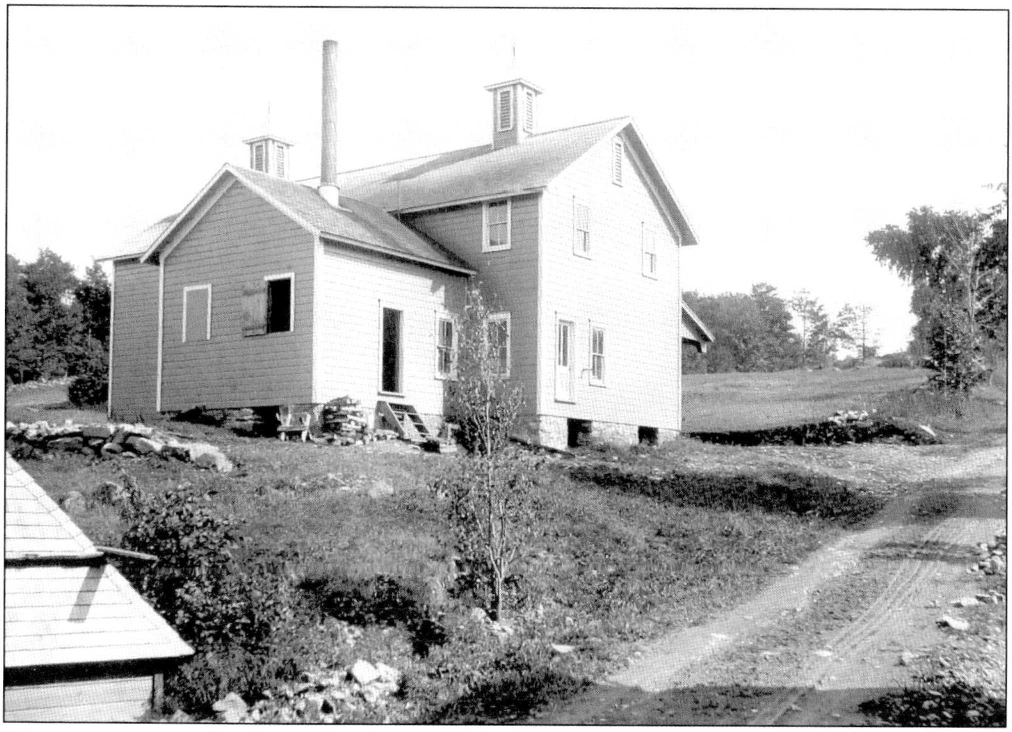

The creamery on the Owen Road was later converted into the first St. John Francis Regis Catholic Church.

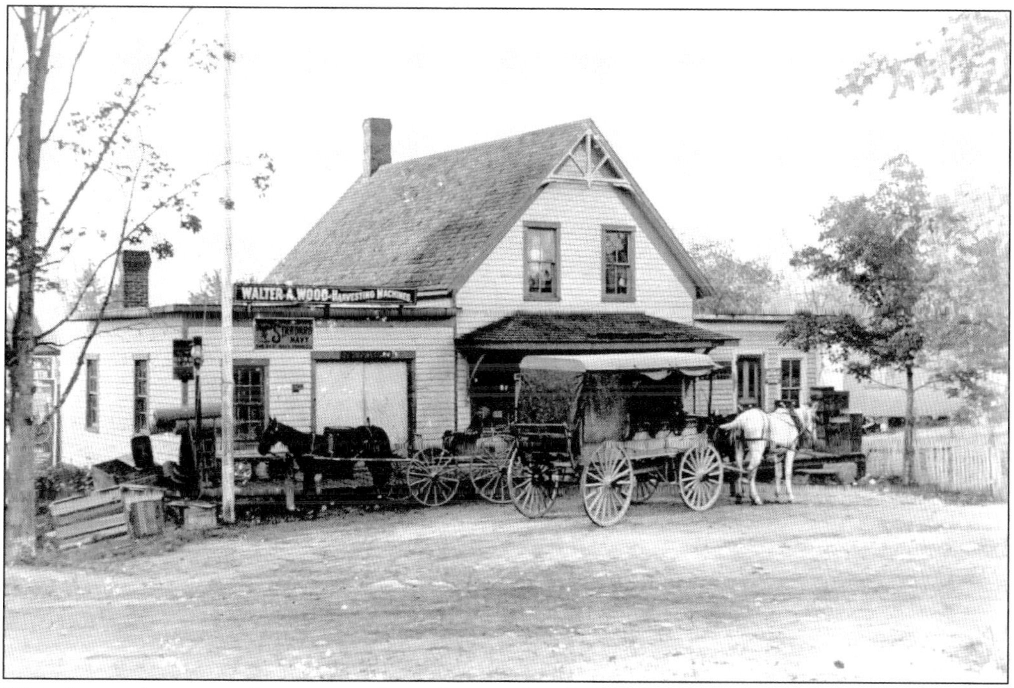

Waite's popular general store stood on the south side of Main Street (Route 2) just west of South Road.

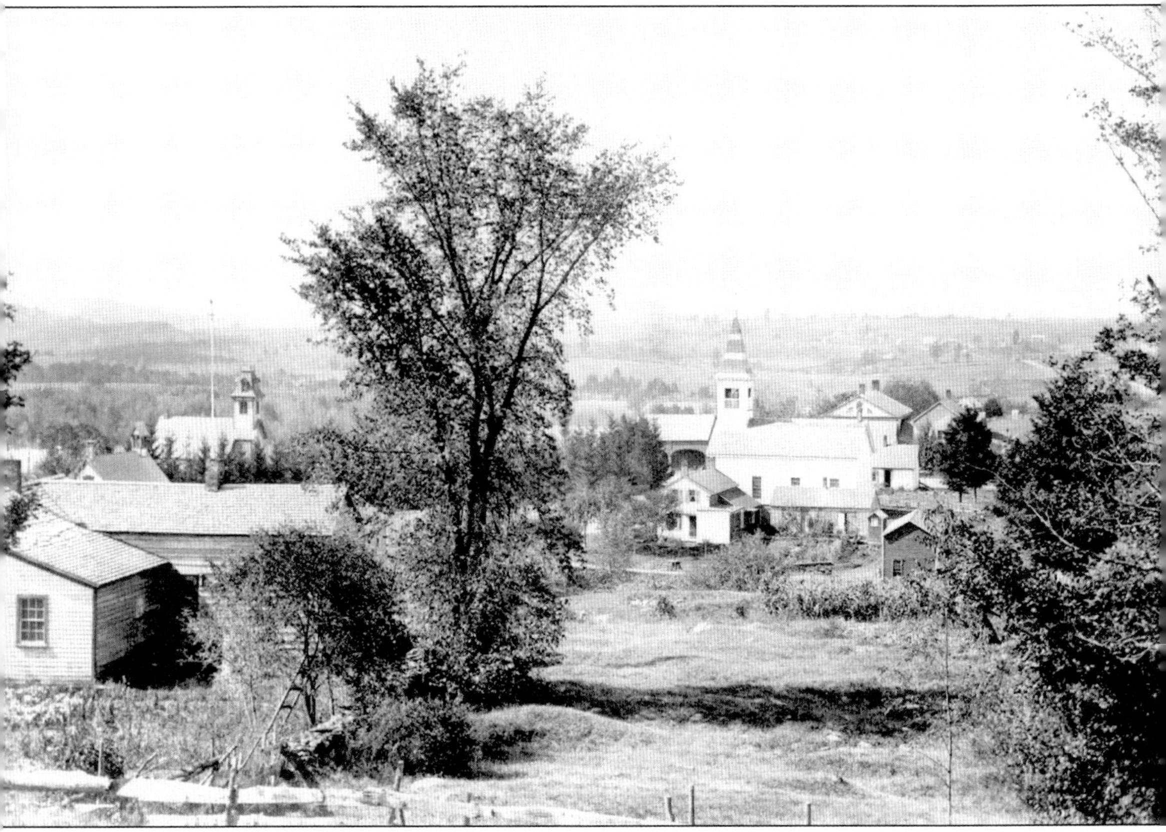

This view of Grafton from the west shows both the Methodist church (left) and the Baptist church. James E. West stood just off Owen Road when framing this scene; this was part of the original road of the 1780s connecting Grafton with Petersburgh. A few portions of this early road can still be driven or hiked today.

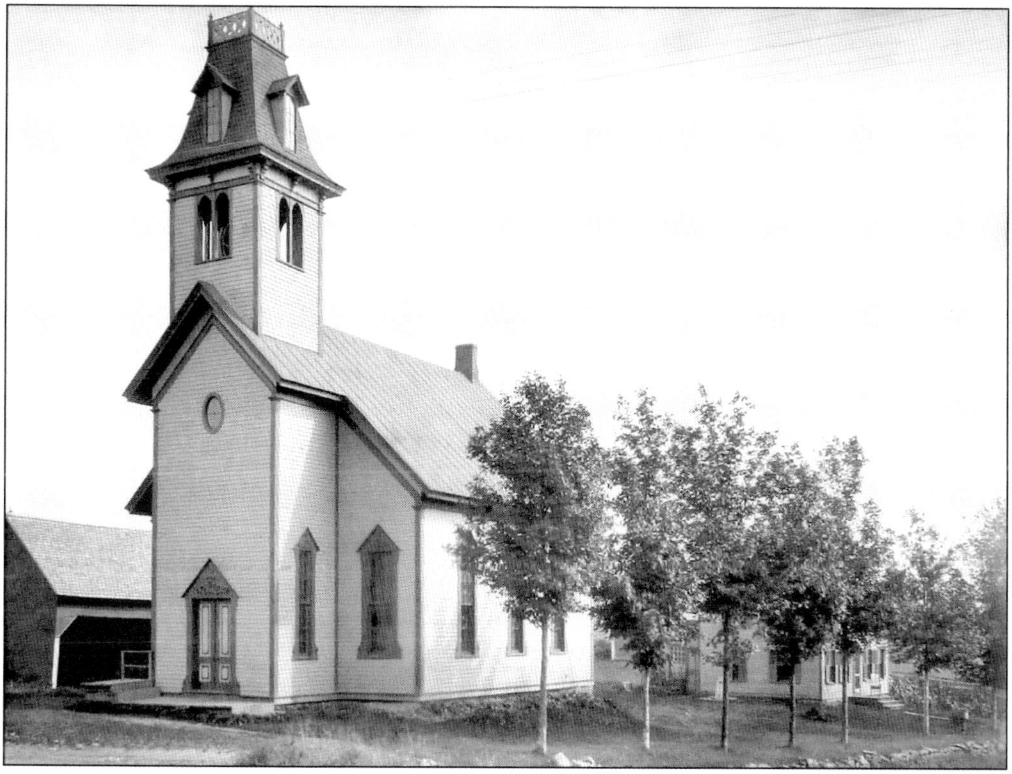

The Grafton Methodist Church, on the corner of the current Main Street and South Road, was constructed in 1875, and largely retains its original exterior appearance today.

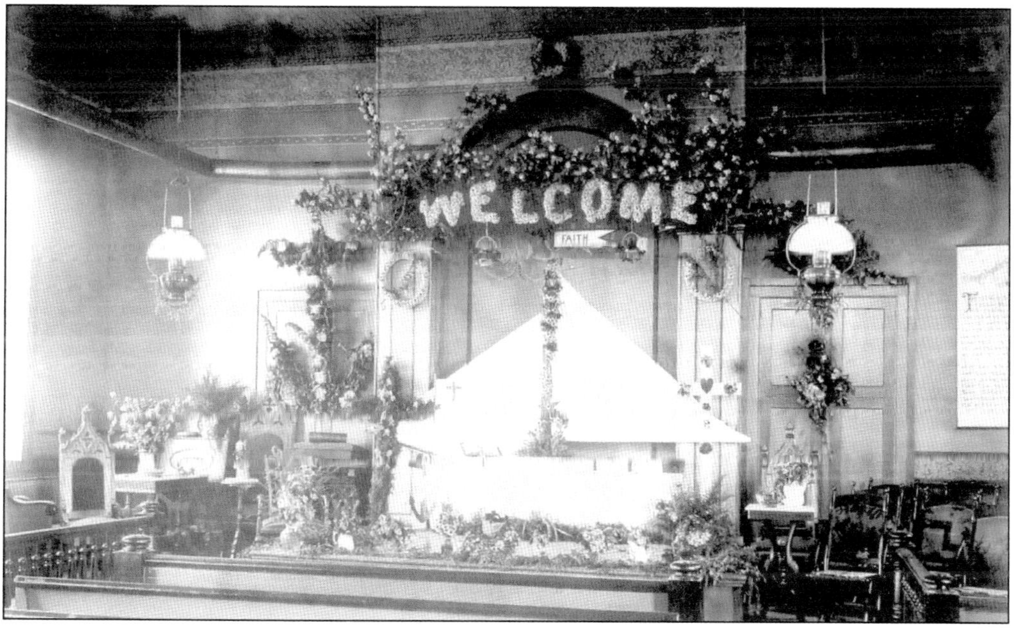

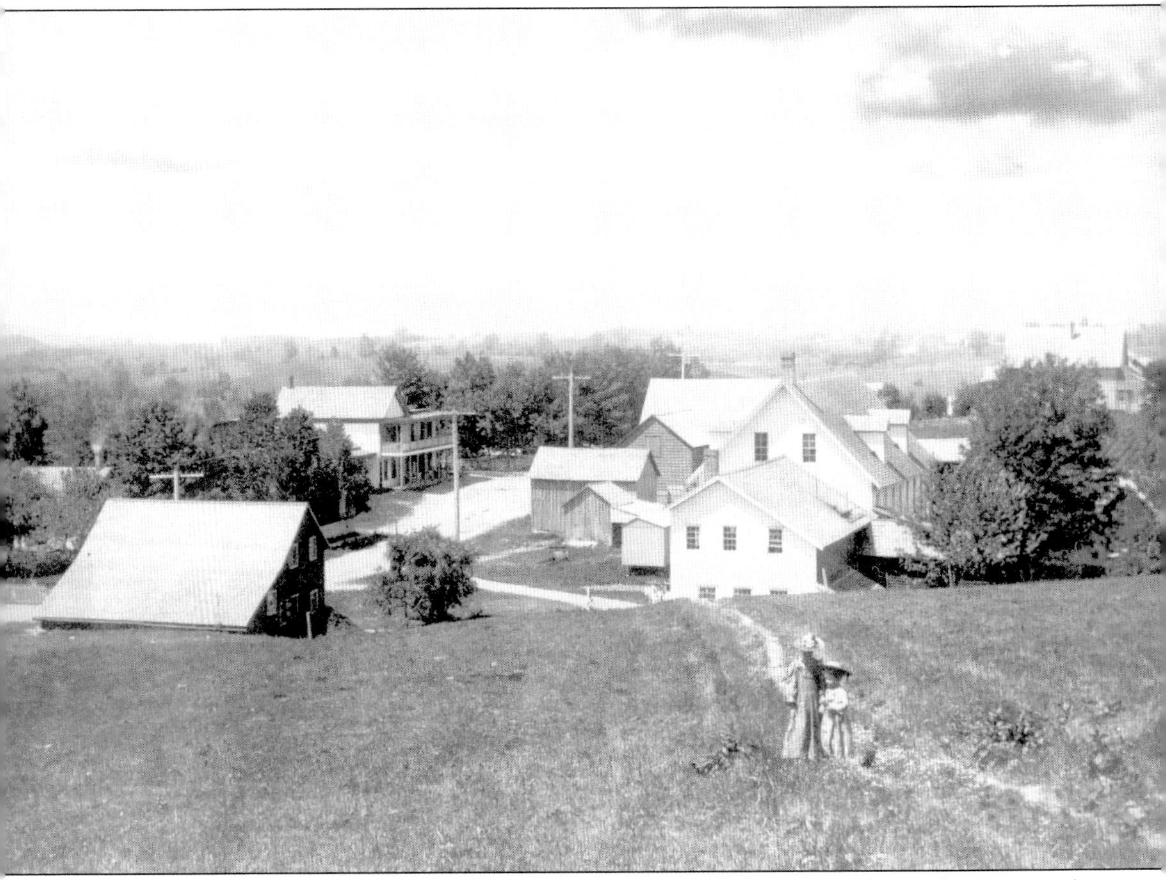

Looking west from behind the Grafton House, James E. West's view shows the Scriven shirt factory behind a short street known as "Lovers Lane." When the factory was destroyed by fire on June 25, 1926, the owner, J. Anderson Scriven, used it for a warehouse.

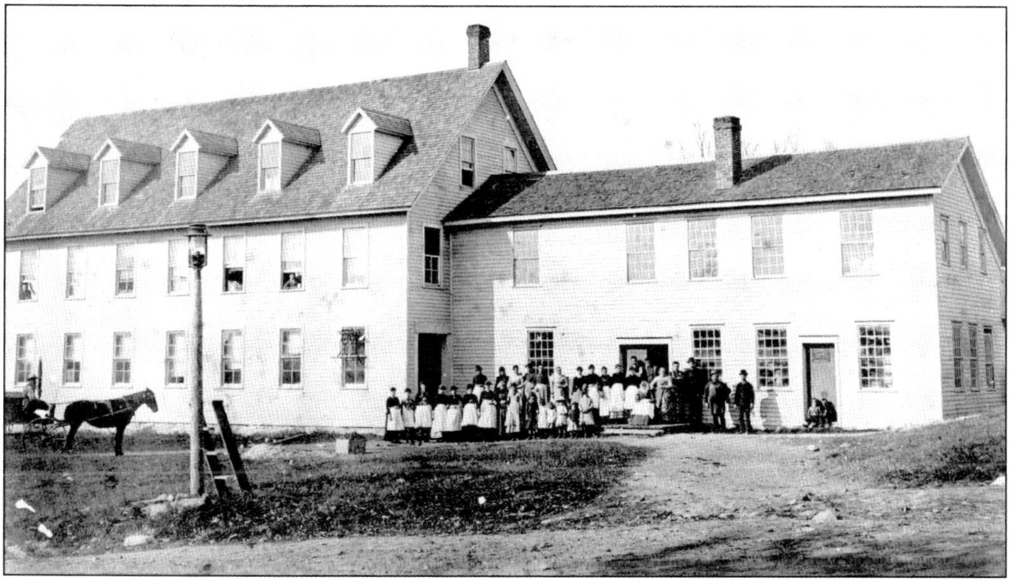

The Scriven shirt factory was an impressive two-story wooden building and employed a number of persons of various ages, as this 1894 photograph below testifies. See also pages 94 and 95 for additional views of the factory.

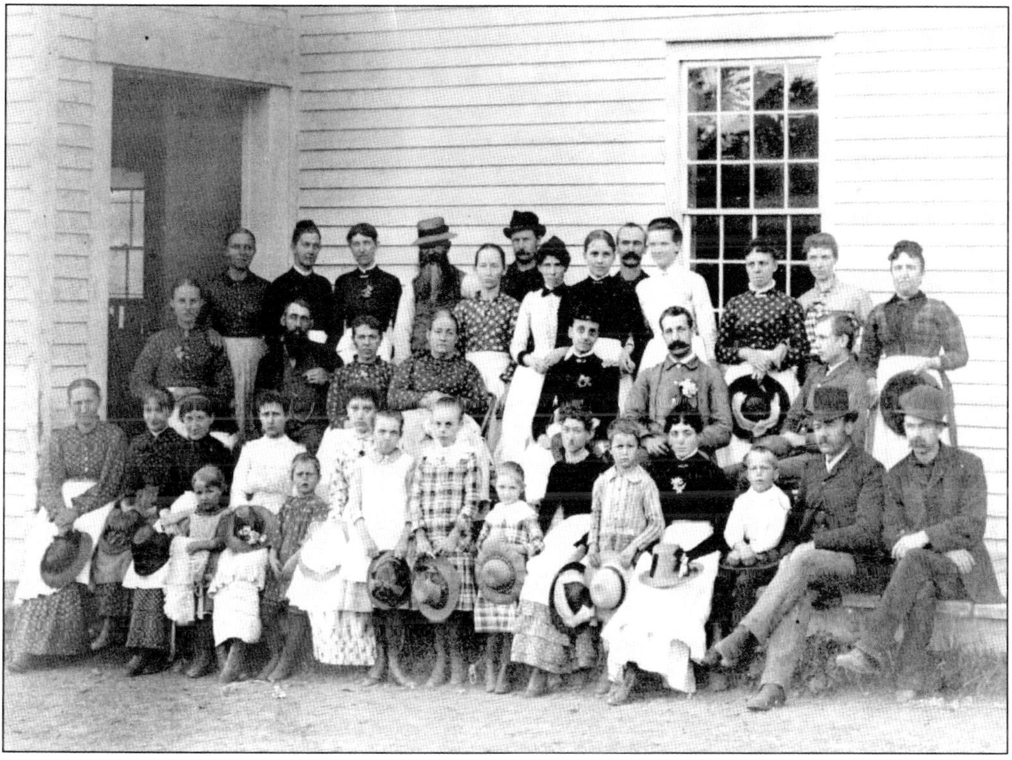

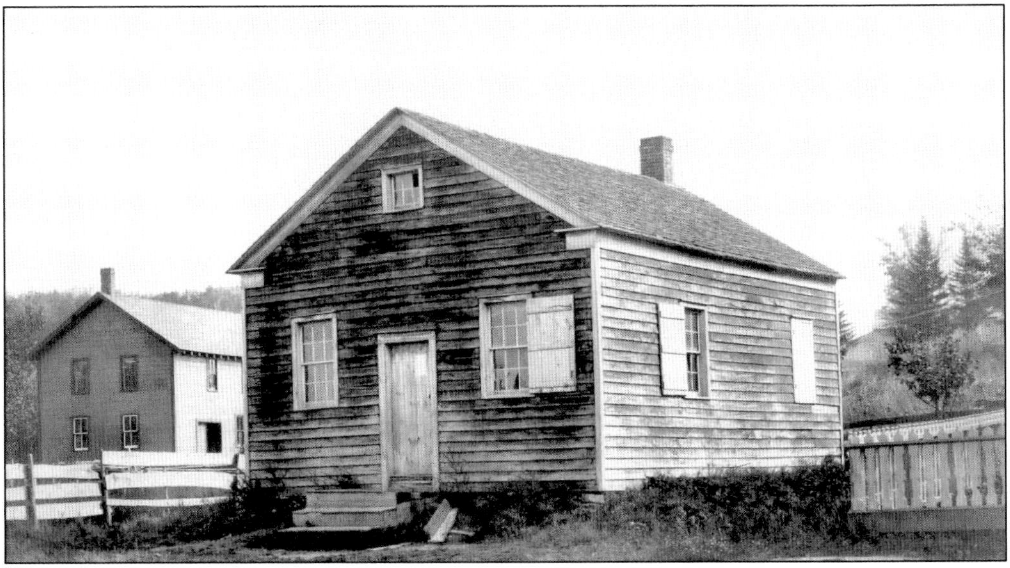

School No. 5 in the center of Grafton (above) had become dilapidated when it was replaced in 1887 by the more modern school building, which now serves as the post office. When the 1895 photograph below of the new school was taken, Adelbert Wilcox was the teacher.

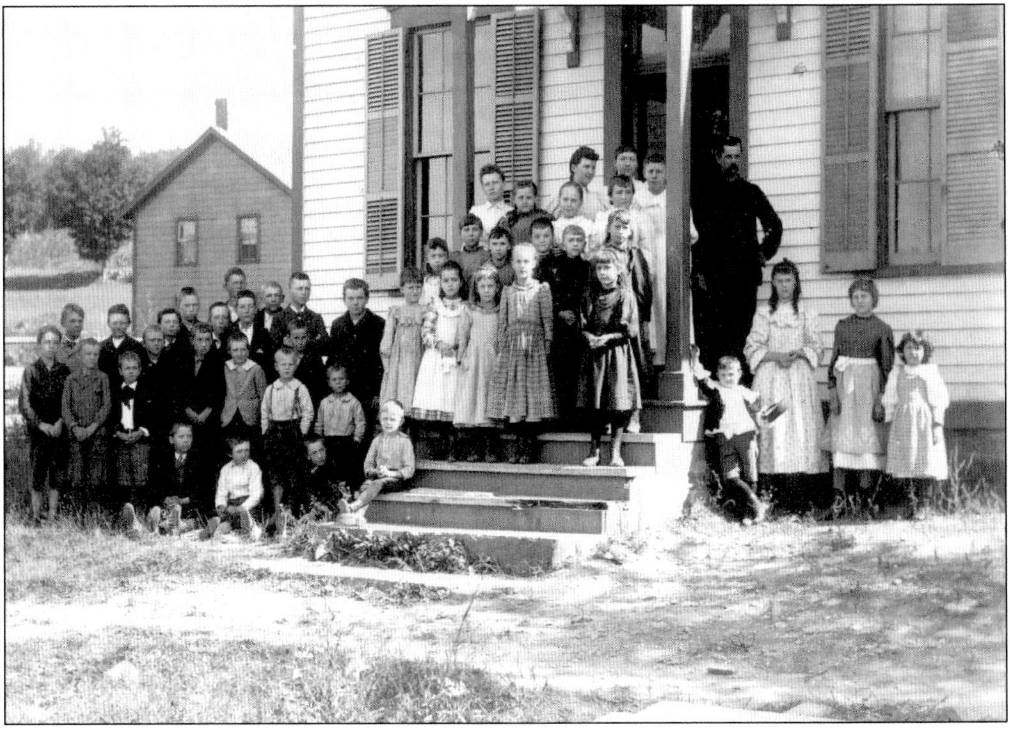

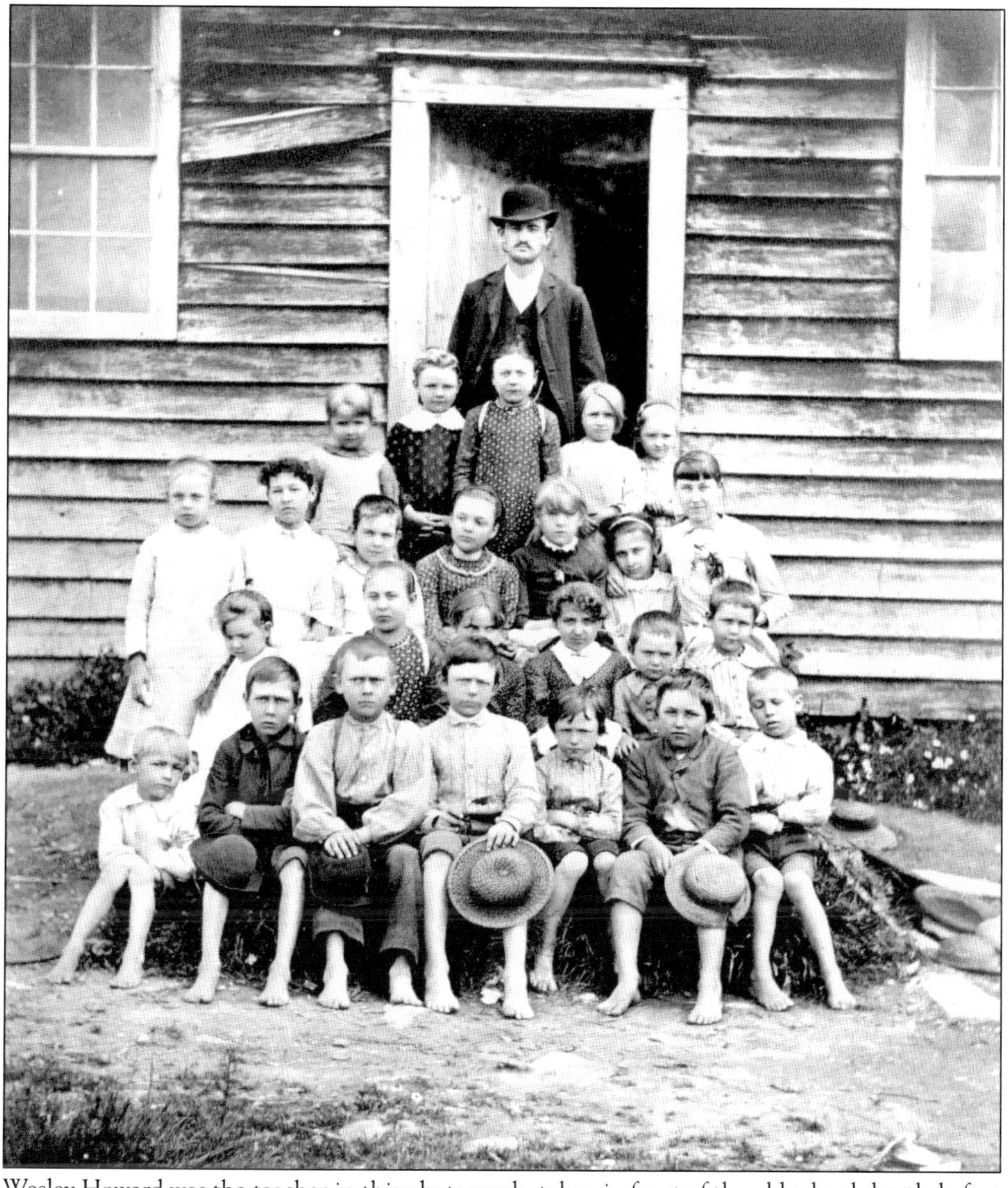

Wesley Howard was the teacher in this photograph, taken in front of the old school shortly before its abandonment. Later in life, Howard was elected Rensselaer County Supreme Court judge.

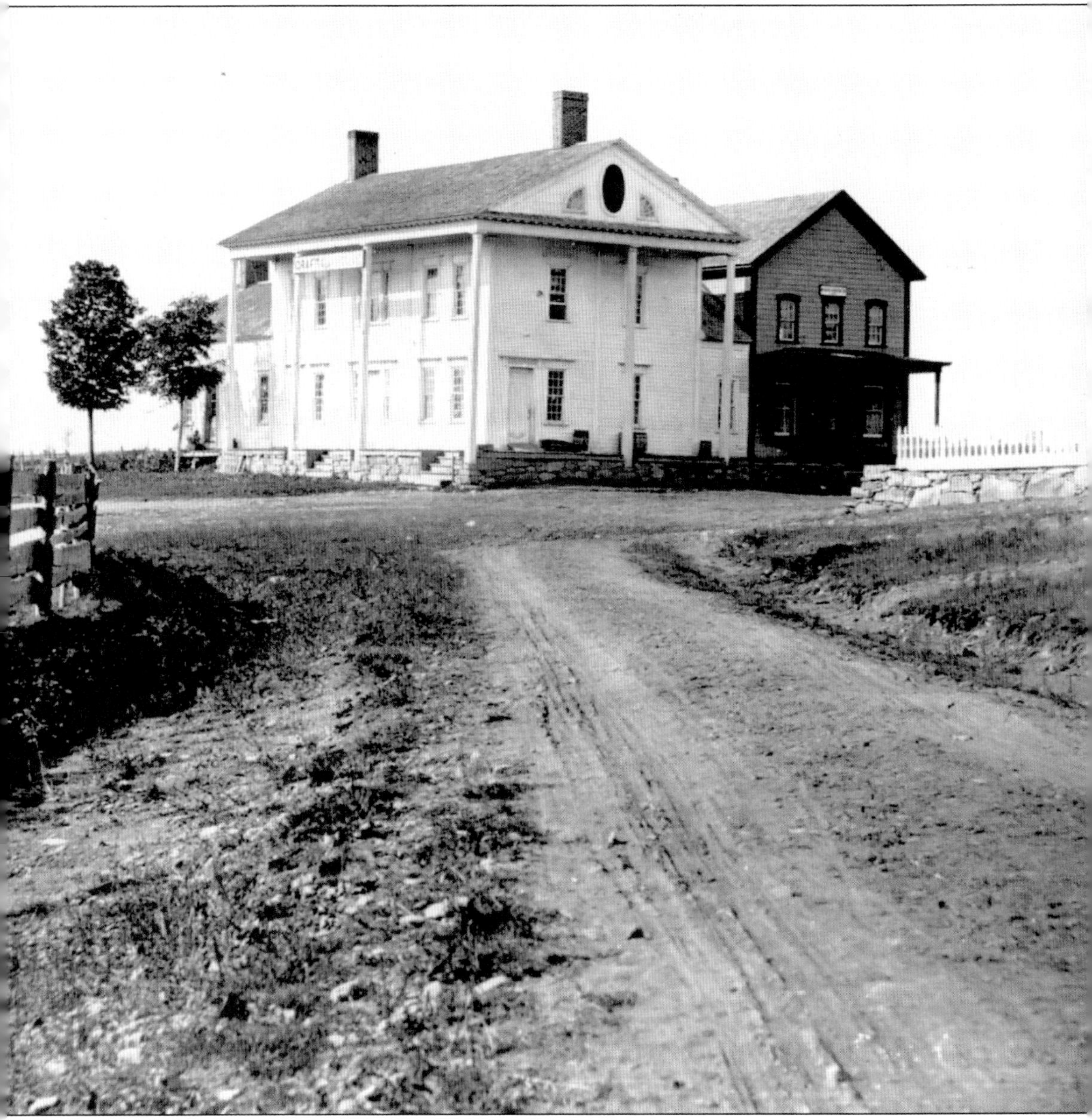

The Grafton House stood just northwest of the village green. This impressive hotel had been constructed in 1838 by the Van Rensselaer family; it was extensively remodeled in 1905, but was demolished in the 1920s.

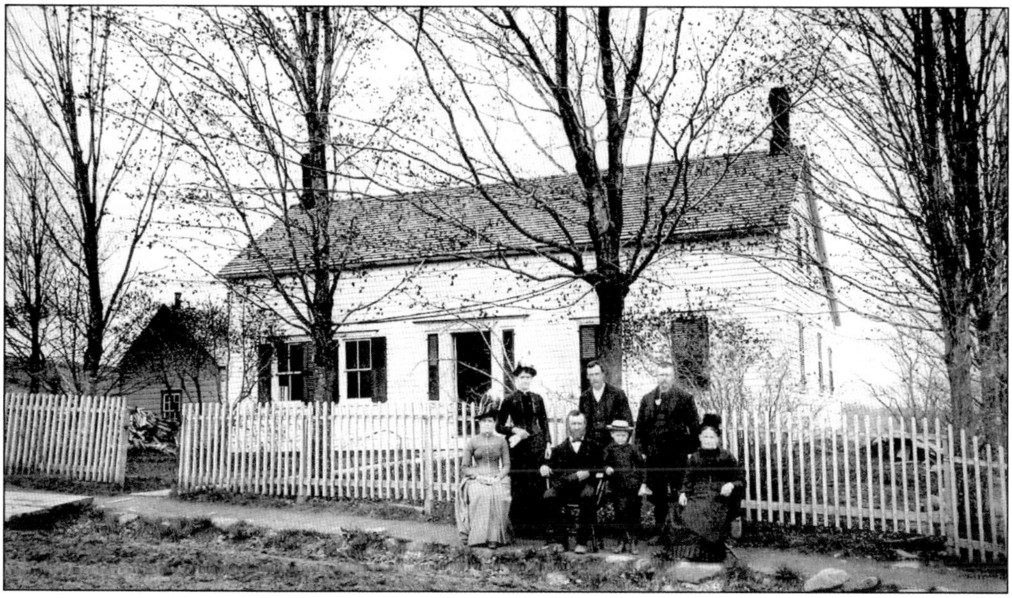

The former William Waite house still stands on the south side of Main Street, just east of the Grafton Community Library.

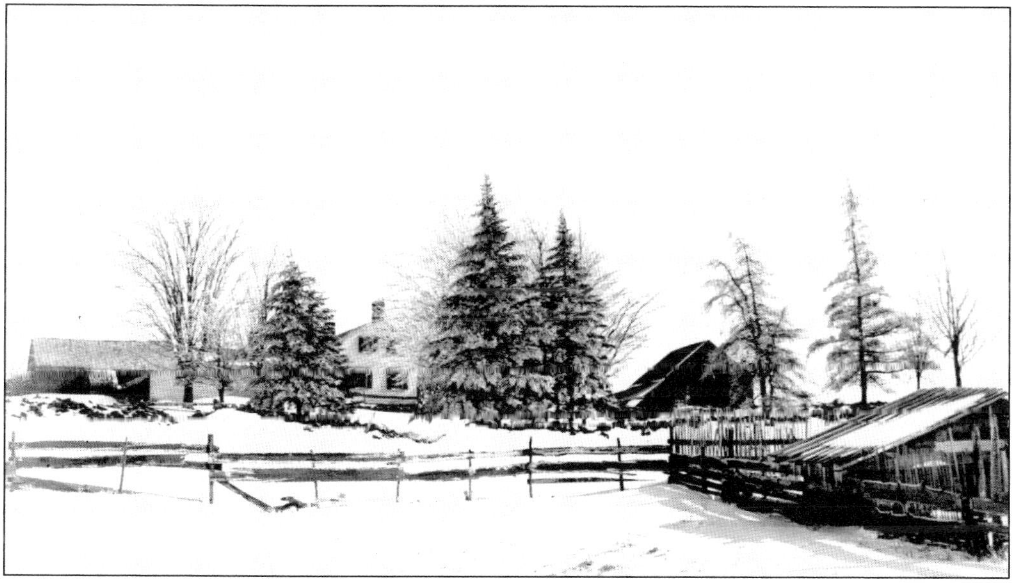

The Jabez Hakes house and outbuildings, captured after a fresh snowfall, are not located on a rural road as one might presume, but are found on the north side of Main Street across from the Grafton Town Hall in downtown.

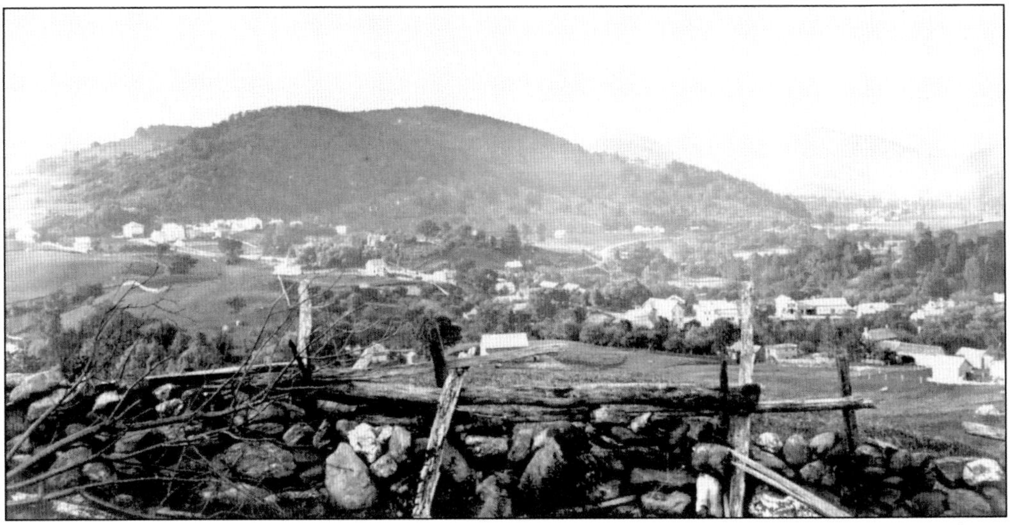

These views overlooking Petersburgh are not visible today due to reforestation. The scene above looks from Stewart Road to the east, and the scene below, showing the lower or northern covered bridge and the mill yard, was taken from Duffy's Hill just northeast of the village.

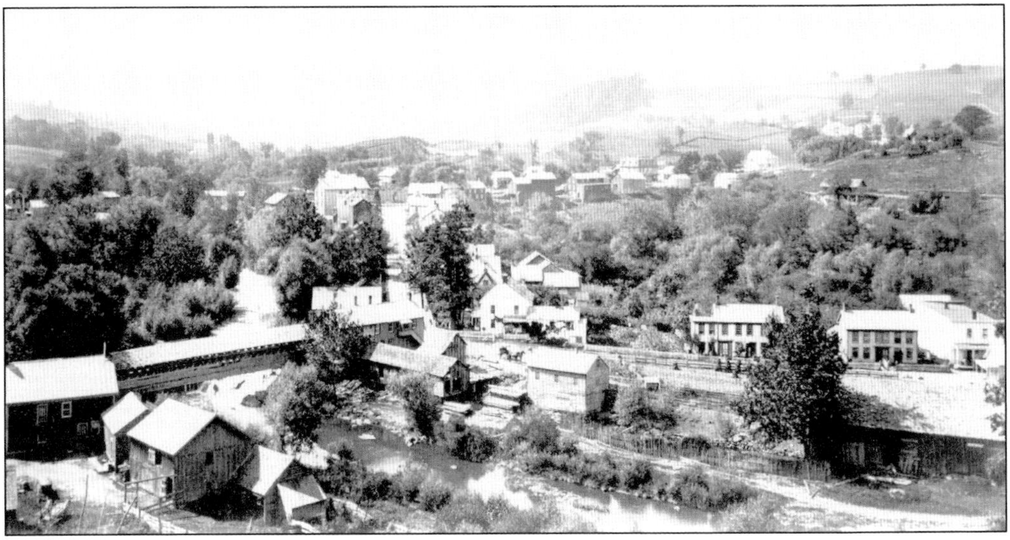

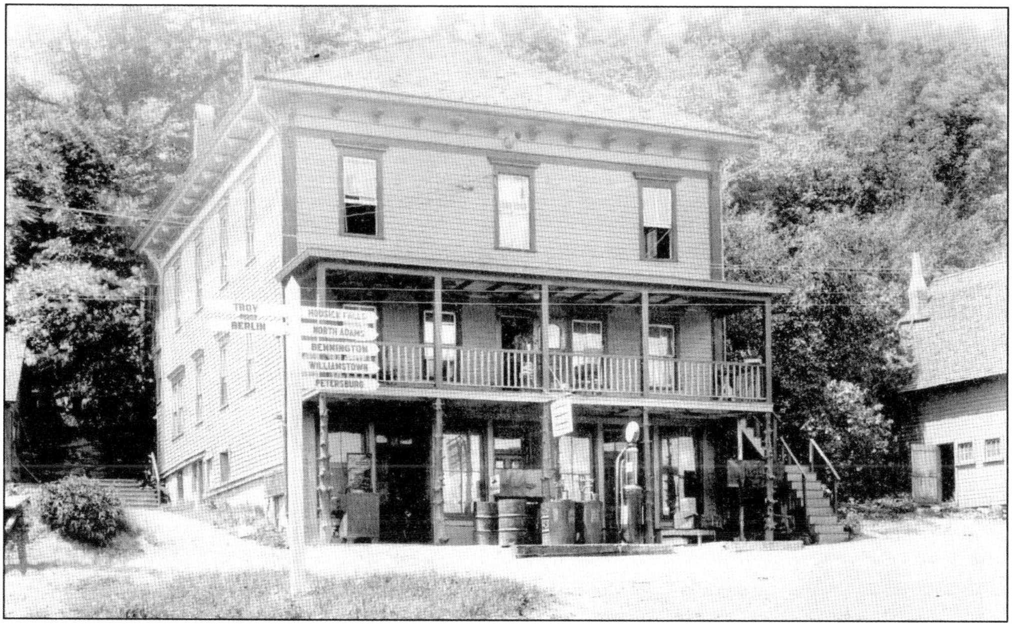

All roads seemingly led to Petersburgh. Located on the west side of the current State Route 22 in Petersburgh, the Eagle Opera House housed a hotel as well as an early service station.

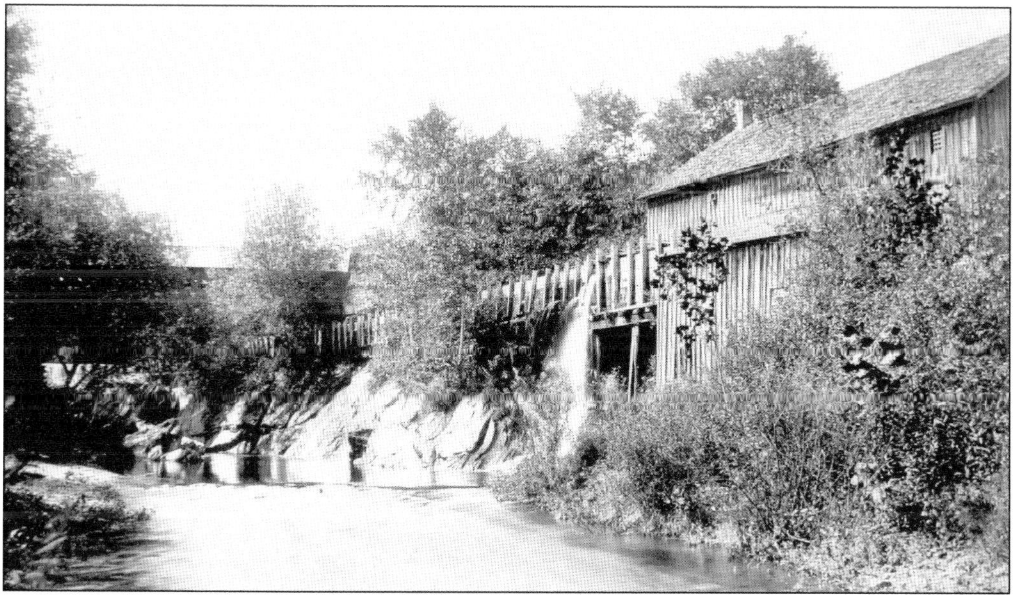

The old Van Rensselaer mill in Petersburgh was located just north of the upper or southern covered bridge.

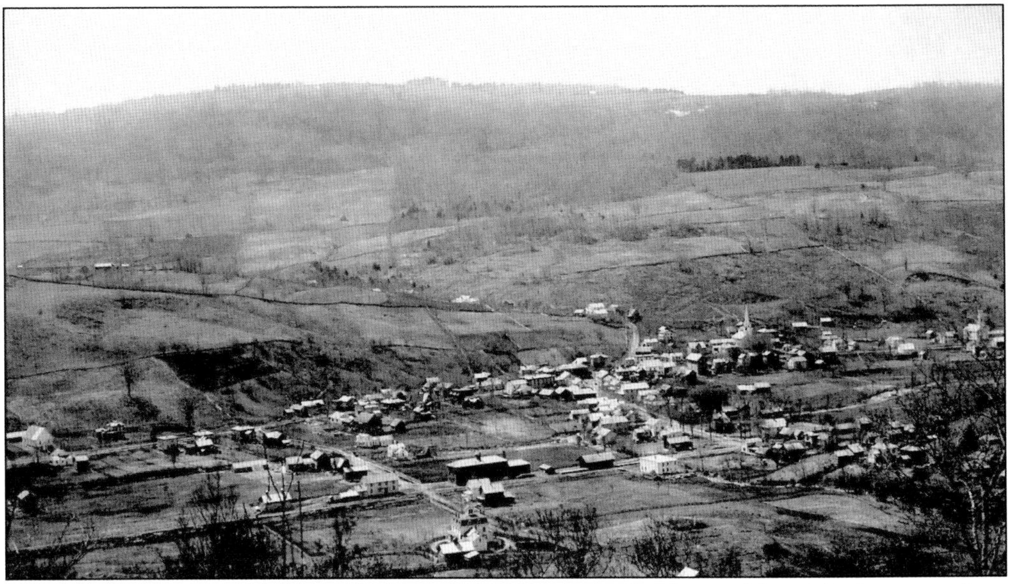

The entire village of Berlin is visible in a treeless early spring landscape (above) looking west from the "Crow's Nest" behind the present elementary school toward the Rensselaer Plateau. The view of the laundry and creamery on Community Avenue and the Lebanon Springs Railroad (below), later the Rutland Railroad, was taken from part way up the hill on Plank Road.

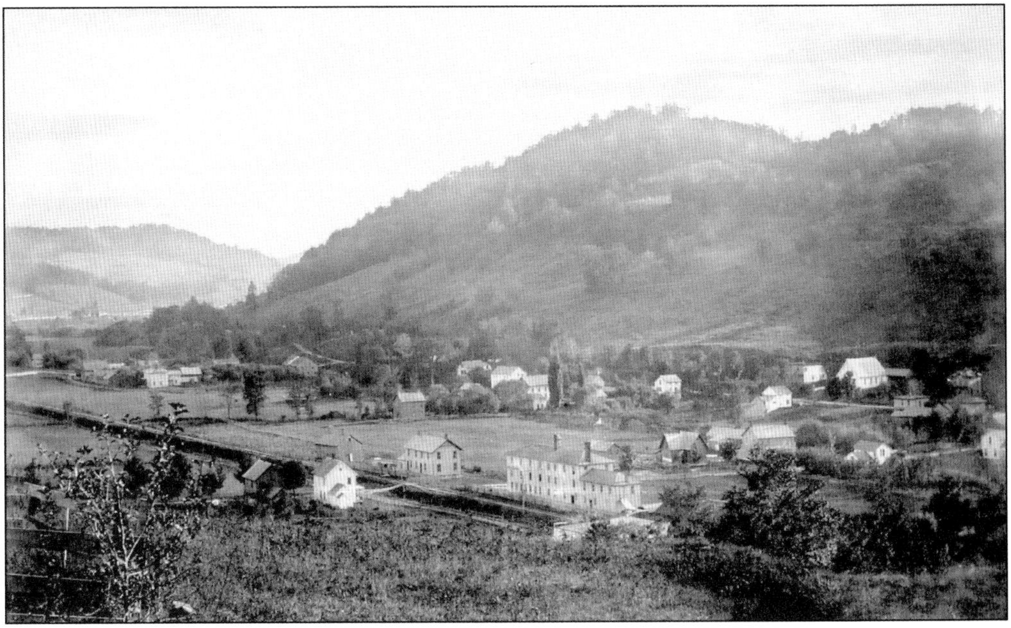

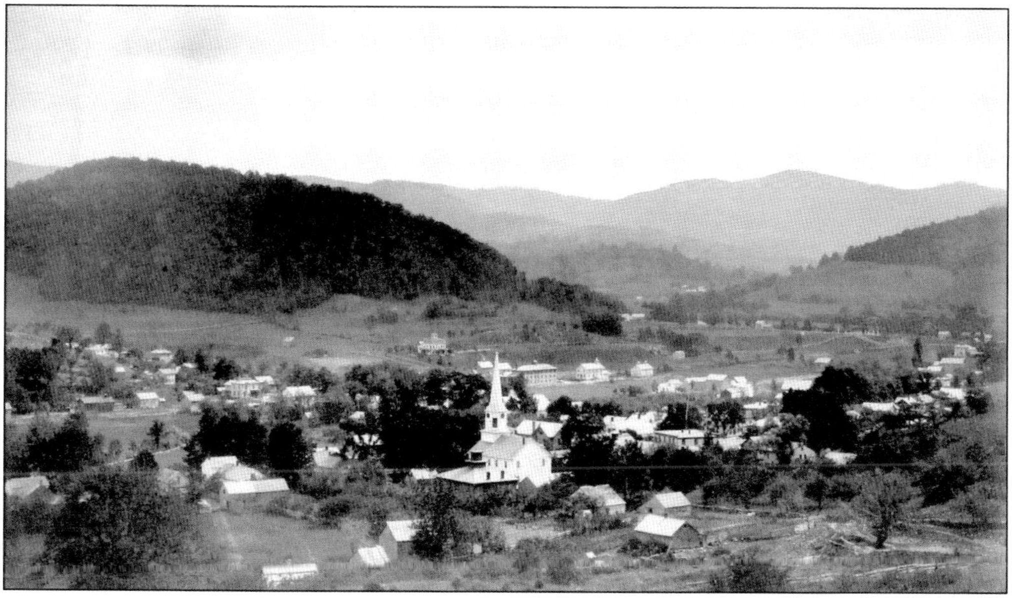

Another view from Plank Road (above) in which the First Baptist Church is prominently visible looks east into Southeast Hollow toward the Taconic Range. In the photograph reproduced below, a man strolls south on North Main Street toward the Seventh Day Baptist Church early on a sunny morning.

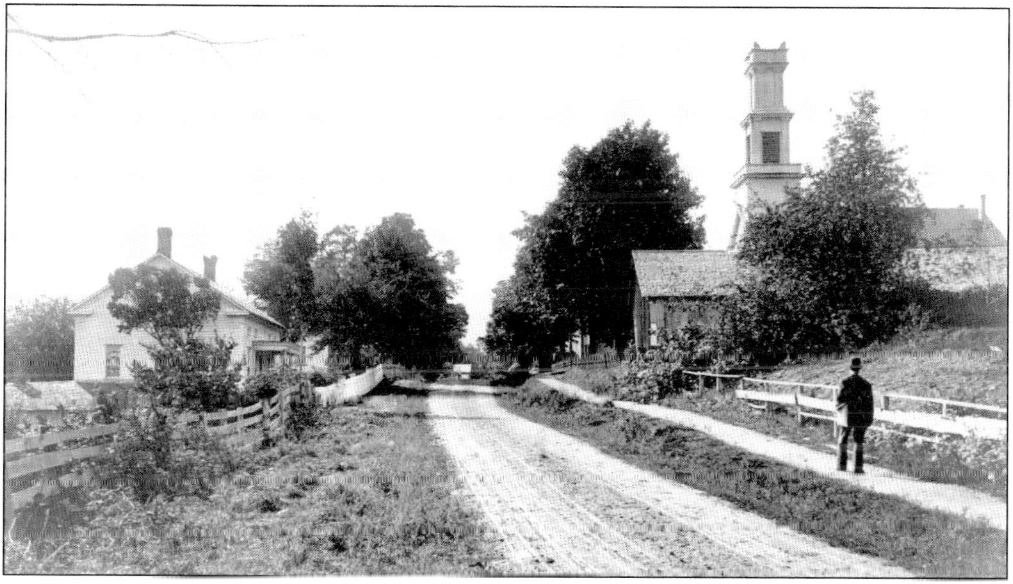

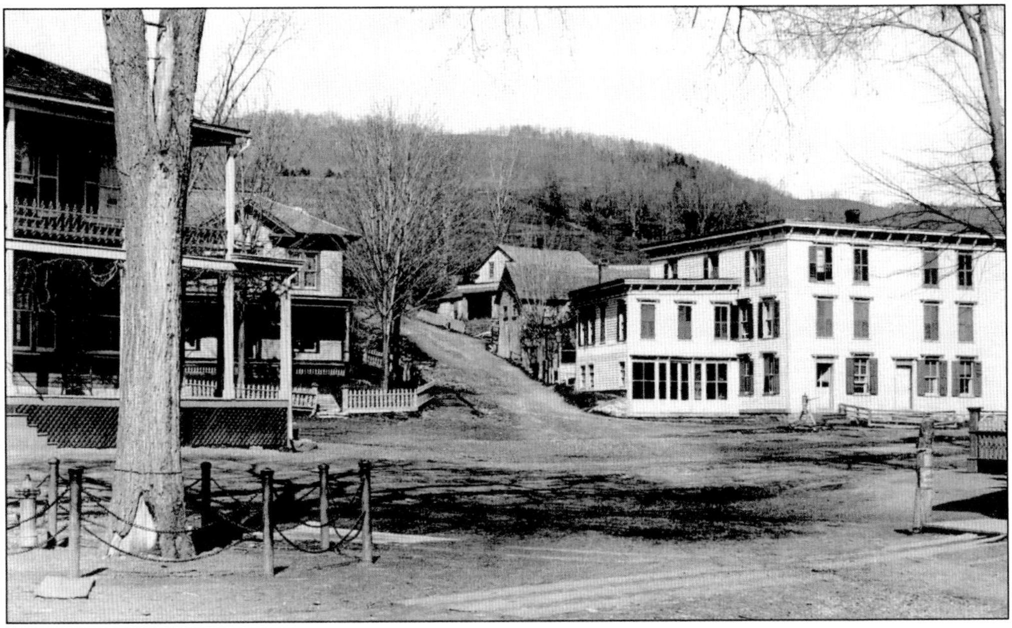

The intersection of Main and Elm Streets was the center of activity in Berlin. In the view (above) looking west up Plank Road, the Colonial Inn, an early tavern constructed in 1806 by Burton Hammond, is visible behind the elm tree, across Plank Road from the Rogers home. The view below looks south on Main Street and shows the Stillman Brothers' store and the Wadsworth Hotel on the left. James E. West maintained a small studio behind the hotel in the 1880s and 1890s.

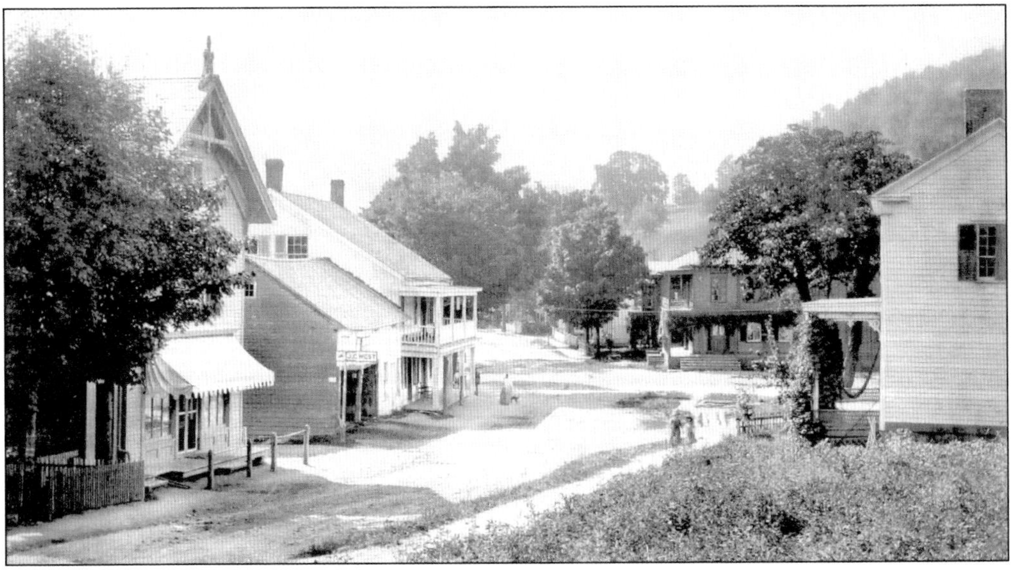

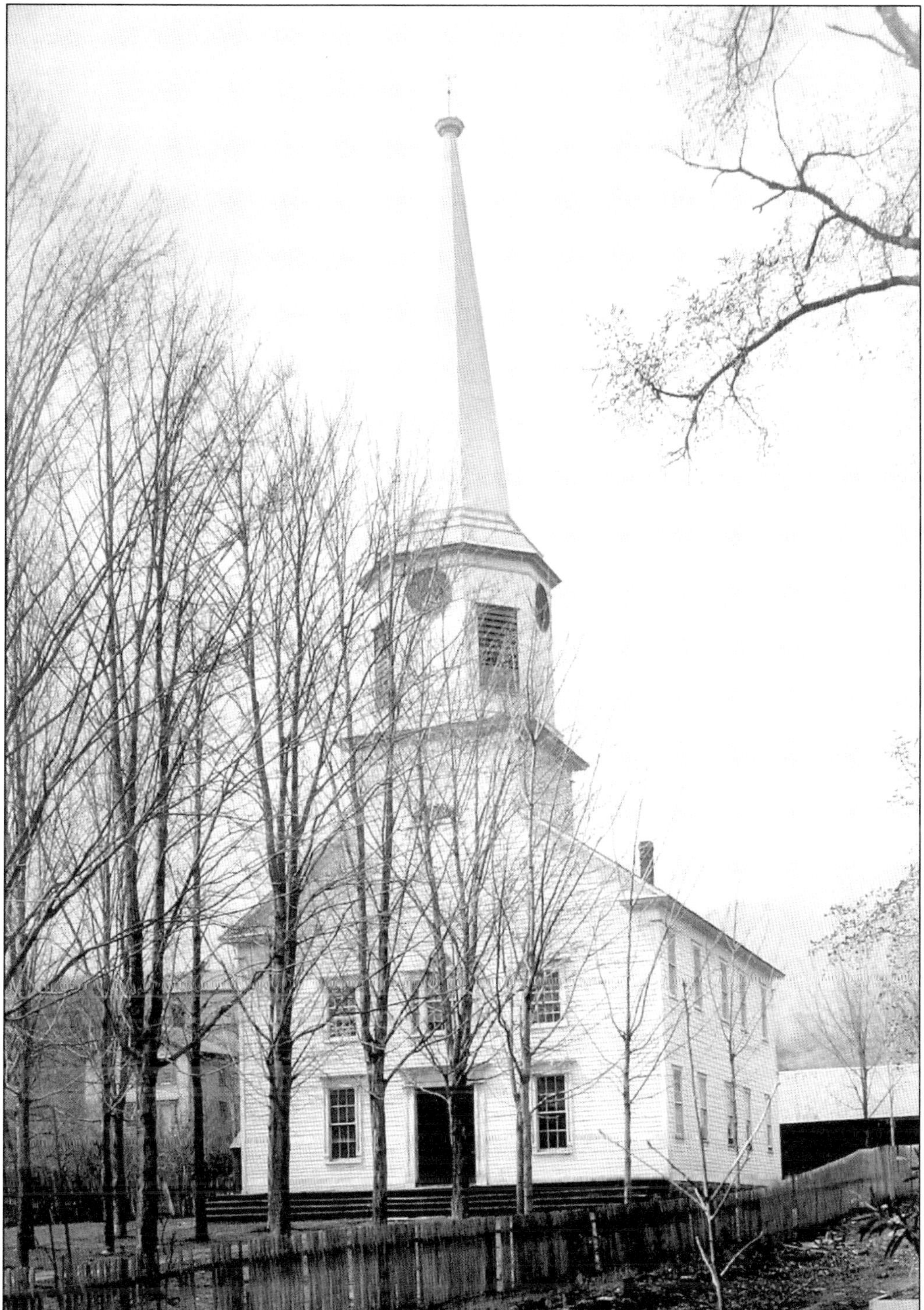

The elegant First Baptist Church was the principal downtown Berlin landmark. Constructed in 1830 and beautifully maintained, it was destroyed by fire in the devastating propane tanker explosion on July 25, 1962.

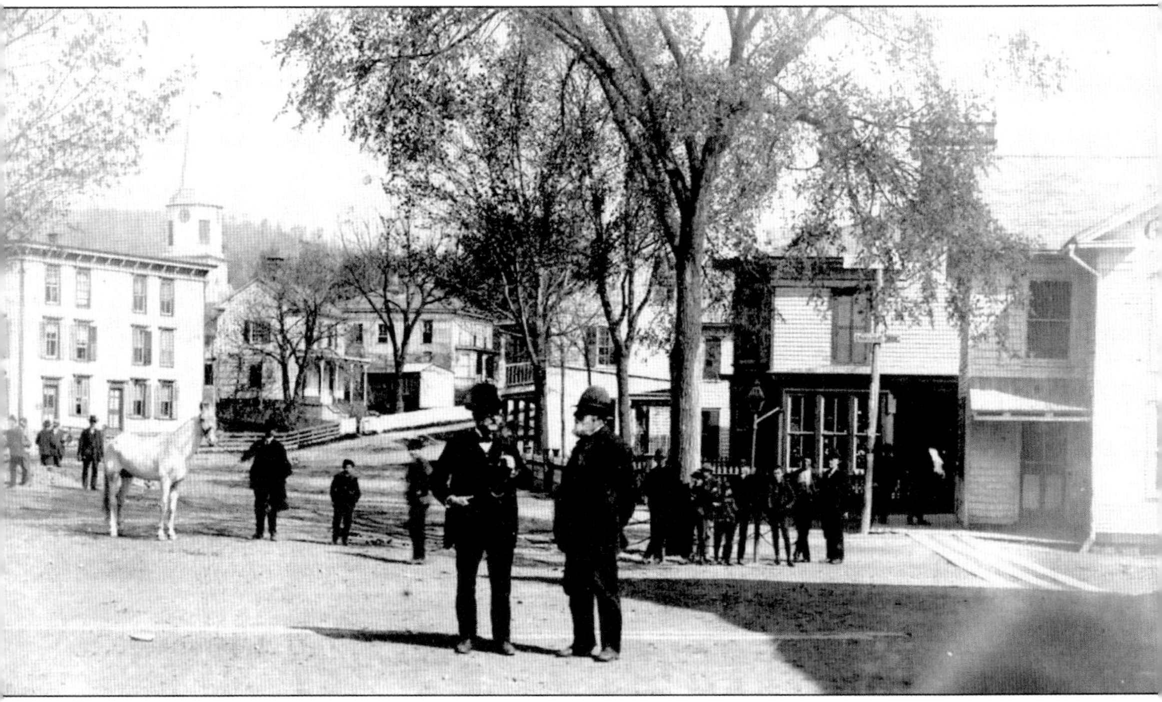

Men and boys enjoy a sunny spring afternoon at Main and Elm Streets in Berlin in this view, which looks north past the famous elm known as the "Ring Tree." Gifford's cash market, on the right, was later converted into Maxon's shirt shop.

Two

Rural Scenes

While traveling between the three towns and adjoining communities taking the portraits of individual and family groups and their homes that composed the vast majority of his output, James E. West often took the time to capture scenes of rural beauty. Creating artistic photographs in the scenic countryside probably brought him little financial renumeration, but West clearly took great care in composing these views.

During the 19th century, much of the forest that covered the Rensselaer Plateau and Taconic Range was cut to open more pasture land and also for the production of charcoal, firewood, and lumber. The open expanses shown in many of his panoramic scenes taken a century ago are no longer visible today. The steep-sided valleys, small mountain streams, waterfalls, lakes, and other scenic features of this region continue to attract both tourists from busy urban areas and new homeowners as they did a century ago.

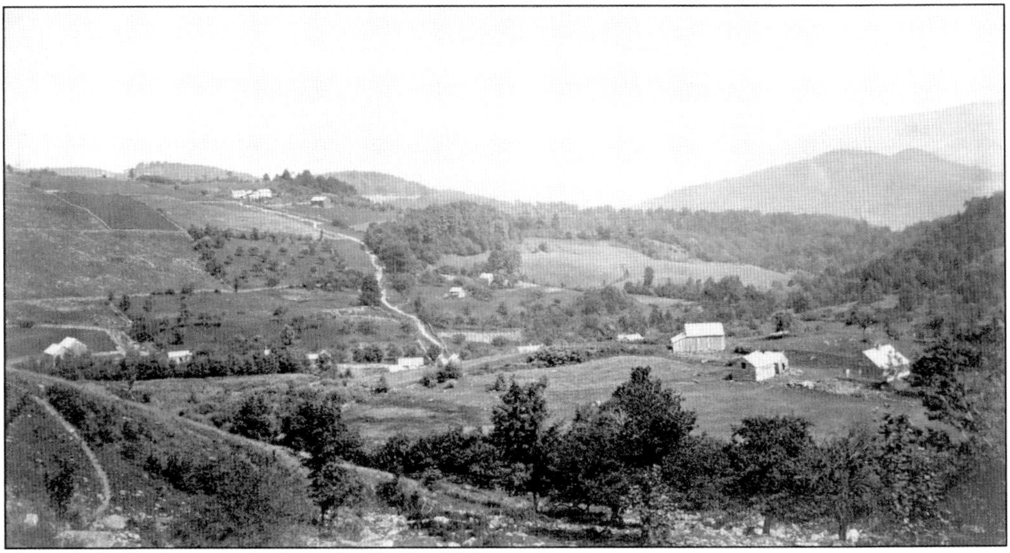

Looking north from the present Route 2, James E. West captured the view (above) of a Petersburgh locale known as Stillman Village and sometimes whimsically as "Puckertoot;" the old John Green farm shows on the right. The striking late afternoon autumnal scene (below) was taken from the hill above the Frank Maxon farm and looks north with Petersburgh visible in the distance.

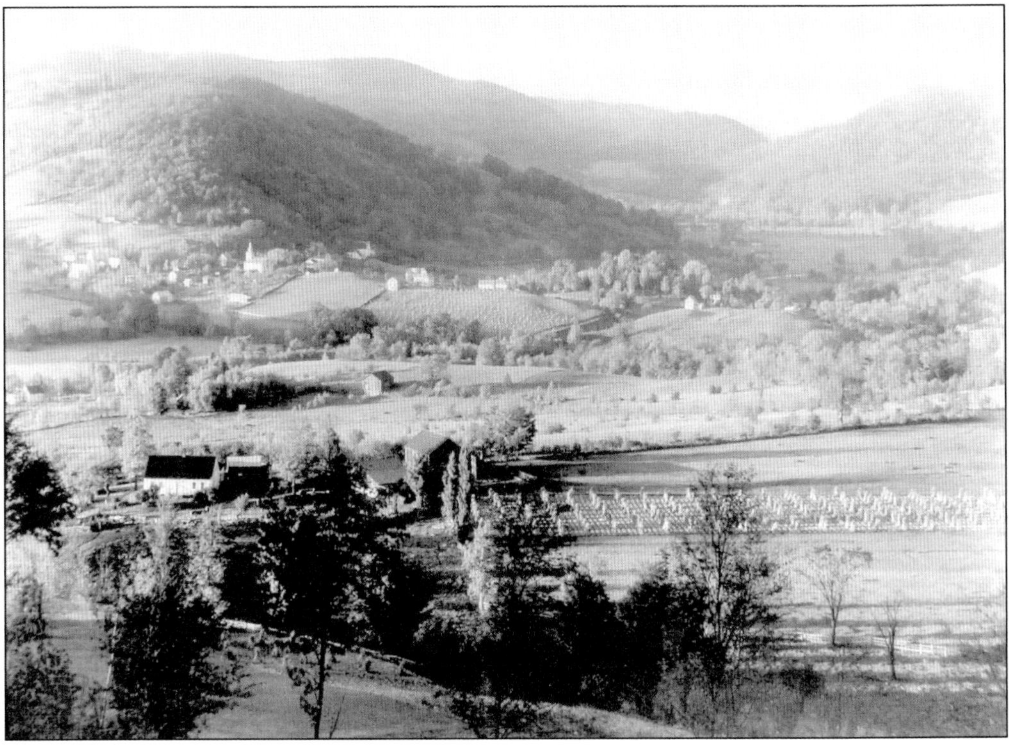

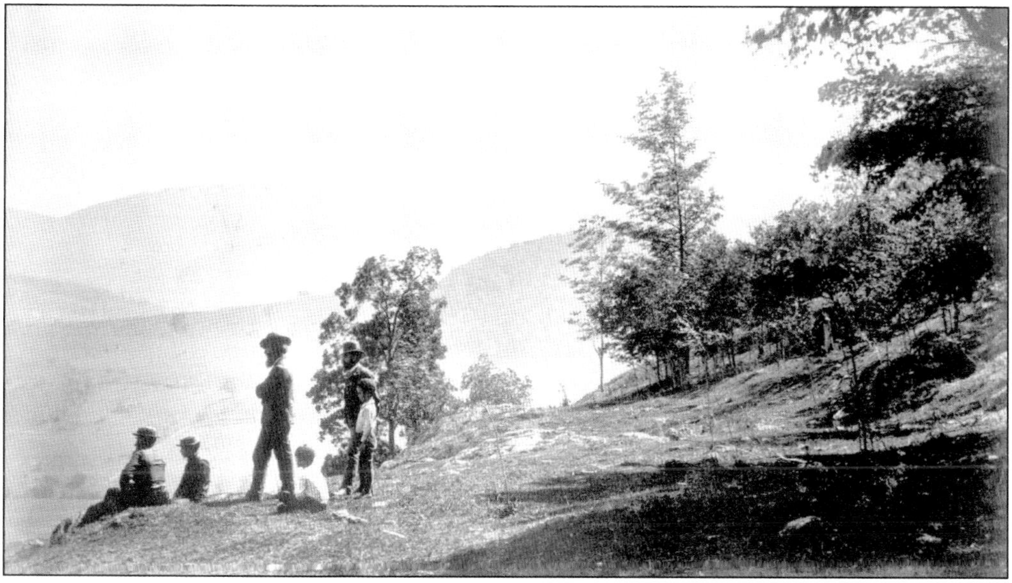

From open ledges west of Potter Hill Road and north of Stillman Village in Petersburgh, one can still gaze across the wide valley of the Little Hoosic toward the "White Rocks" on the Taconic Range.

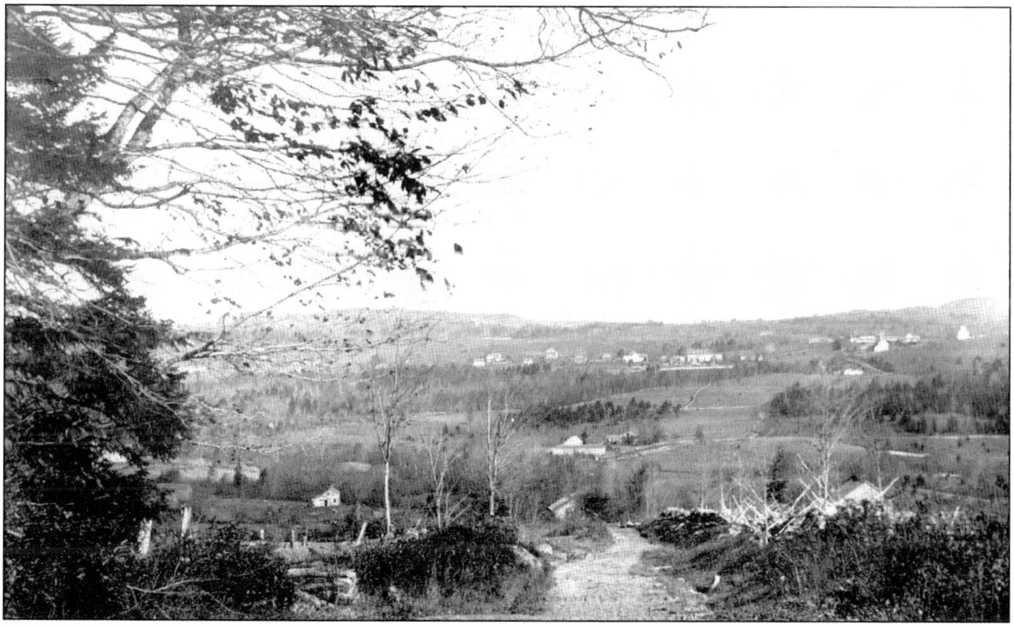

In a largely treeless landscape in the early 1890s, West was able to capture a distant view of Grafton Center from the south from a high point of land known as "the Pinnacle."

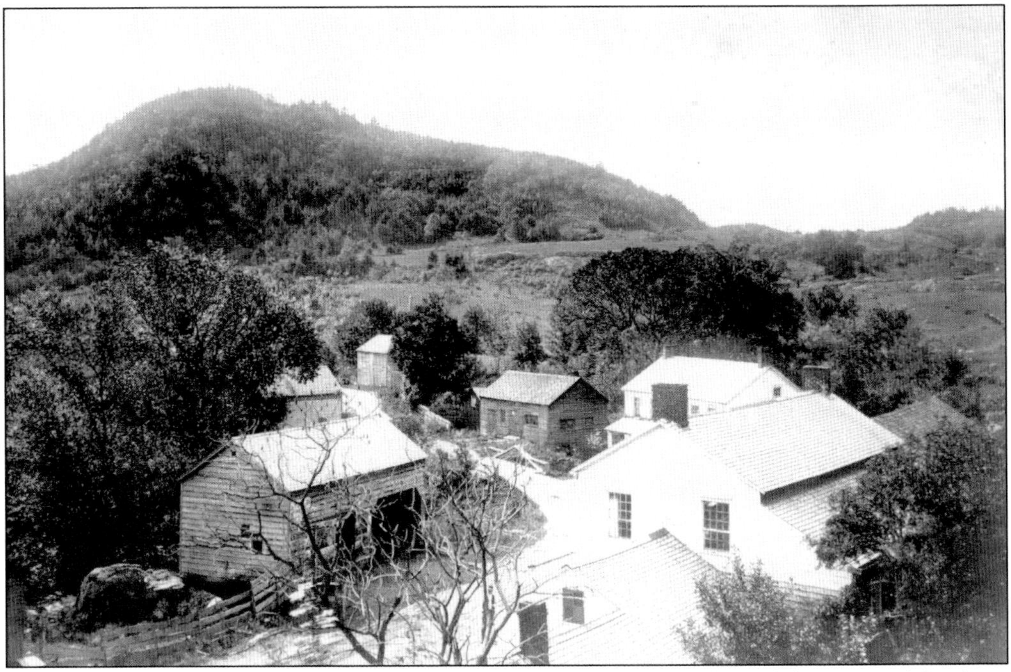

The hamlet of Quackenkill (above) is found on the western boundary of the town of Grafton; Camel Hill, in the background, has been greatly altered by stone quarrying operations. In the view below, the photographer's daughter, Maude, relaxes on exposed rock ledges, possibly at "the Pinnacle."

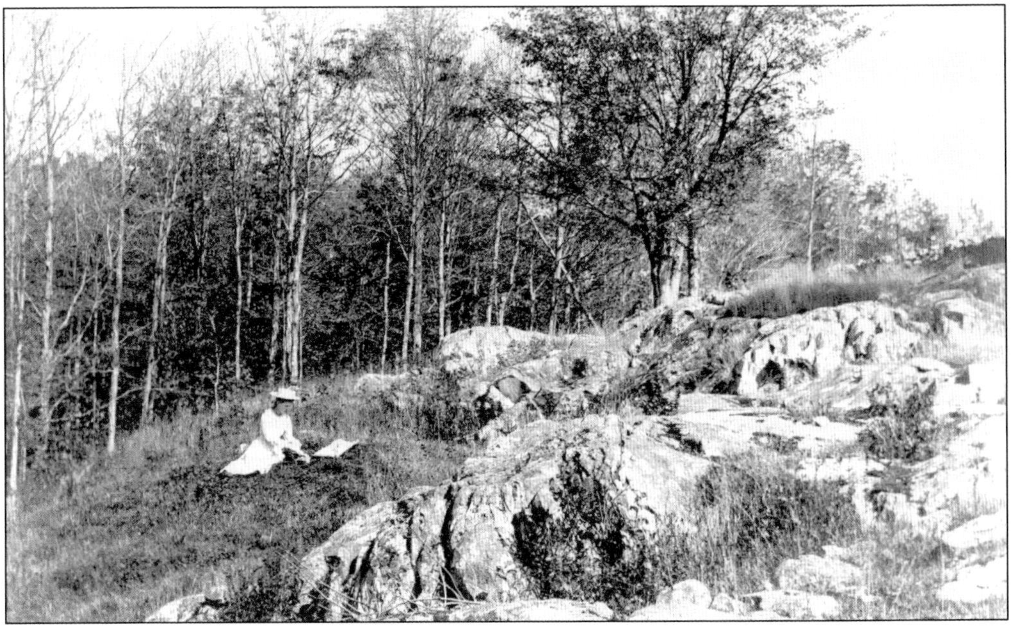

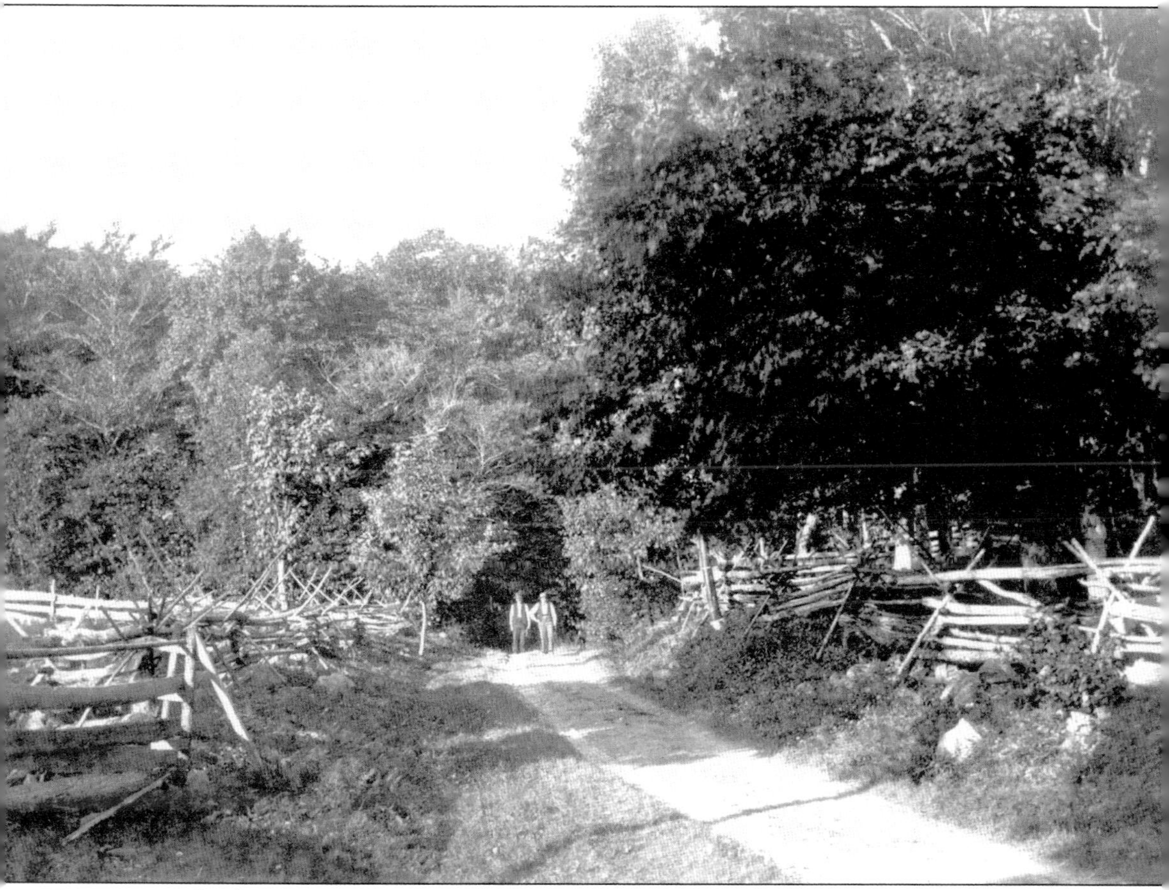

Two men walk along the old Ward Hollow Road north of Shaver Pond, which connected Grafton and Pittstown to the north. Wooden rail fences were still in common use in the late 19th century.

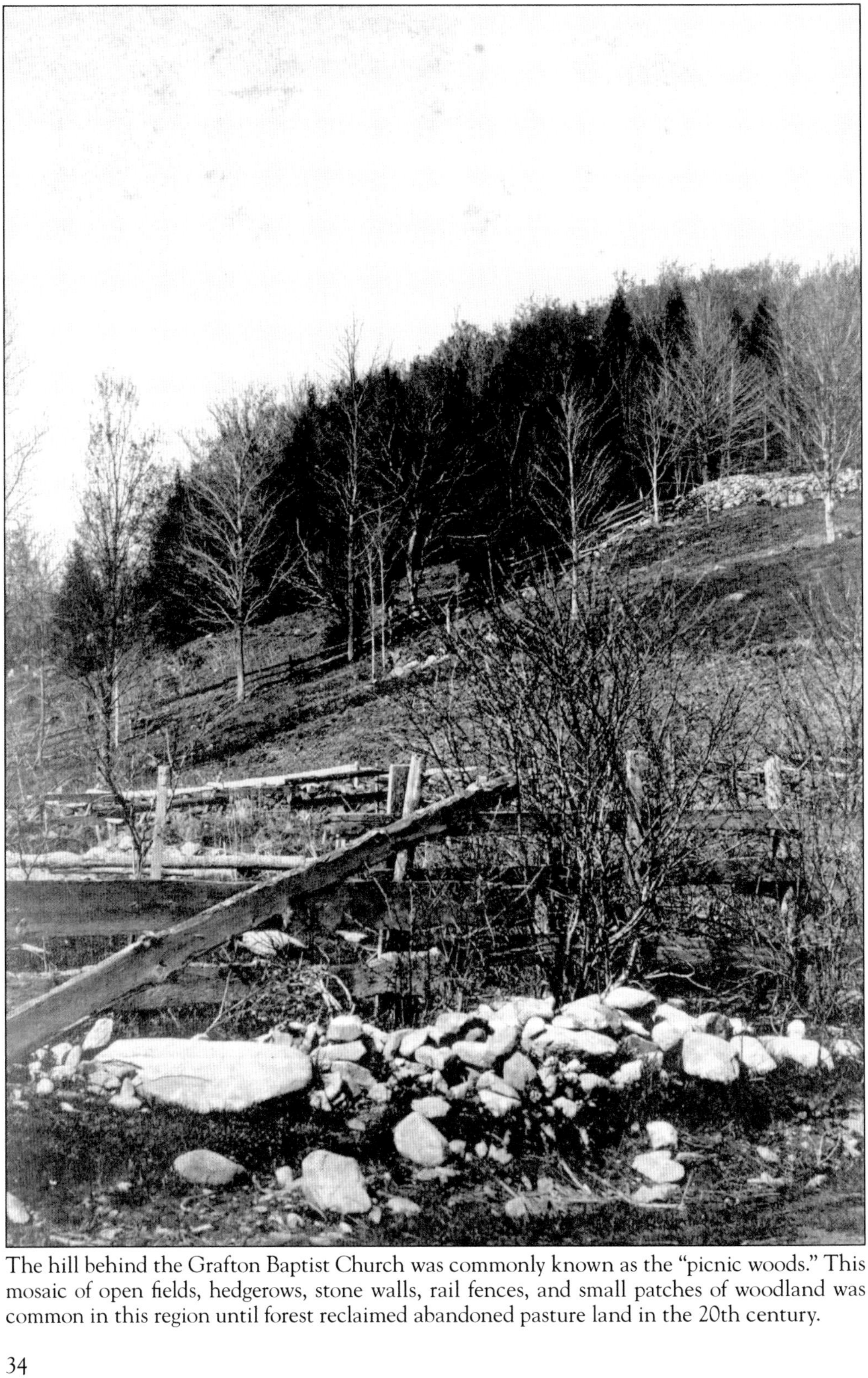

The hill behind the Grafton Baptist Church was commonly known as the "picnic woods." This mosaic of open fields, hedgerows, stone walls, rail fences, and small patches of woodland was common in this region until forest reclaimed abandoned pasture land in the 20th century.

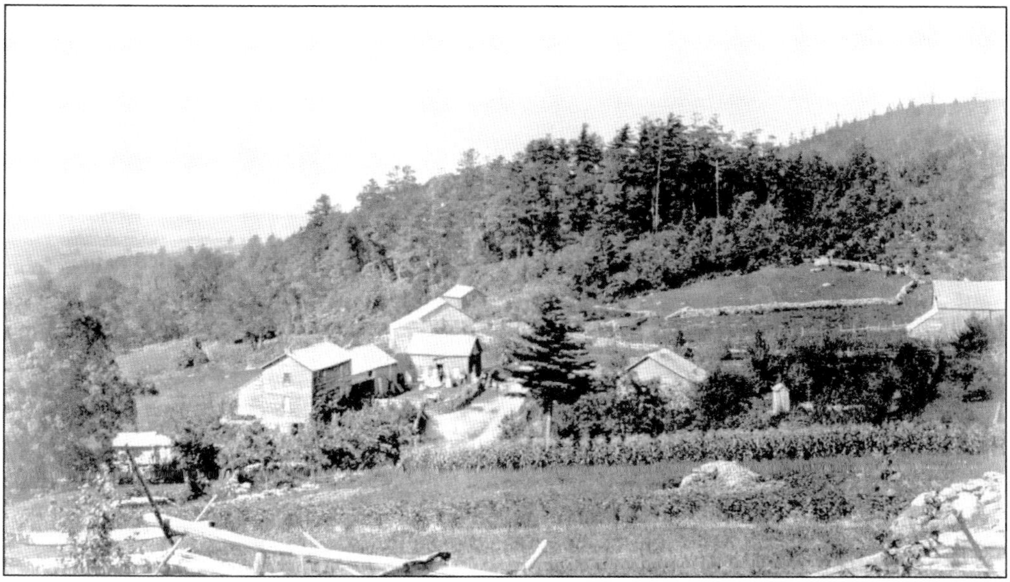

Little remains in the Pittstown State Forest today of the once-thriving Agan and Phillips farms (above) in Ward Hollow near Grafton's northern boundary. The old Francis West house (below), later owned by the Agan family, and in the 20th century by noted author Granville Hicks, survives today on Shaver Pond Road. Much of this landscape is wooded today, and has become part of Grafton Lakes State Park.

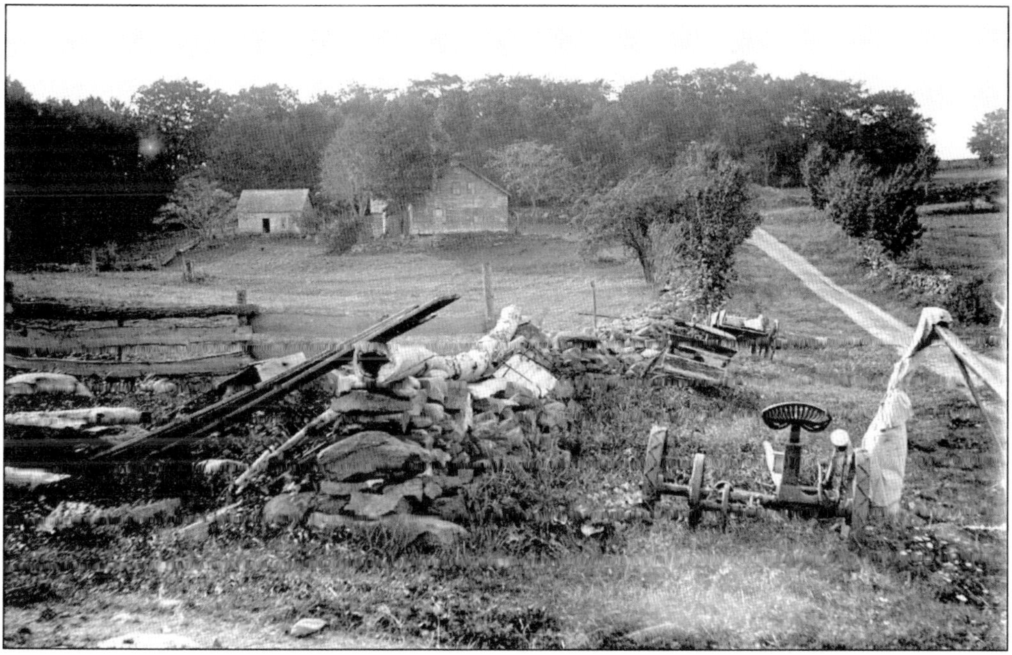

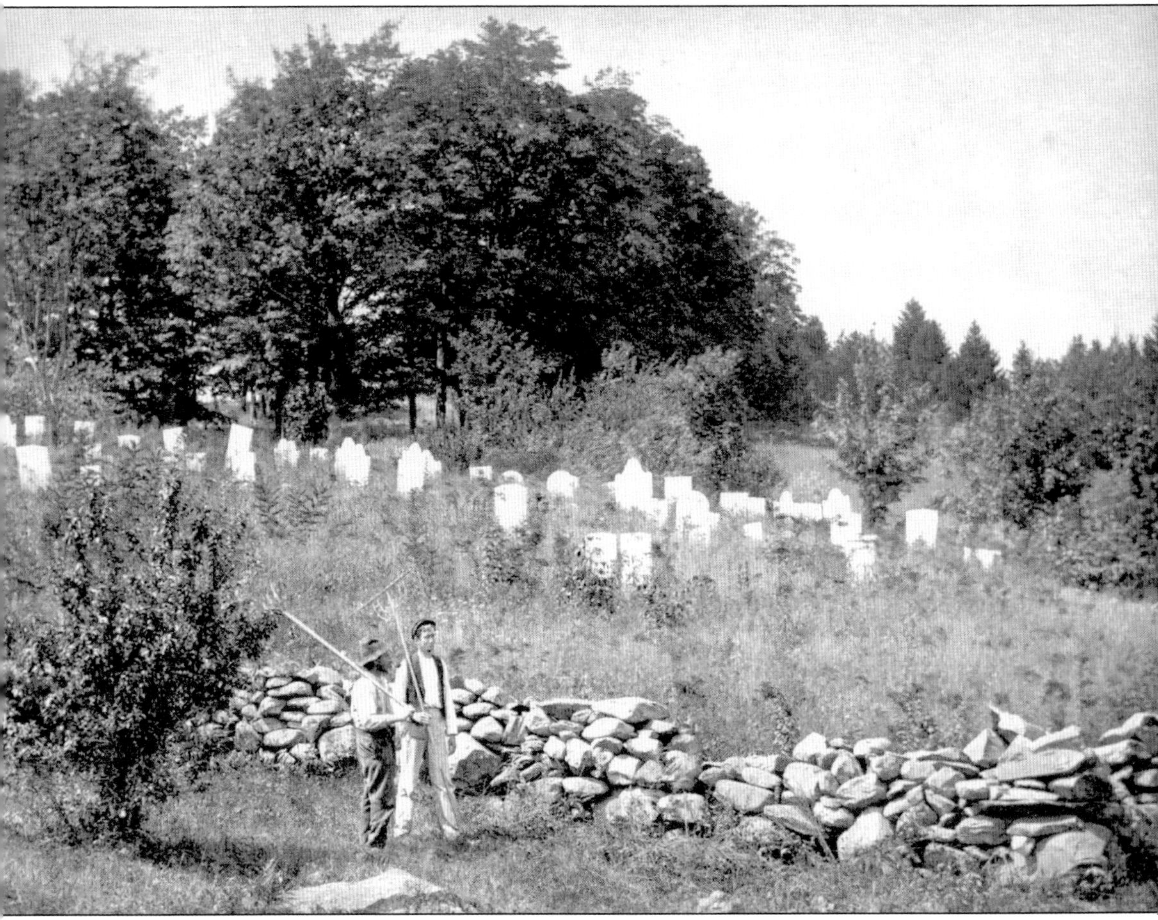

The early Scriven or Ziba Hewitt burying ground is well maintained today at the intersection of Crandall and Hagen Roads in the eastern part of Grafton. The latter road is part of the former Owen Road. The Scriven family and other early settlers from New England followed this road up the mountain west of Petersburgh when they emigrated to Grafton in the years following the American Revolution.

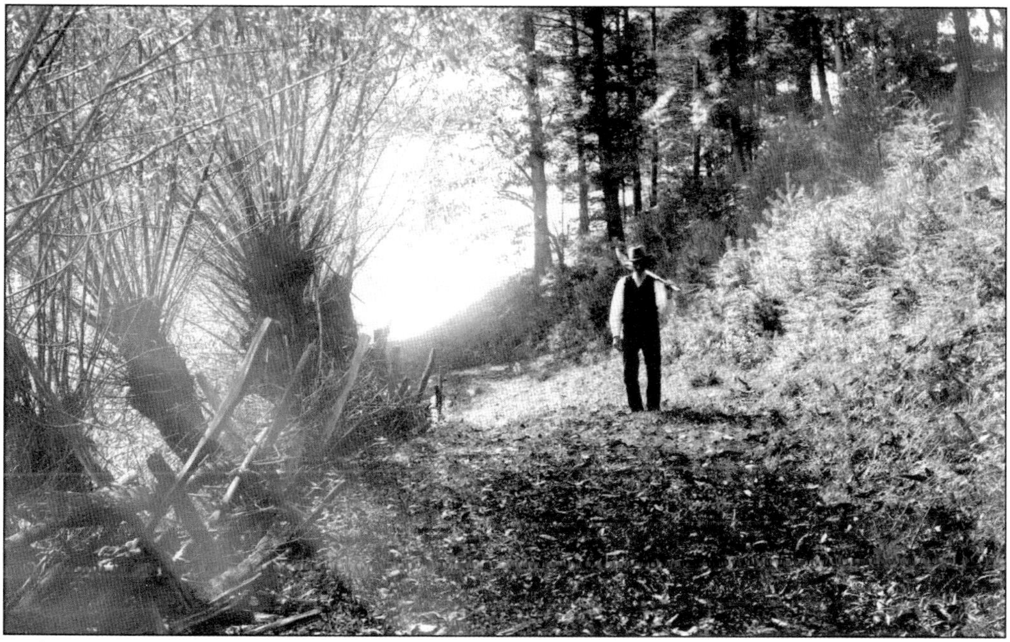

Early morning sun highlights a farmer carrying a shovel along an old road (above) near Shaver Pond in Grafton, then known as the Beltway, now found in Grafton Lakes State Park. The simple wooden queen-post truss bridge (below) spanned Dill Brook in Petersburgh near its junction with the Little Hoosic River.

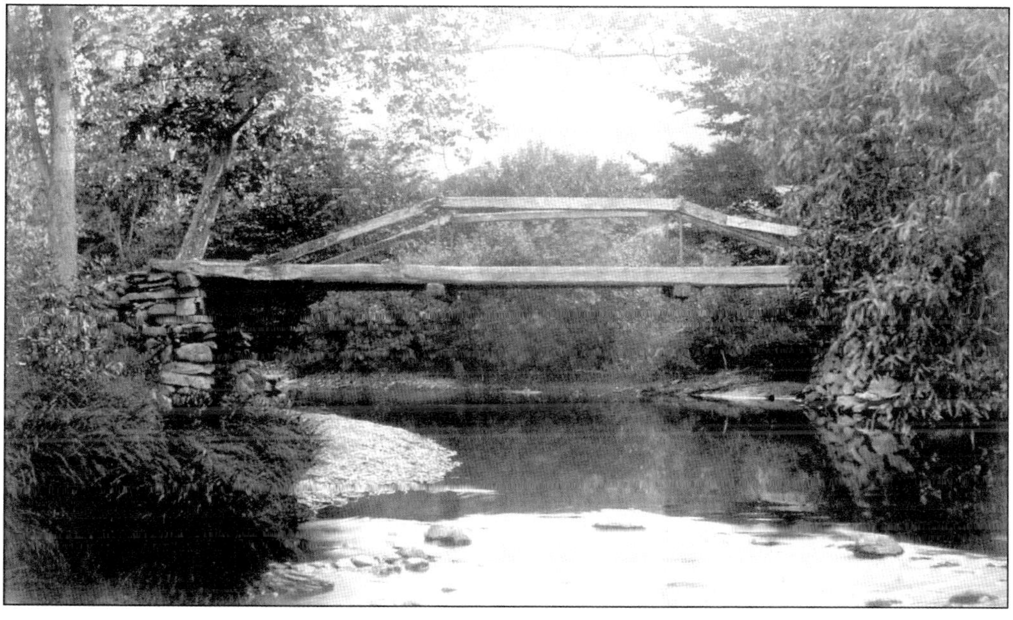

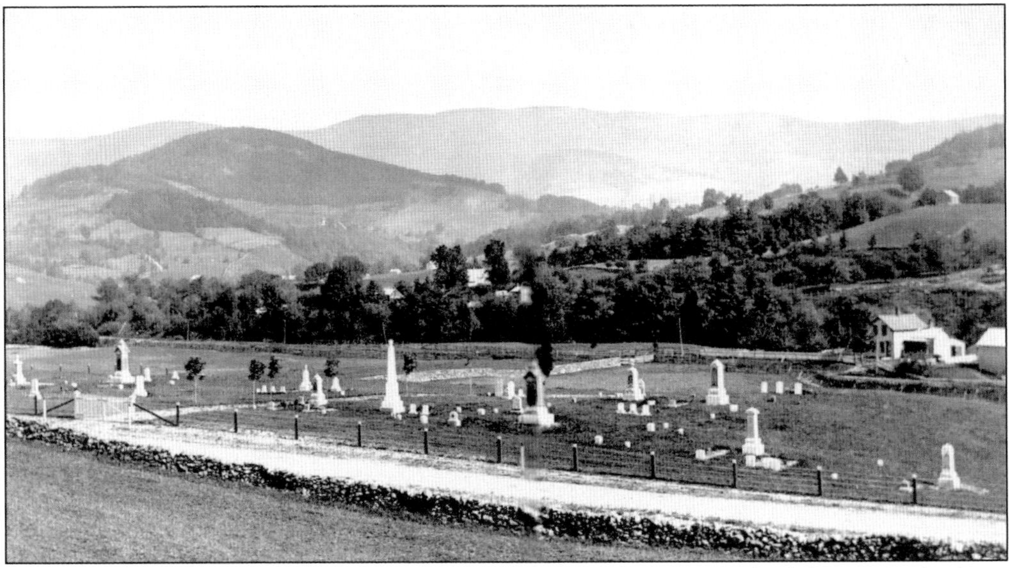

Two cemeteries in use today in the Taconic Valley have scenic mountain backdrops. Meadowlawn Cemetery in Petersburgh (above) was established in the middle of the 19th century, while the Berlin Community Cemetery (below) incorporated an earlier Baptist church burying ground.

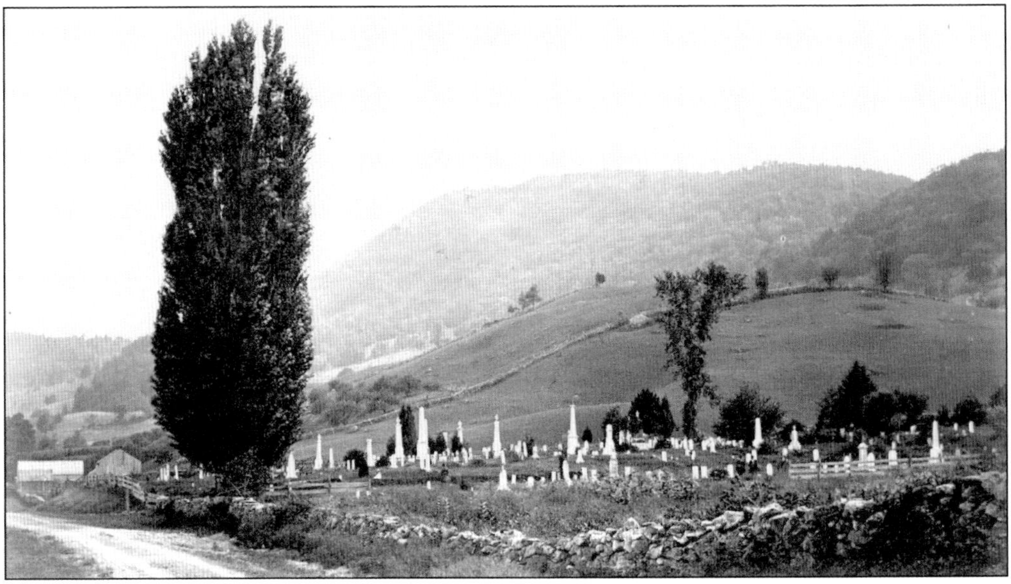

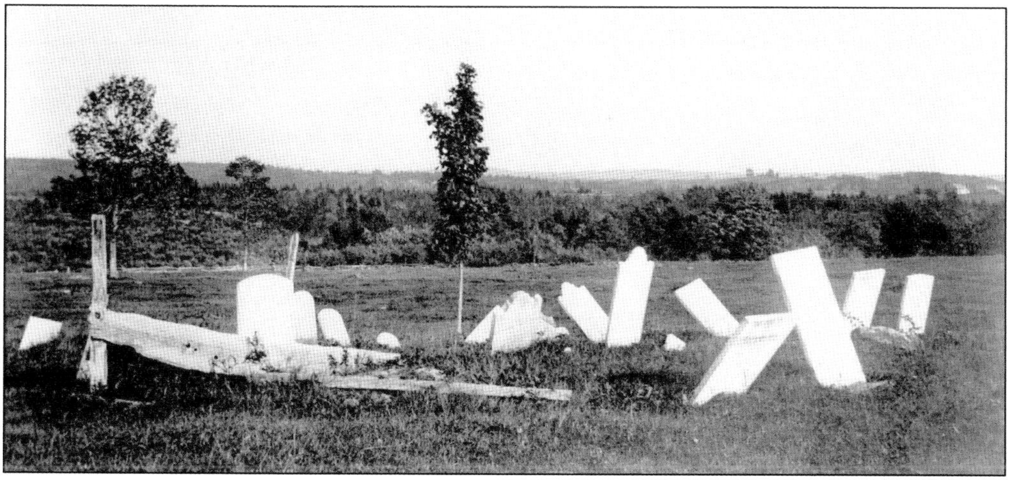

The private burial ground of the Francis West family in Grafton (above), now part of Grafton Lakes State Park, has been surrounded by second-growth forest. The view below atop the flat Rensselaer Plateau appears to show the early Littlefield burial ground on Old Road in Grafton.

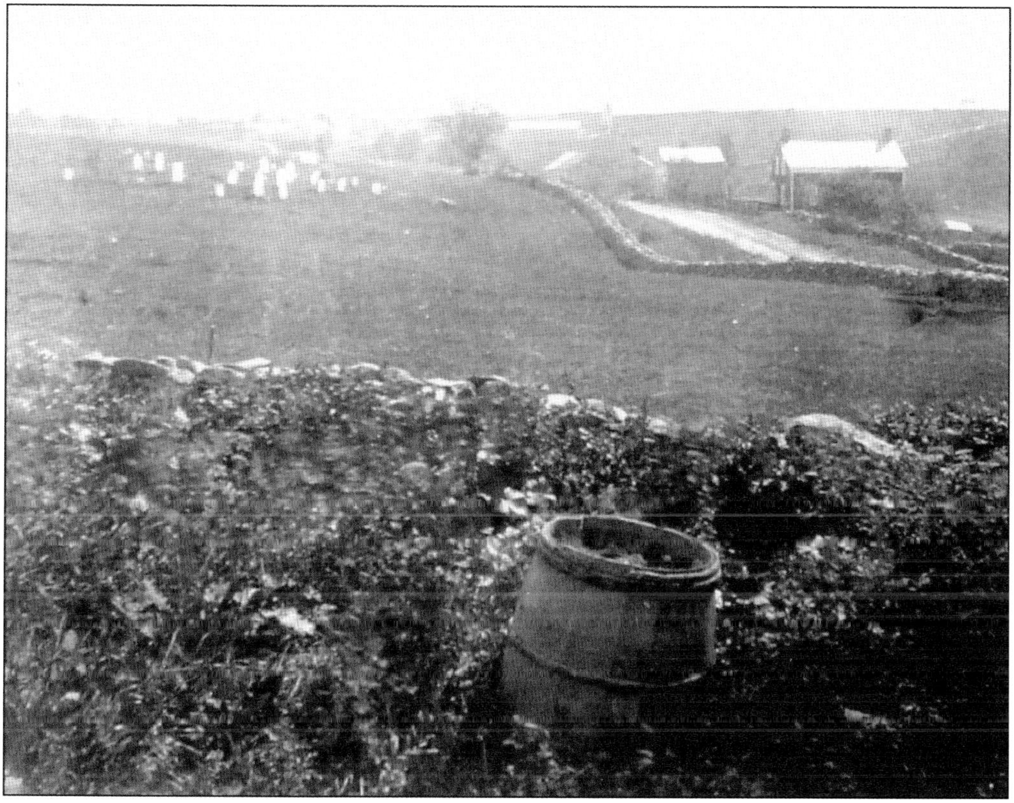

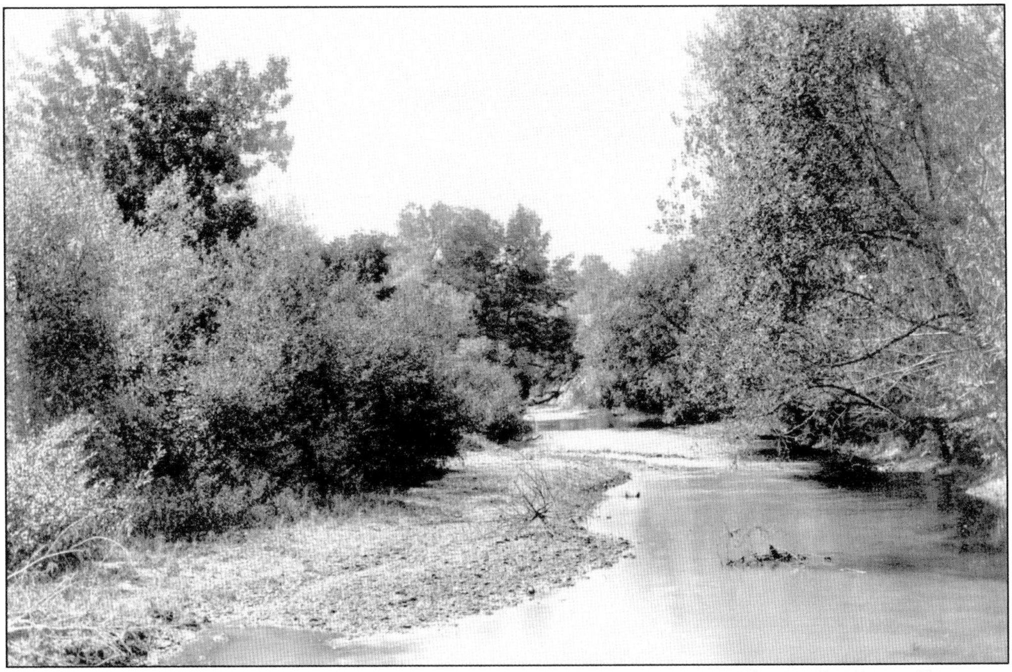

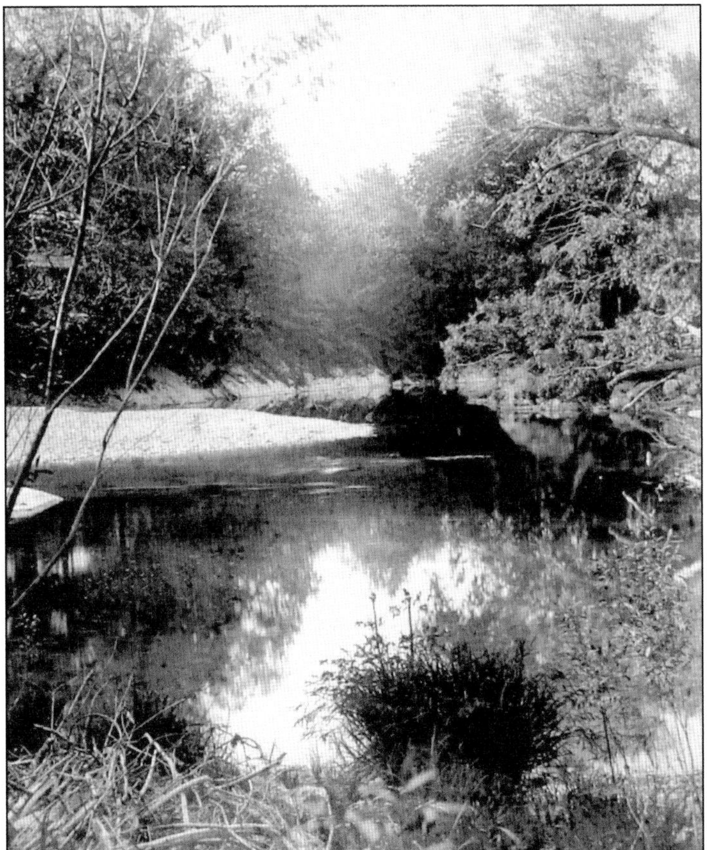

The Little Hoosic River, for a long time favored by fishermen, appears very placid at low summer water levels in these views taken between Petersburgh and North Petersburgh.

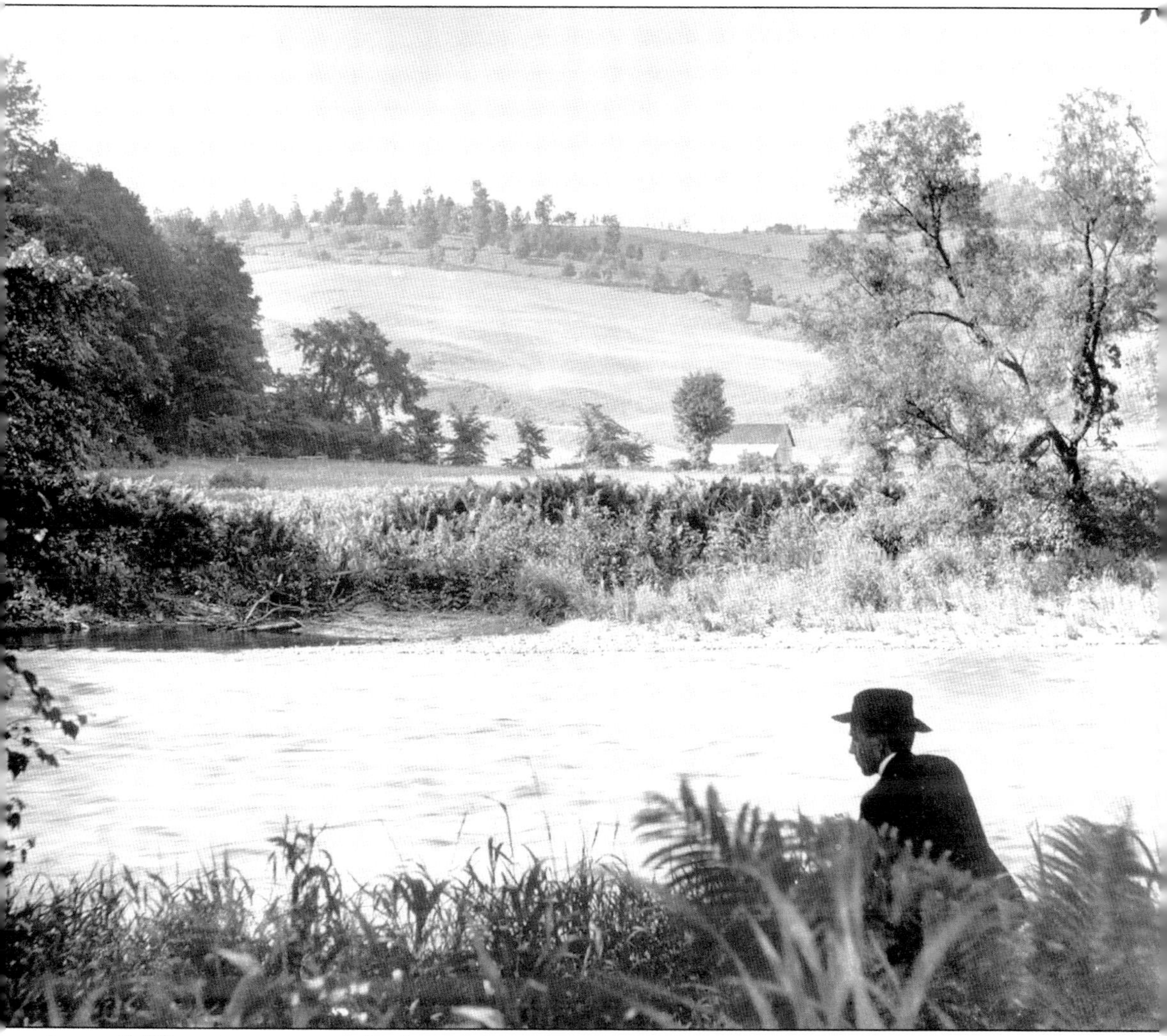

James E. West also captured the larger Hoosic River, a canoeing as well as a fishing stream, in the vicinity of North Petersburgh and Hoosick, during the summer.

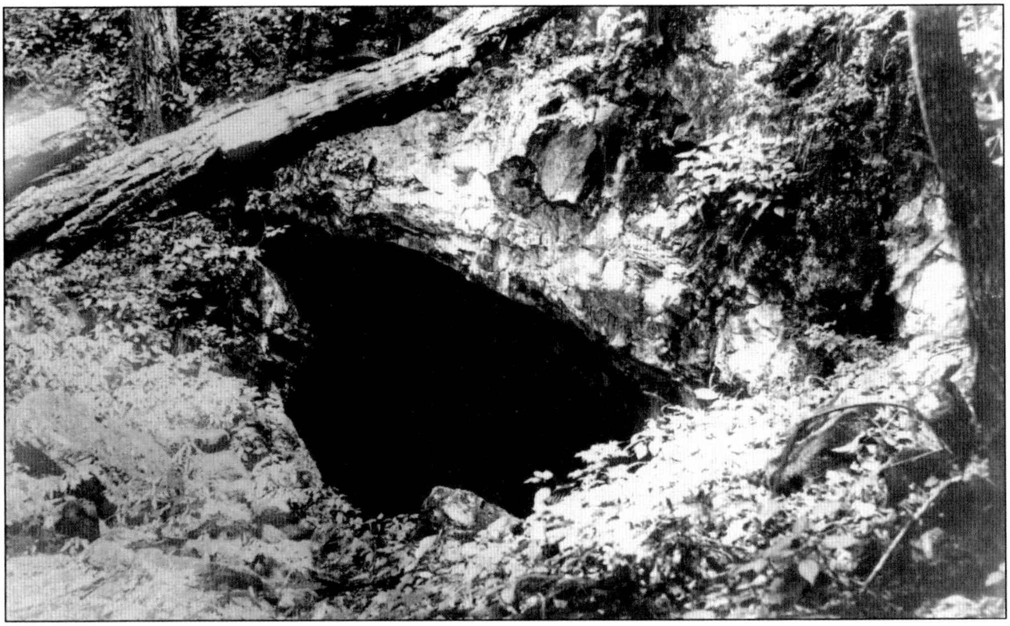

James E. West enjoyed capturing the area's natural wonders with his camera. Bear's Den (above), the most accessible of Berlin's two caverns, has been preserved by a local land trust. The waterfalls on Kronk Brook in nearby Mattison Hollow (below) are found along side a public hiking trail in a protected state forest preserve.

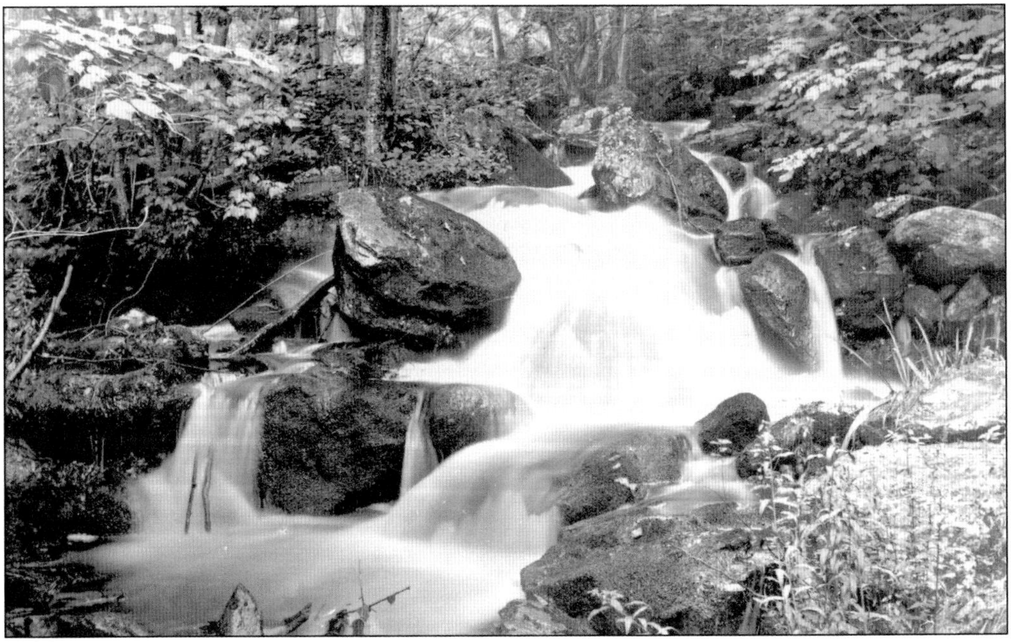

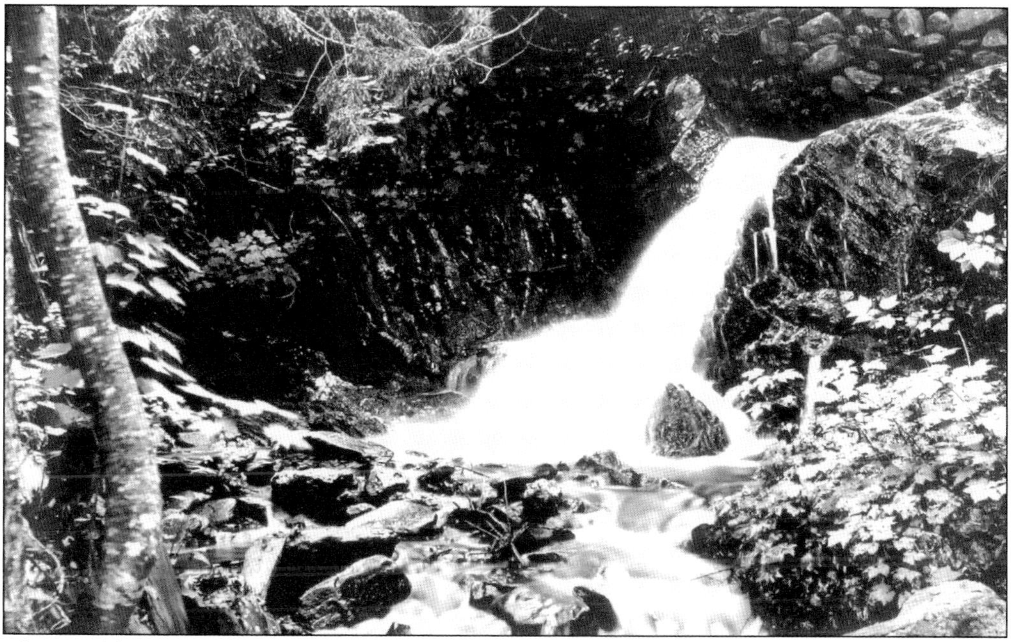

The small but scenic waterfalls (above), known as Davis Cascade, are found in Satterlee Hollow in Berlin. The tiny waterfalls on Coon Brook (below) can be seen from Toad Point Road just to the north in Petersburgh.

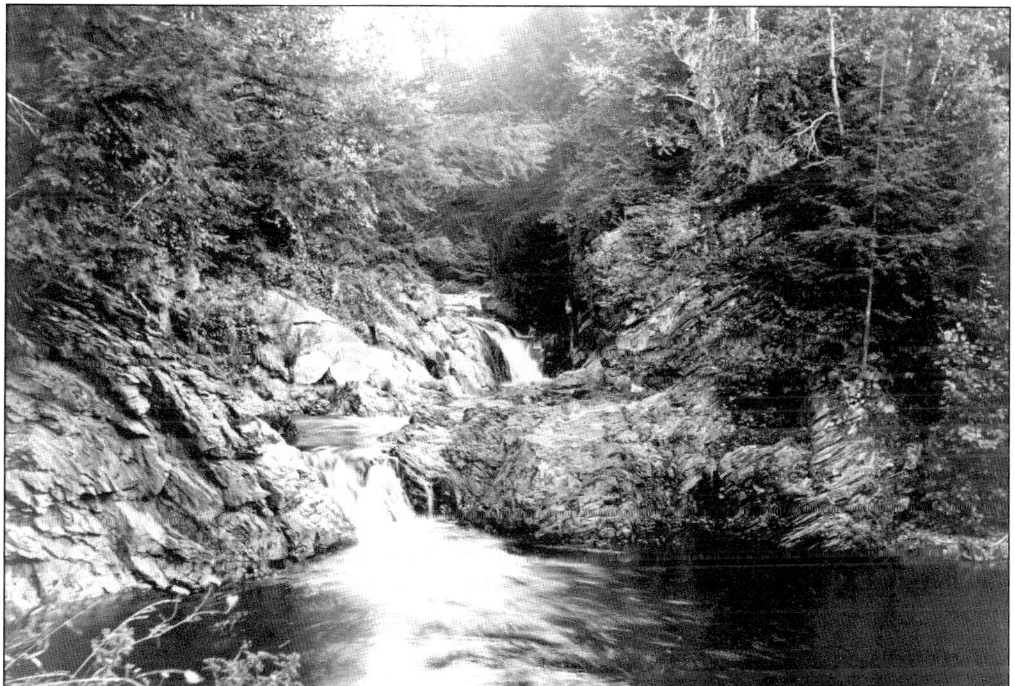

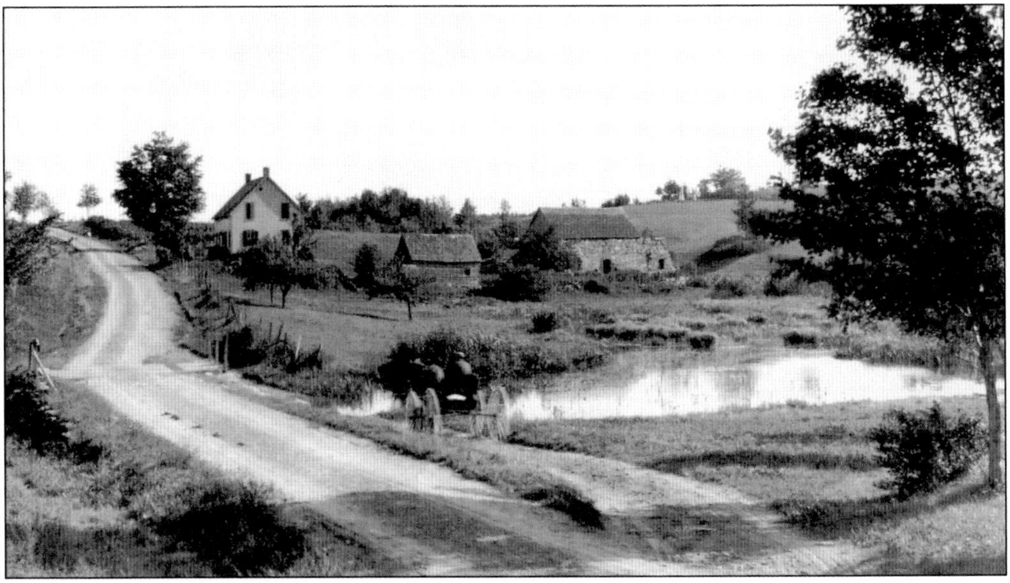

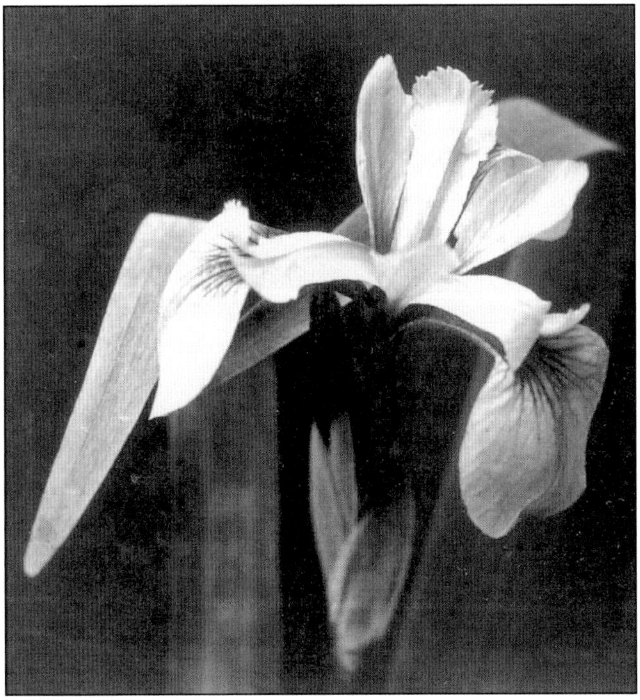

Snyder's Bridge in Grafton (above) was located on North Road; this view looking north shows the ruins of the old Van Rensselaer gristmill behind the house and barn. The blue flag iris (Iris versicolor) blooms in summer in many wetlands in the region, such as the marsh along Grist Mill Brook just above the bridge.

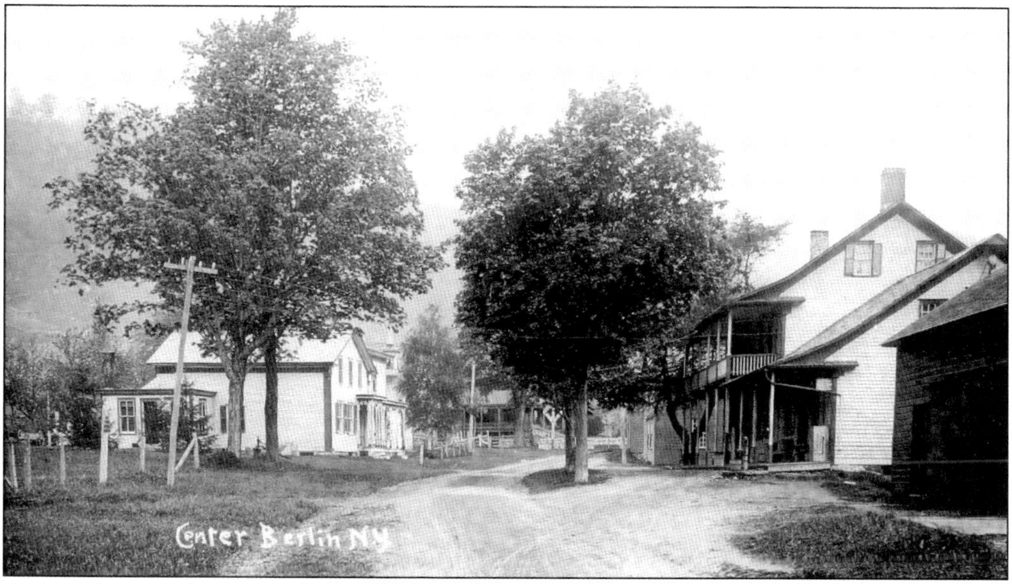

A few of the old homes in Center Berlin shown in these two photographs stand today, but the appearance of the hamlet was dramatically altered by the widening of State Route 22 in the 1960s.

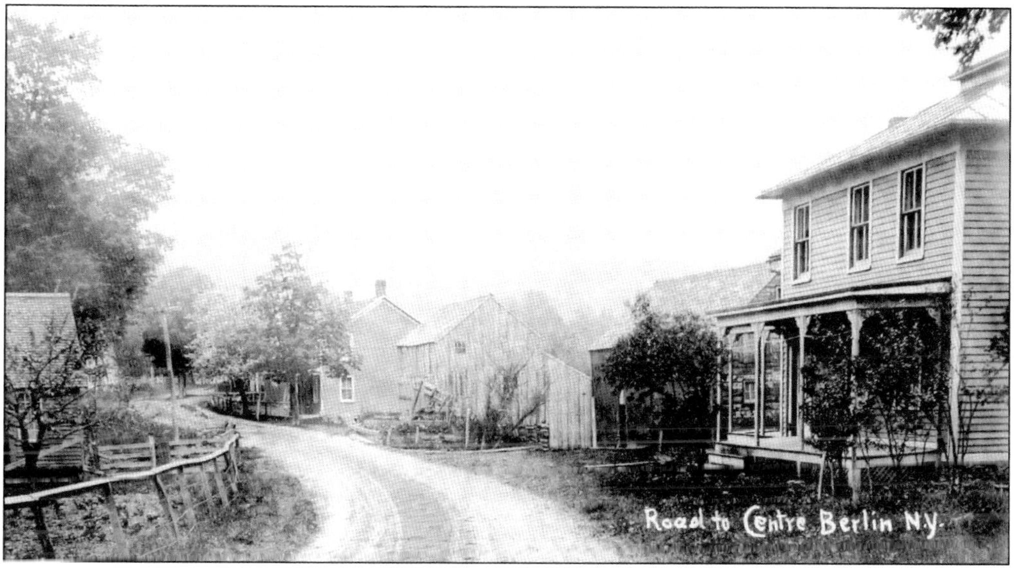

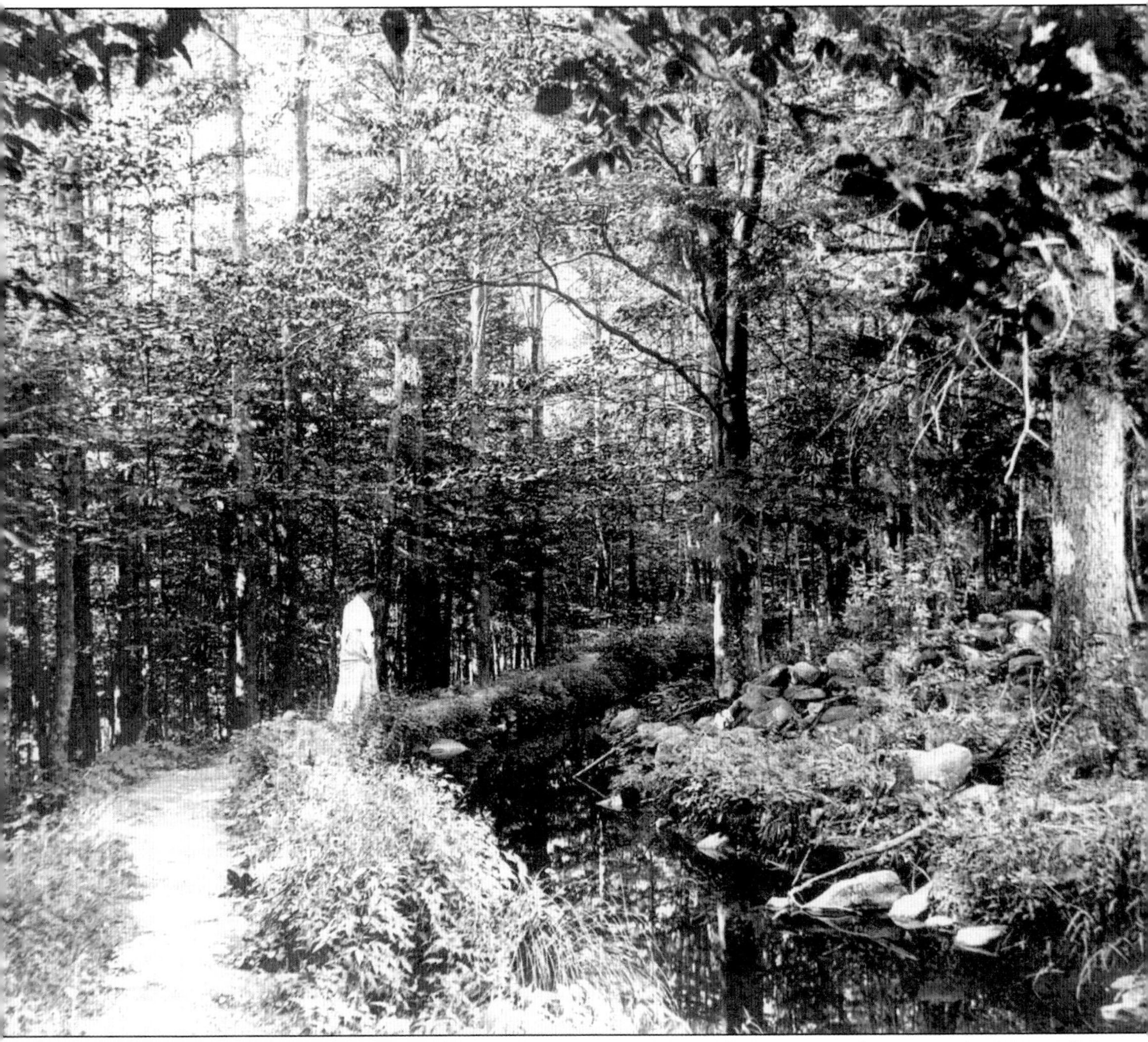

The photographer's wife, Kate West, takes a peaceful stroll down a path alongside Grist Mill Brook in Grafton, just west of Snyder's Bridge.

Three

LAKES AND PONDS

While only four water bodies of any consequence are found in Berlin and none exist in Petersburgh, the mountainous Rensselaer Plateau in Grafton is home to a number of scenic small lakes and ponds, which attracted many summer visitors 100 years ago, when hotels as well as private camps flourished there.

Four picturesque natural ponds featured in these photographs, Long Pond, Mill Pond, Second Pond, and Shaver Pond, have been incorporated into Grafton Lakes State Park. These are now very popular with bathers, boaters, fishermen, and nature lovers alike. James E. West typically included his daughter or other young people in composing his views of lakes and ponds.

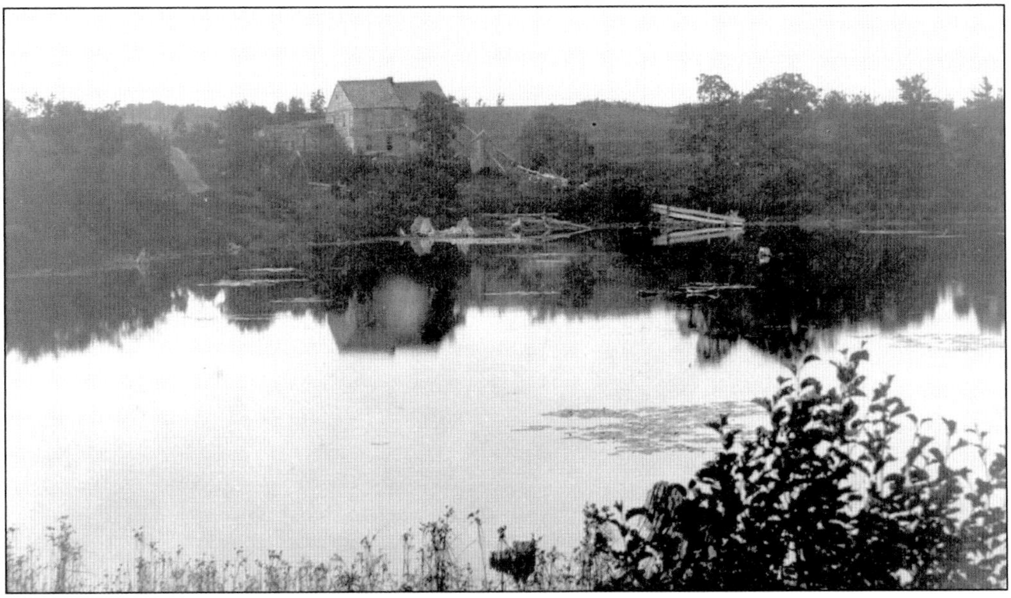

Mill Pond, just north of Grafton Center, was created in the 1840s when a small natural lake was dammed to provide a better water supply for the gristmill. The scene at dusk (above) shows the old Garner Stuart house, long since destroyed. The view below, taken on a rainy summer day, looks south over Mill Pond toward the village.

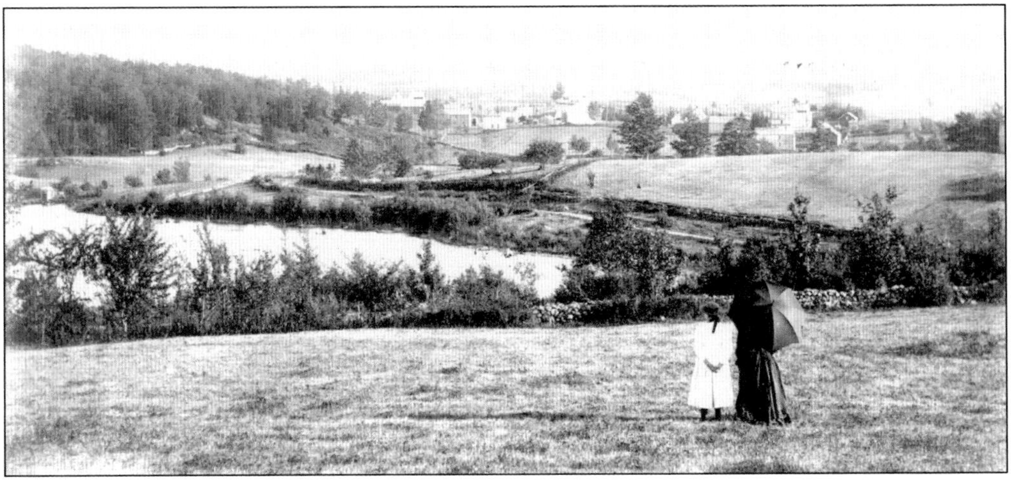

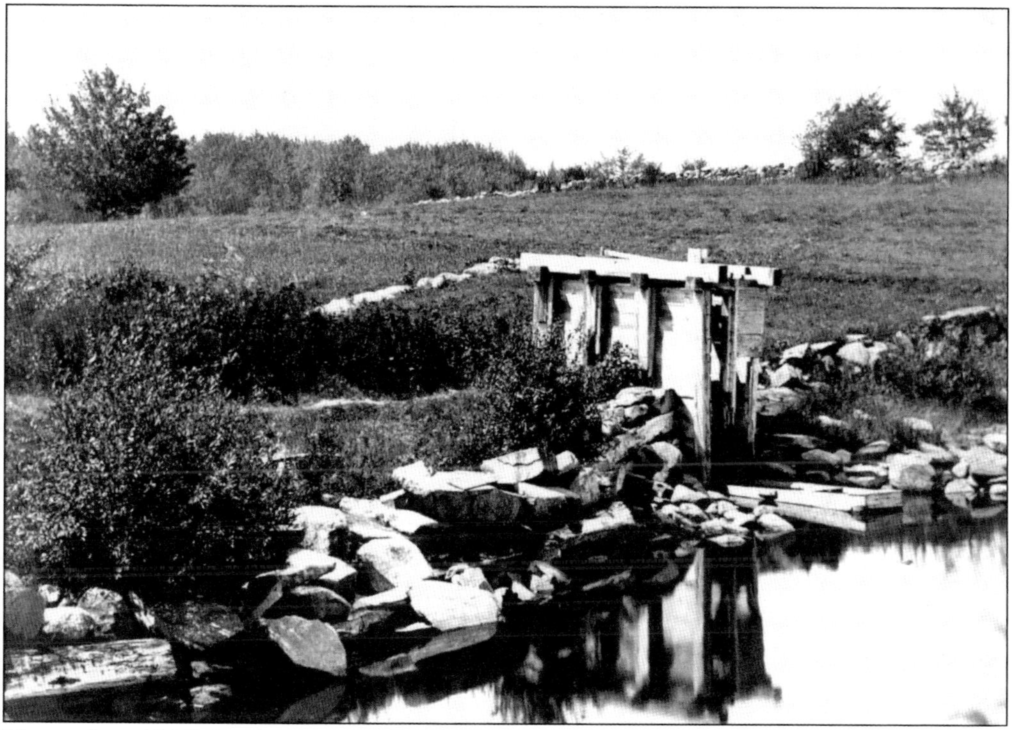

The outlet of Mill Pond was controlled by a primitive wooden sluice gate (above). The early gristmill itself (below) had been abandoned and was in ruins by the late 1800s.

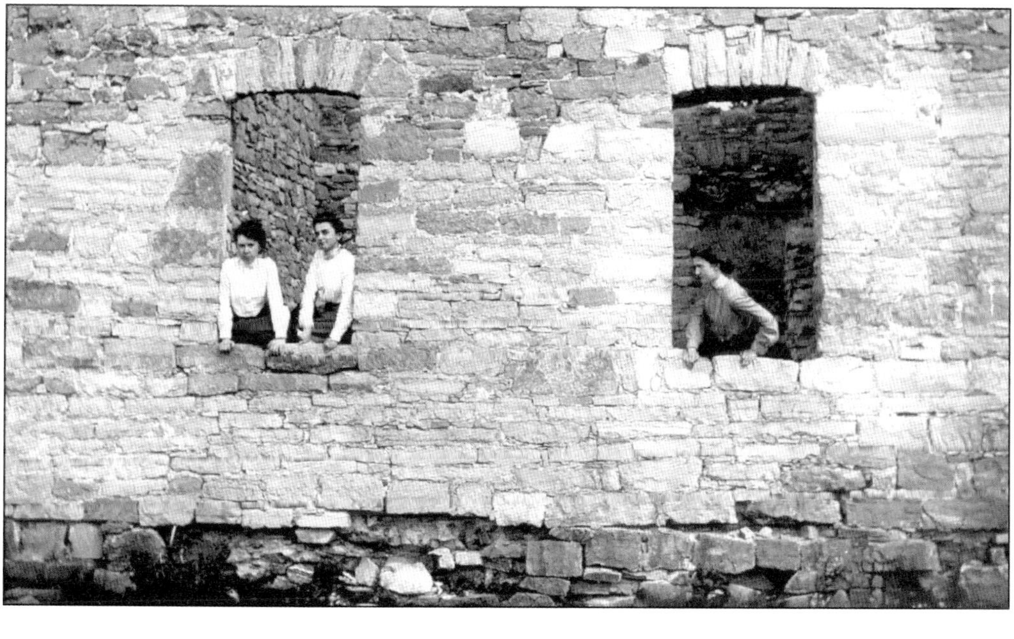

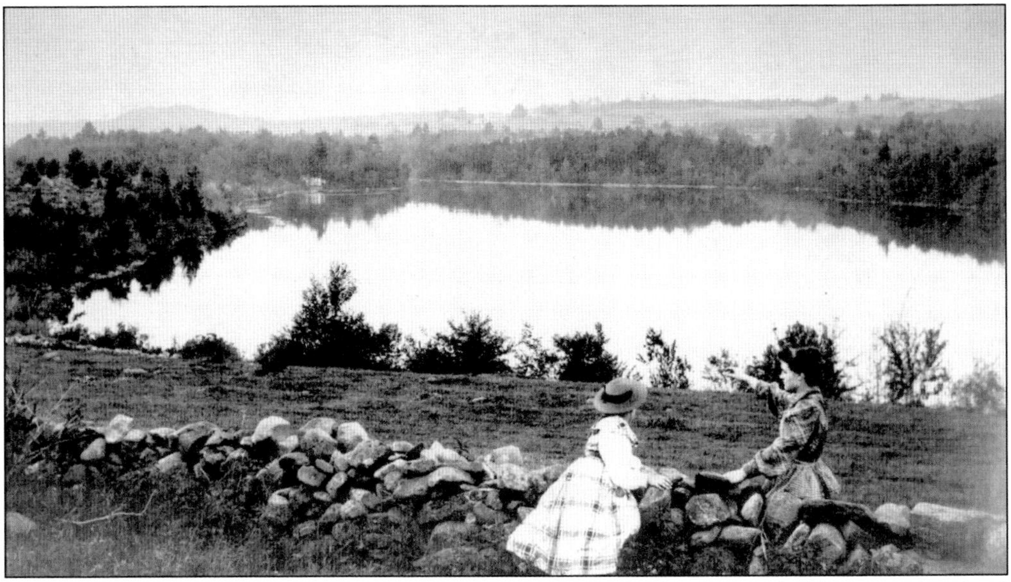

Second Pond, just upstream from Mill Pond, was a natural lake surrounded by open farmland when the photograph above was taken. In the scene below, boaters hurry to avoid an impending summer storm on Second Pond.

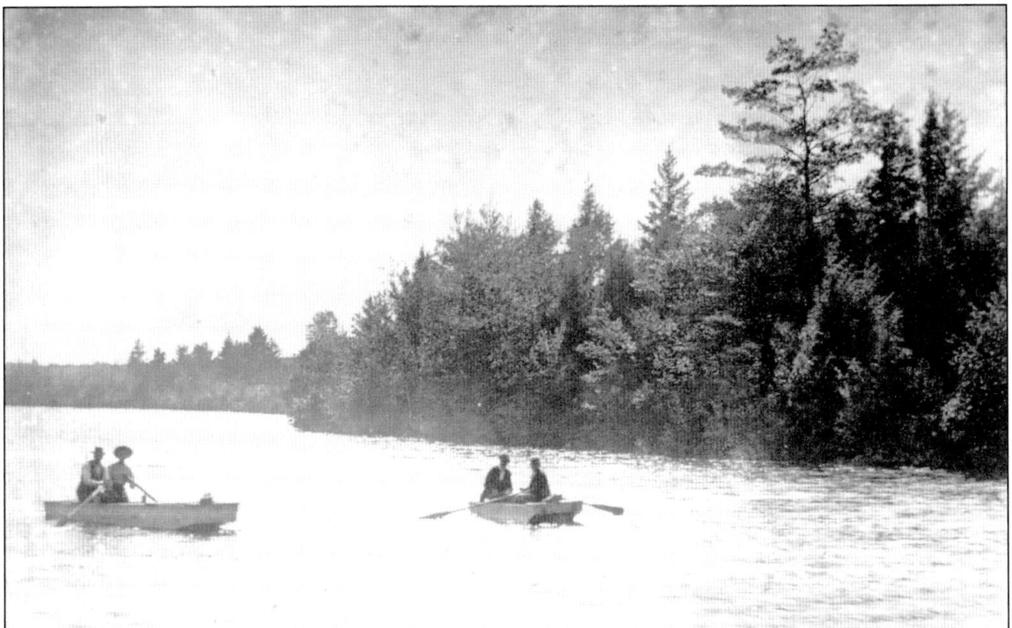

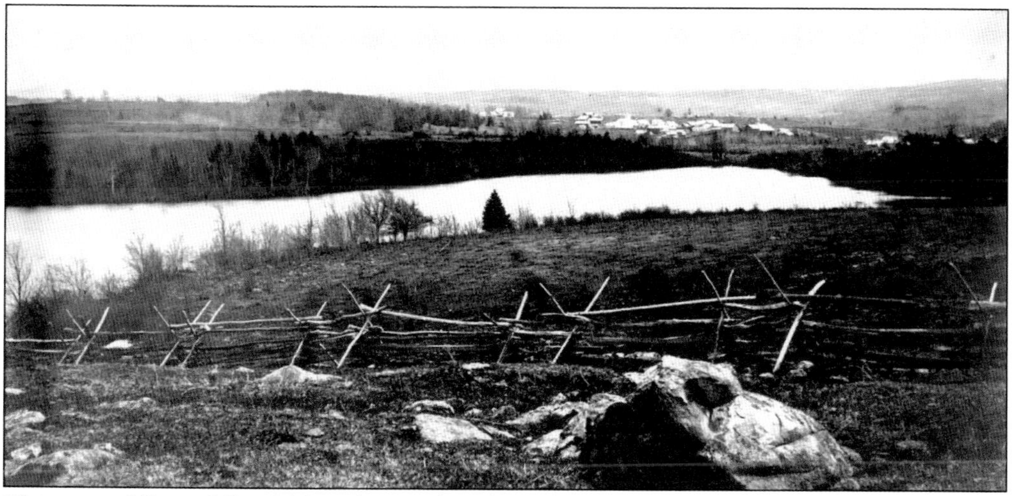

This view of Second Pond (above) was taken from the pasture of the J. A. Scriven farm looking south over Mill Pond toward Grafton Center. While Second Pond was a natural lake, the water from its outlet (below) was controlled to maintain a stable water level in Mill Pond downstream.

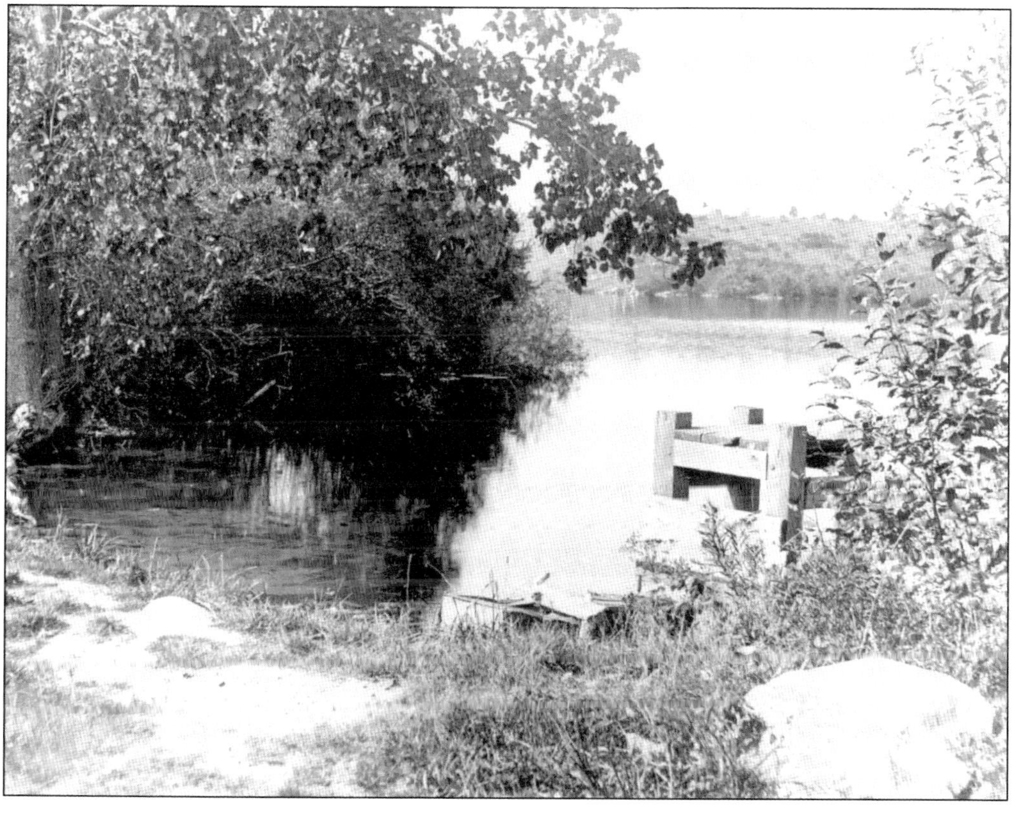

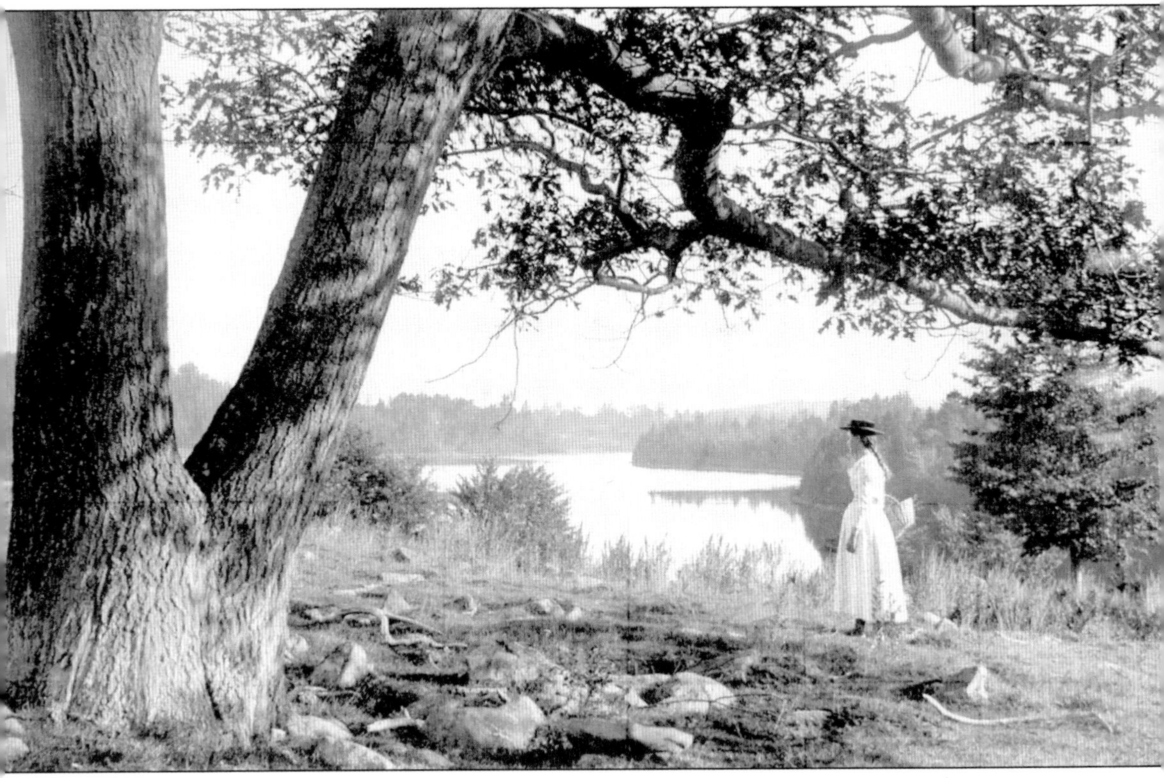

The photographer's daughter, Maude, pauses under a large red oak tree while taking an autumn hike along the south side of Shaver Pond, the most unspoiled of the water bodies found in Grafton Lakes State Park.

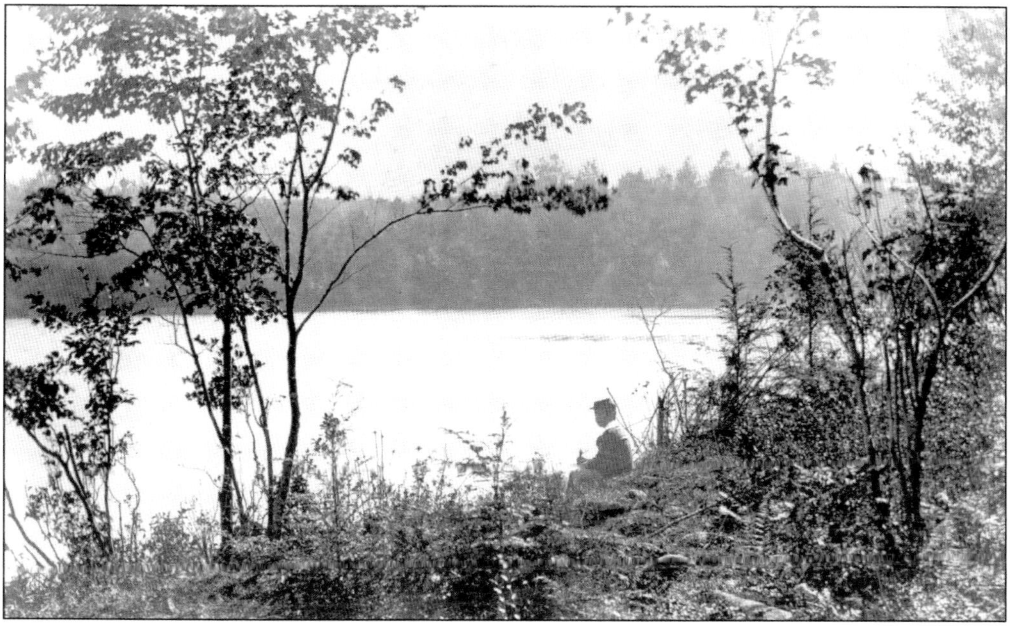

Shaver Pond, a deep lake with a rocky bottom, with no buildings on its shoreline, is a favorite of fishermen and naturalists alike. Seated on the shore is nine-year-old Anderson Scriven (above). Maude West and her friend, Jerry Scriven, Anderson's father, stroll along the south shore on their way to a peaceful picnic.

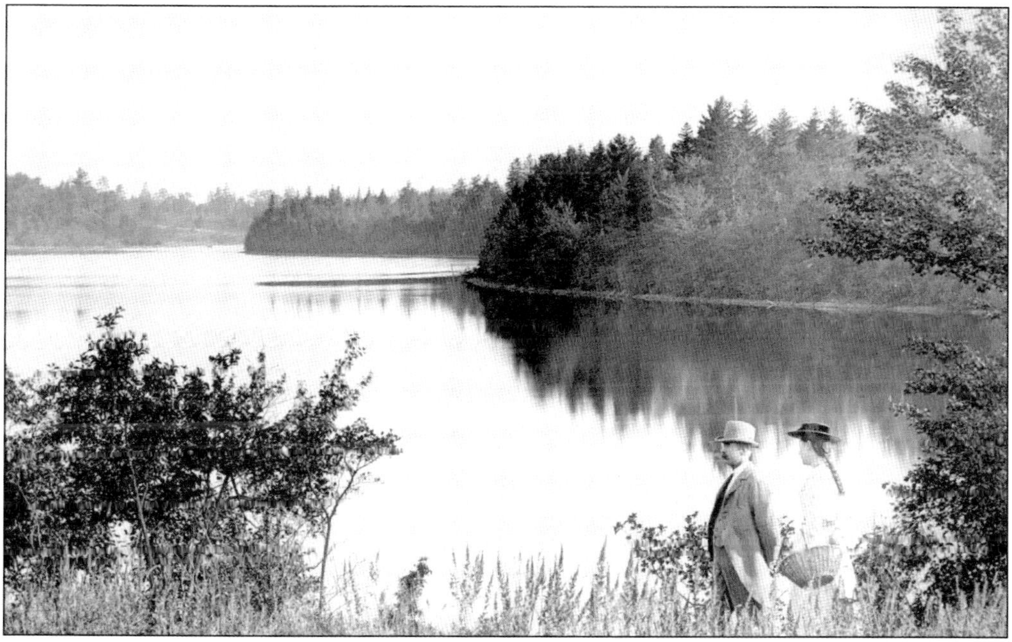

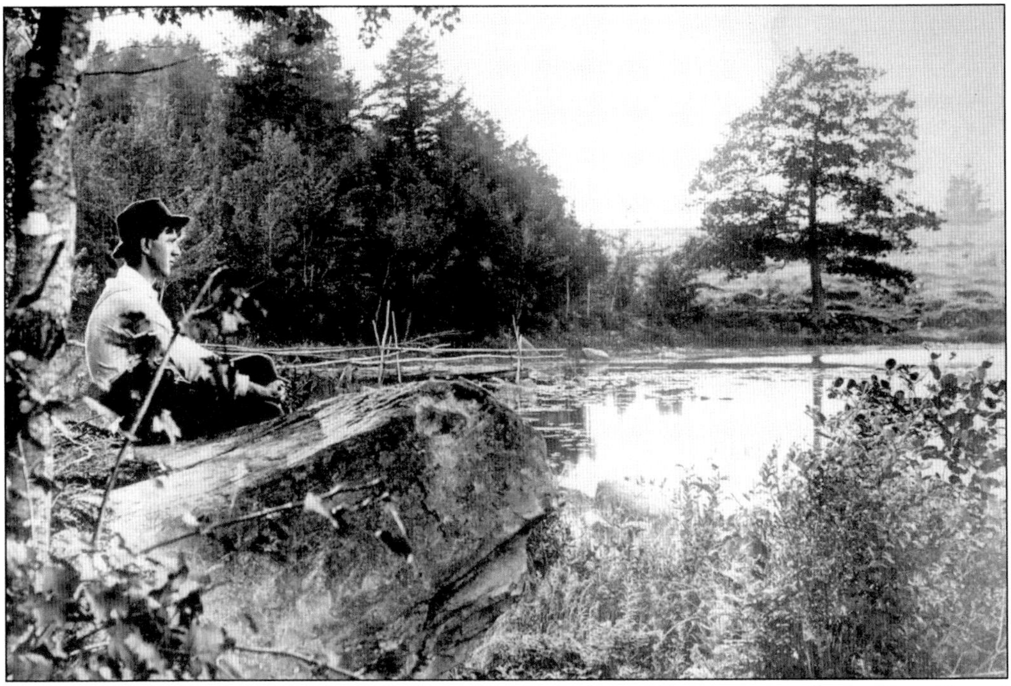

Young Harry Lewis (above) admires Shaver Pond in the early morning stillness. Burt Bristol (below) stands among Steeple-bush (Spiraea tomentosa) at the marshy inlet at the north end of the lake.

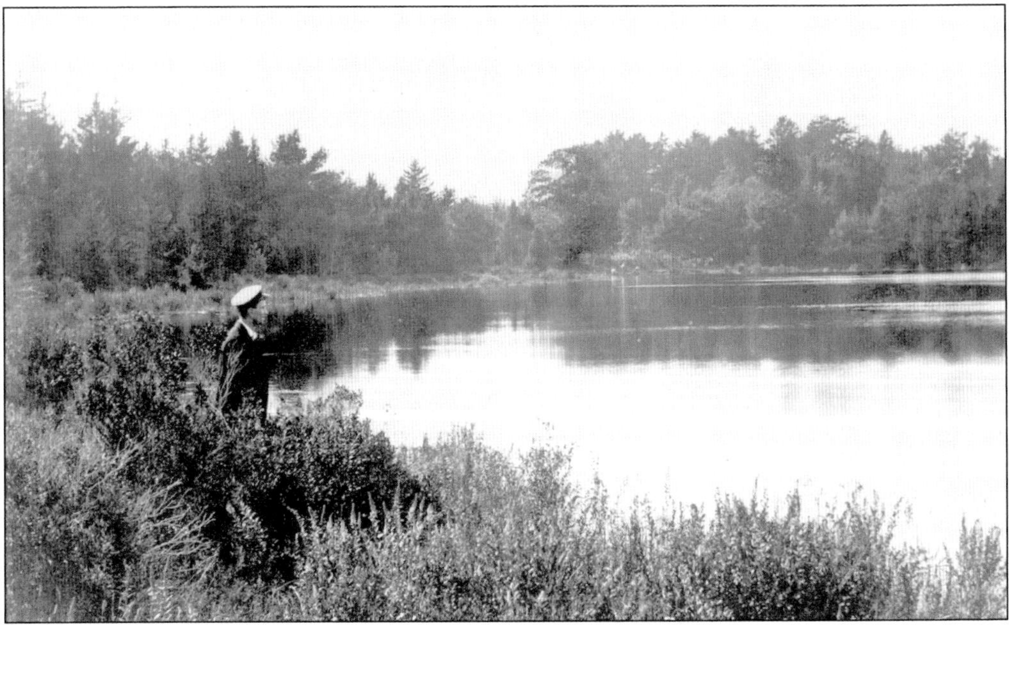

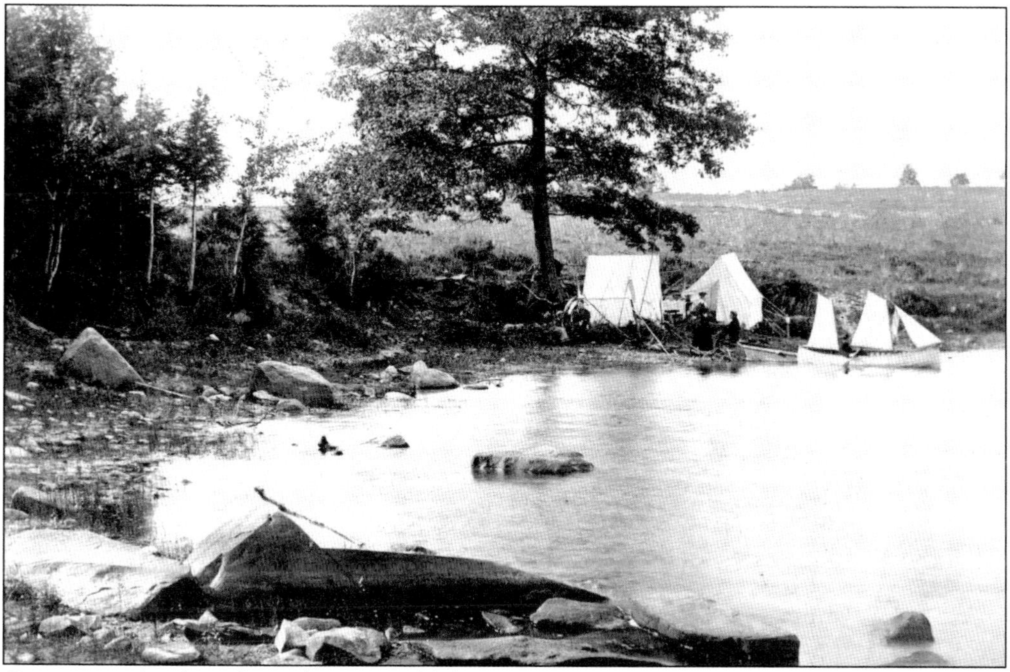

Camping and sailing along Shaver Pond (above) were popular activities for tourists and Grafton residents as well. "Black Rock" (below), an exposed outcropping on the east side of the lake, was a well-known observation point.

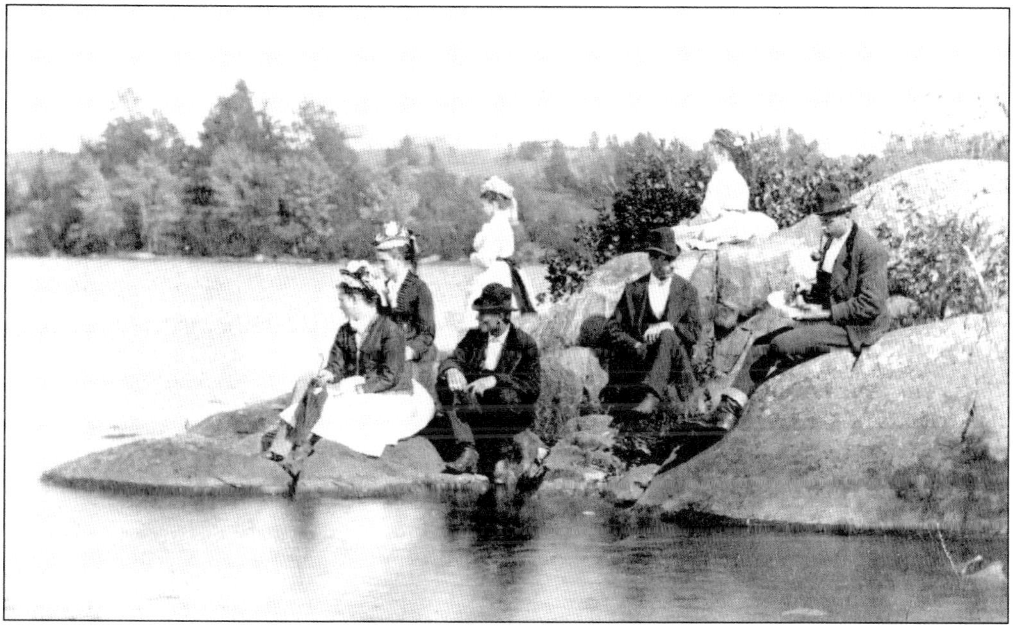

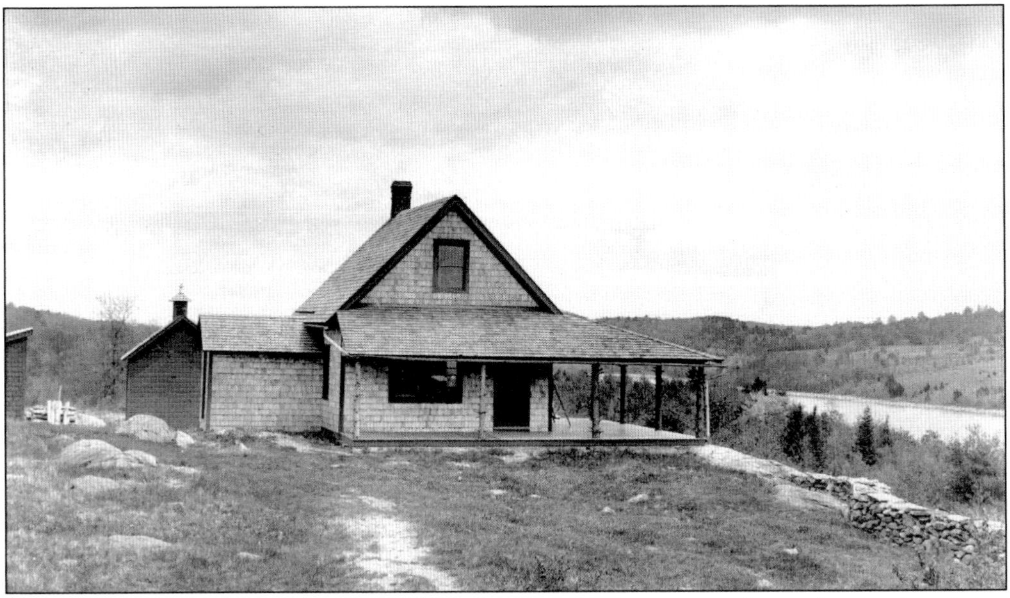

Tibbits Lodge and Chapel (above) stood where the water tower is now located in Grafton Lakes State Park. Swimming in Long Pond (below) was popular around 1900, but styles of bathing attire were rather conservative at that time.

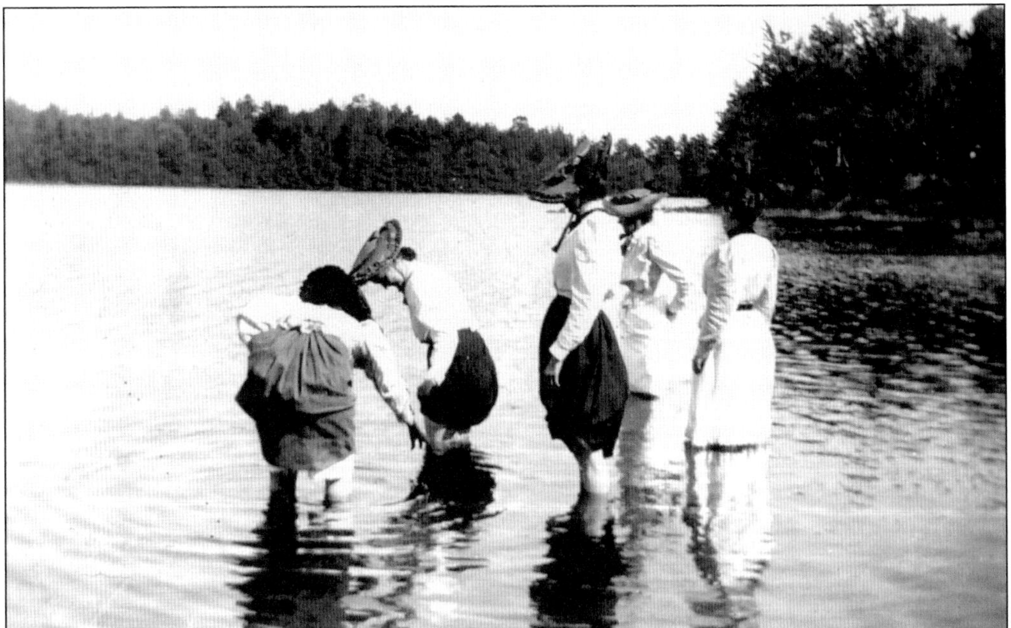

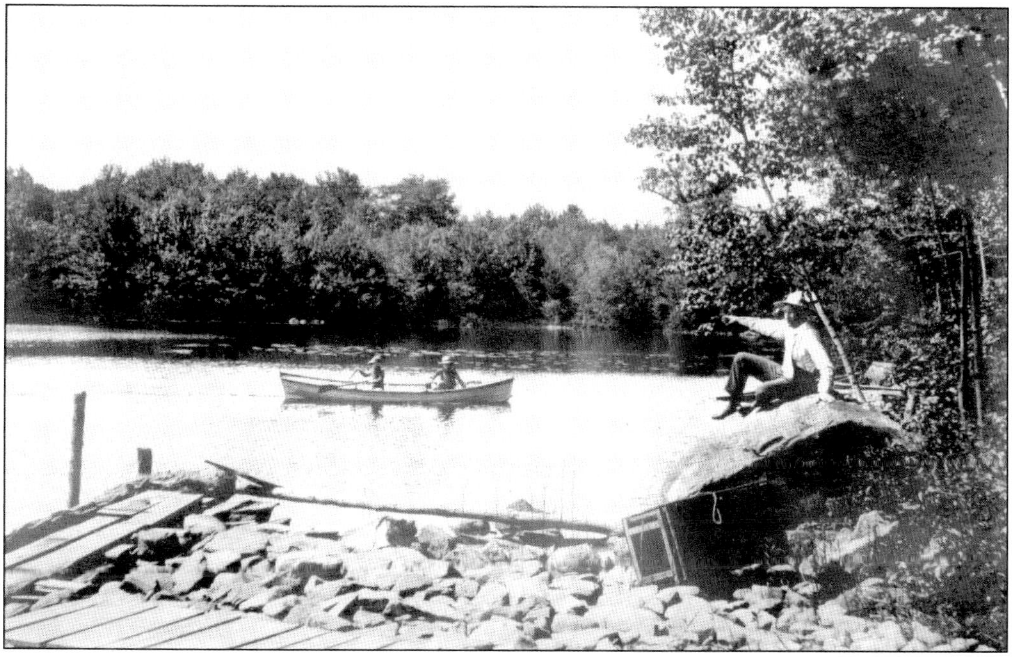

Myron West proudly observes his sons canoeing on Taconic Lake (above), while other boaters enjoy a hot, cloudless summer day on another Grafton water body, Hayner Pond, now known as Forest Lake.

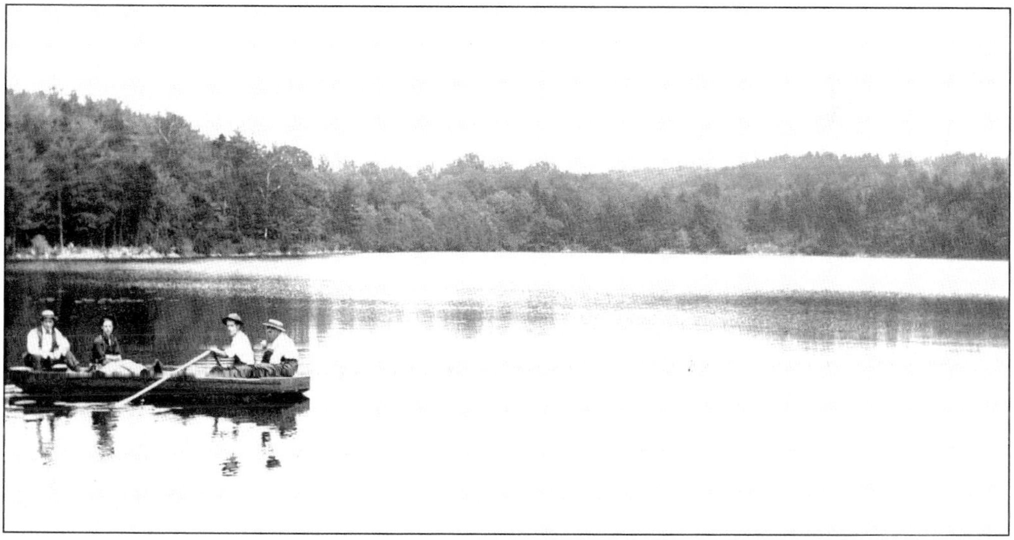

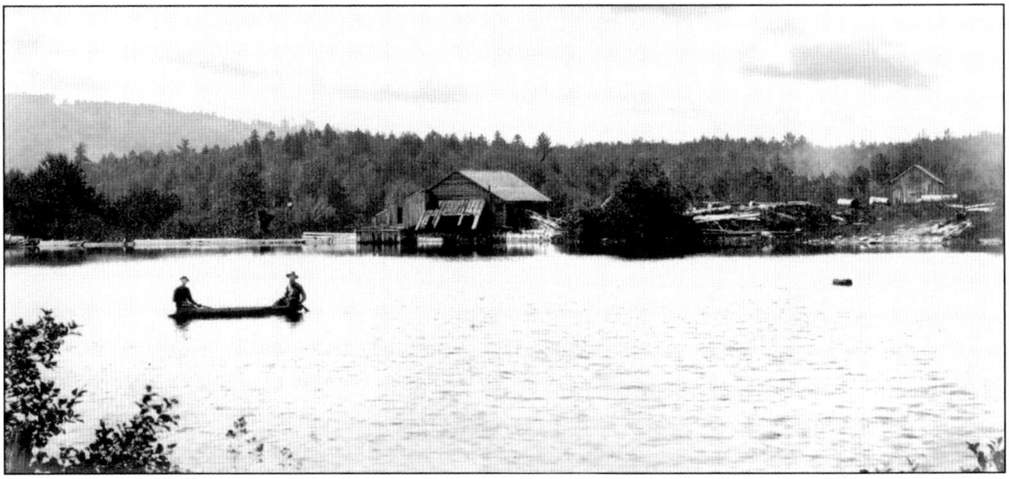

Only the foundation survives today of the sawmill located at the outlet of Cranberry Pond (above), a pristine mountain lake in the southern part of Grafton bordered by a floating bog mat. James E. West captured beautiful reflections at dusk on a placid Mill Pond (below).

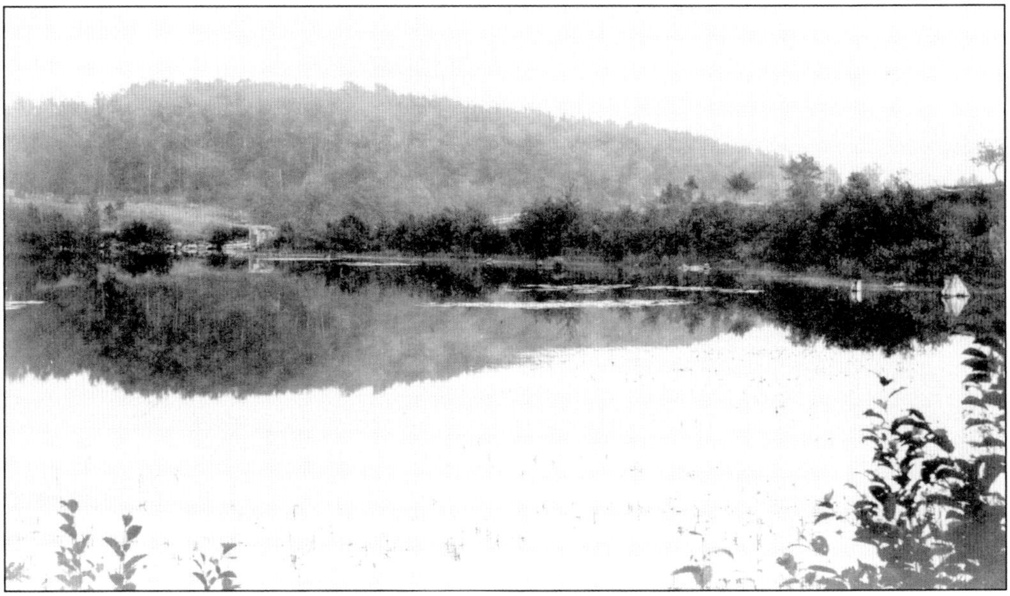

Four

People and Their Homes

Like most photographers of his era, James E. West's primary source of income was the production of individual and family studio portraits. The subjects of these posed portraits often appear stiff due to the length of the exposures necessary employing the technology of the day. He employed gelatin "dry plate" glass negatives, few of which have survived. The resulting albumen and gelatin prints were mounted on stiff cardboard and were very often inserted by their owners in albums with decorative covers. The smaller album photographs were known as "carte-de-visites" and larger ones were called "cabinet photos." Very often these bore the stamp of the photographer. During the early part of his career, West also produced small tintypes (sometimes called ferrotypes), which were printed on sheets of specially coated iron.

On occasion, he was asked to produce group portraits of families carefully posed in front of their homes, their farms, or their businesses. West also took more spontaneous portraits of family members, relatives, and friends, which allowed him greater freedom to express his creativity and artistic ability.

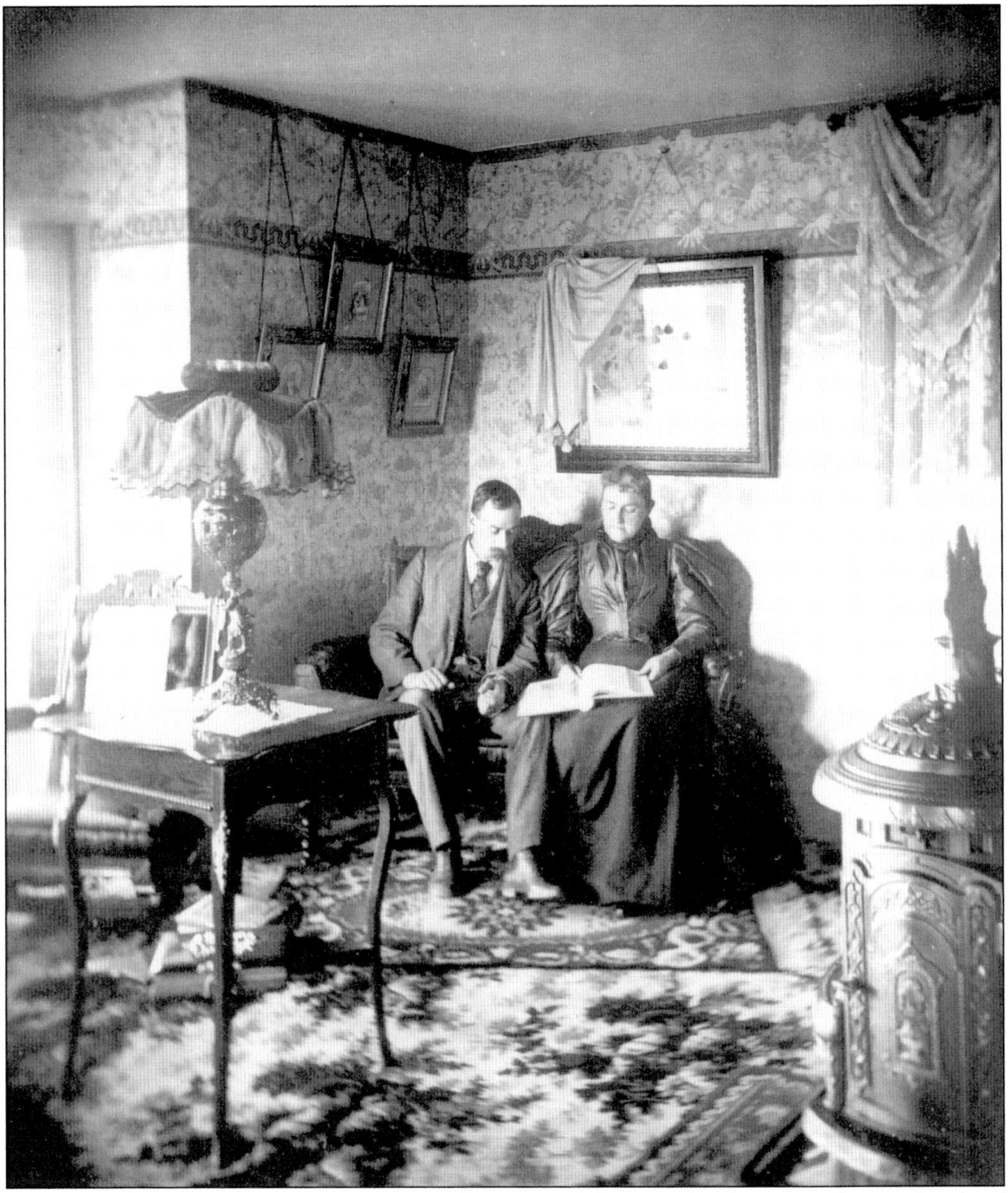

James E. West and his wife, Kate, relax in the parlor of their modest home on the south side of Main Street in Grafton, just west of the firehouse.

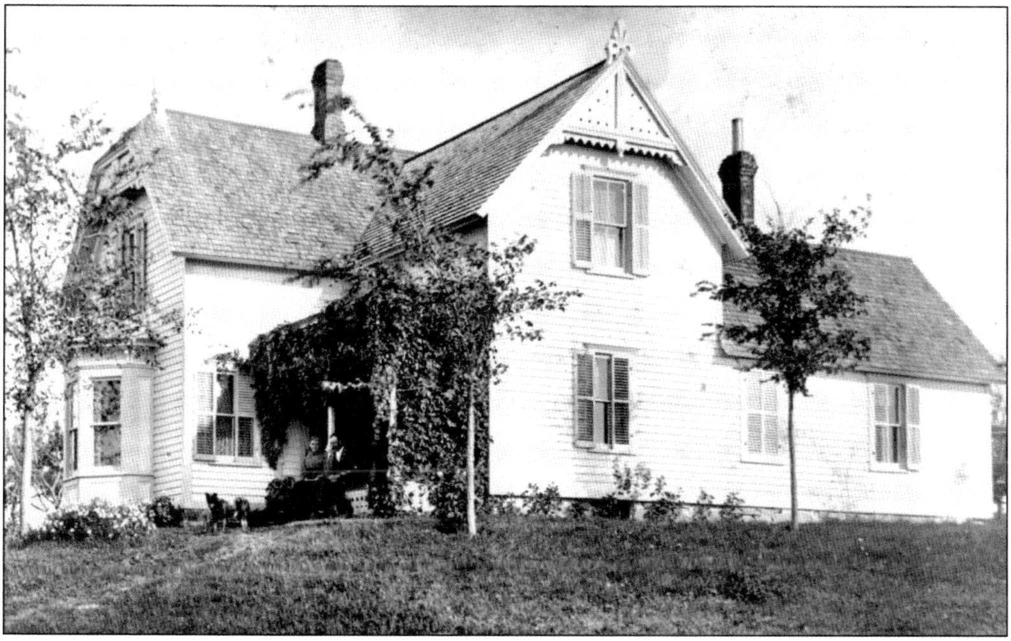

The exterior of their home appears much the same today. At one time, when the Wests lived briefly in Hoosick Falls and Whitehall, it was the residence of the photographer's sister, Sylvia, and her husband, Chester Waite.

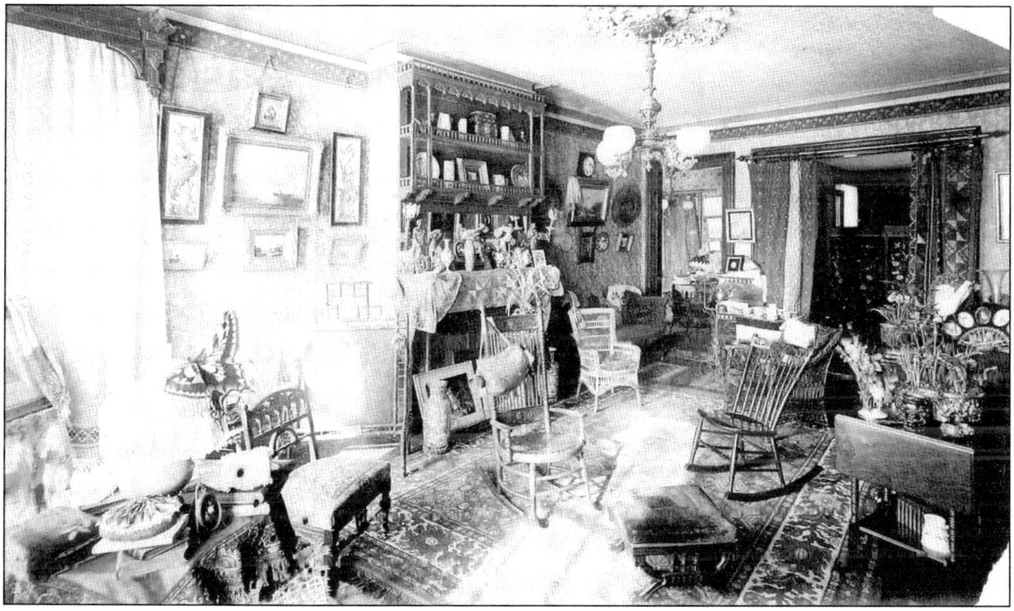

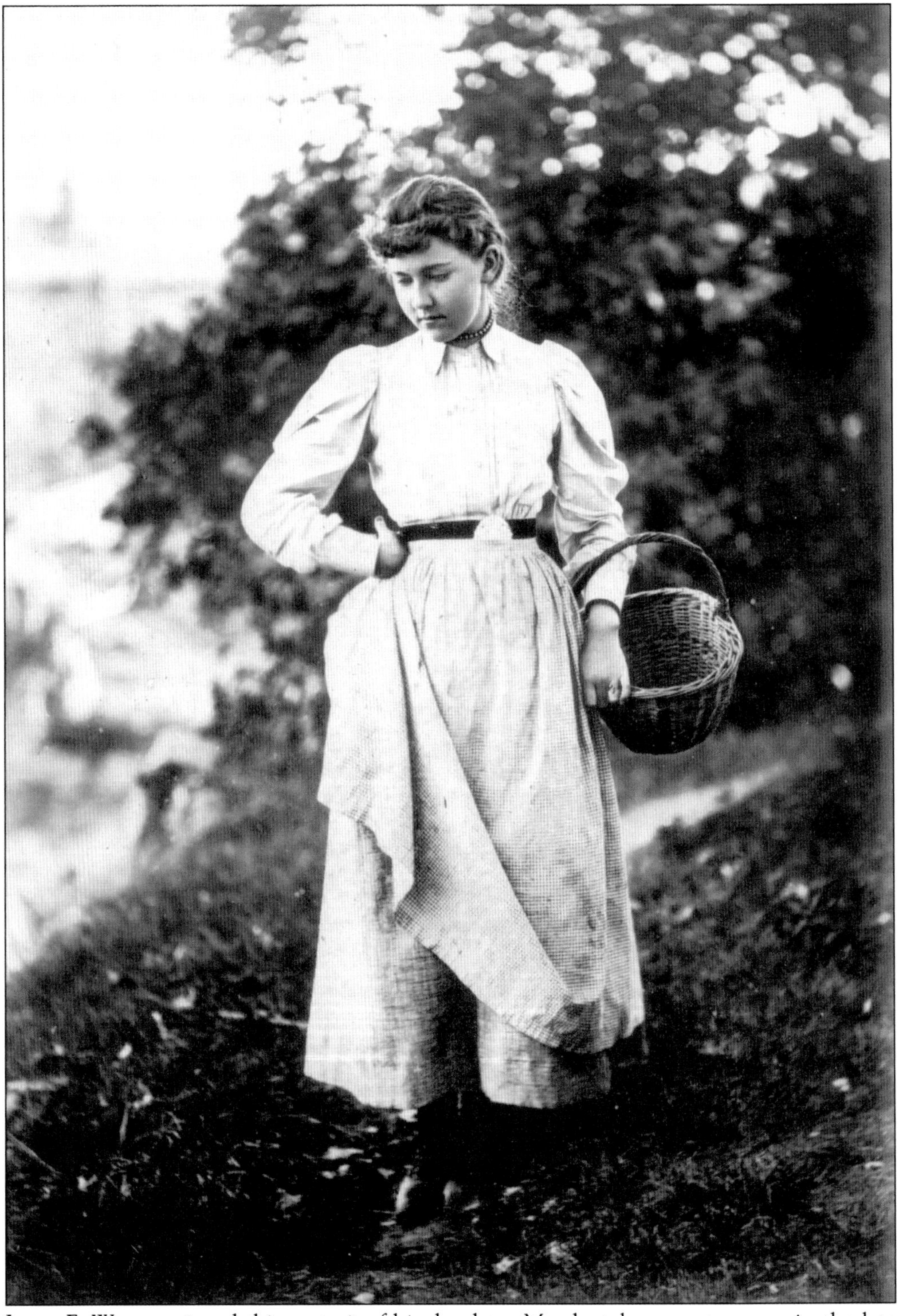

James E. West captioned this portrait of his daughter, Maude, taken as a teenager in the late 1890s, simply as "Dreaming."

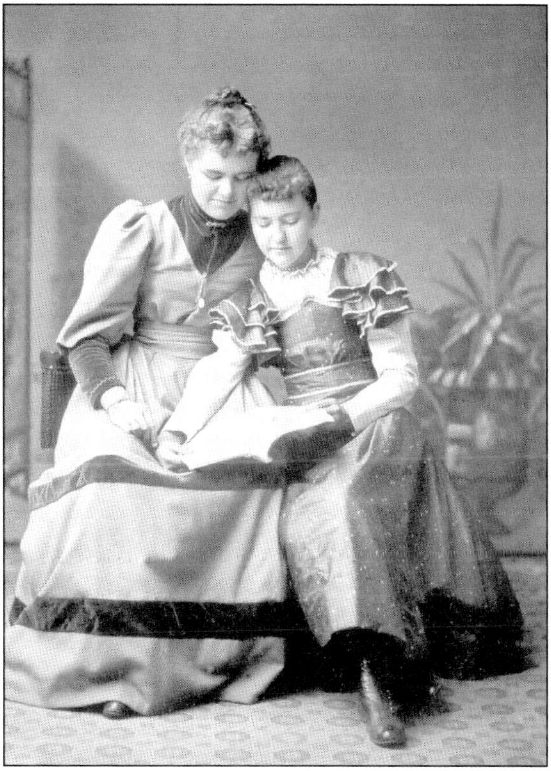

Kate (Bristol) West and her daughter, Maude, enjoy the comfort of their Grafton home.

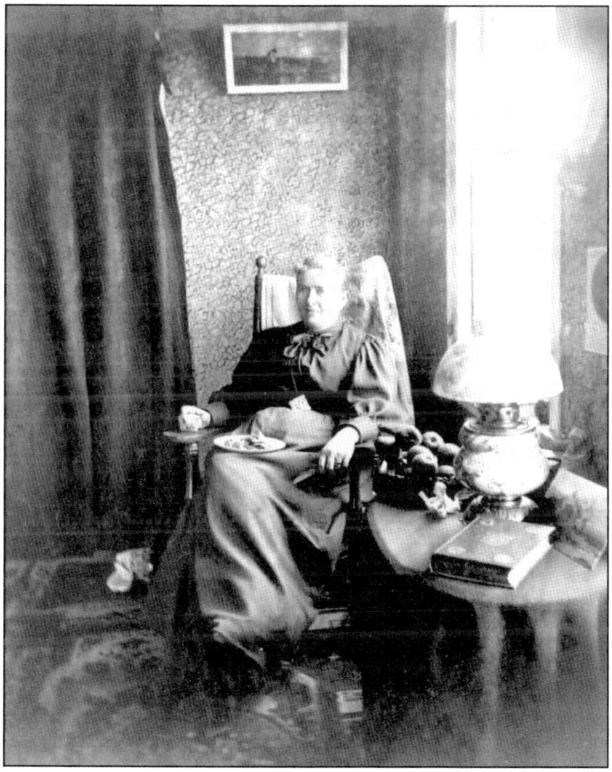

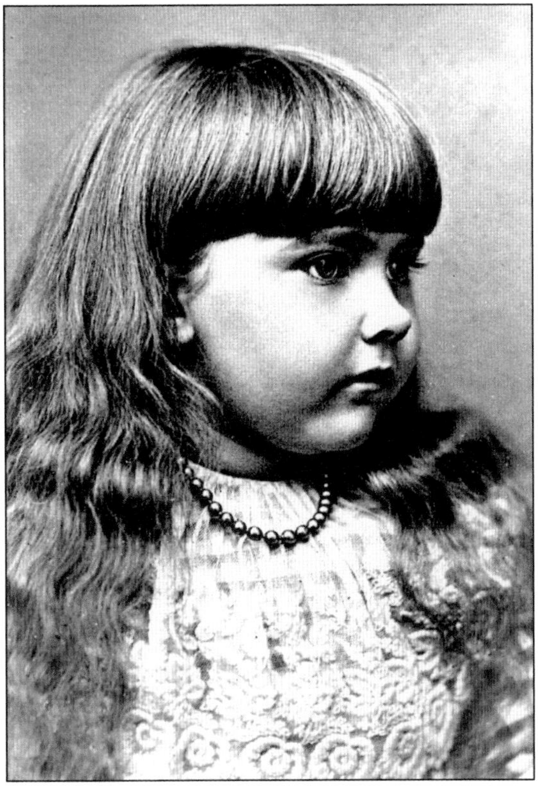

Maude West was the photographer's only child, and he created hundreds of images of her at all ages. Maude wore the "beggar girl" costume in a local theatrical production.

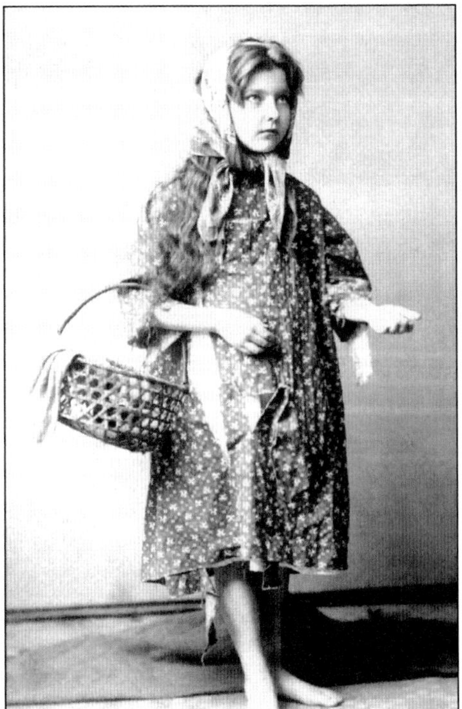

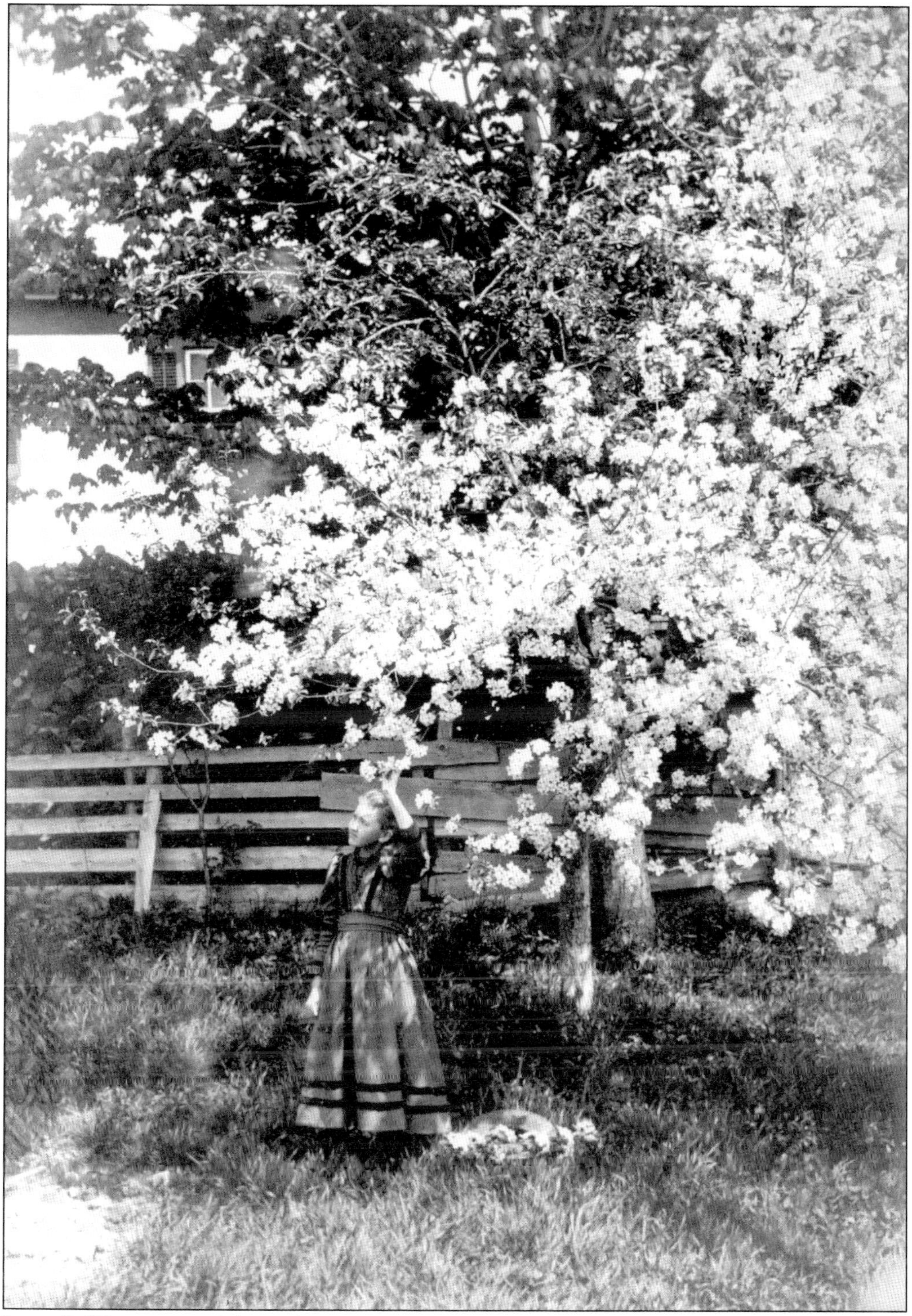

James E. West captured the endearing image of his daughter under a flowering apple tree in their backyard in the early 1890s.

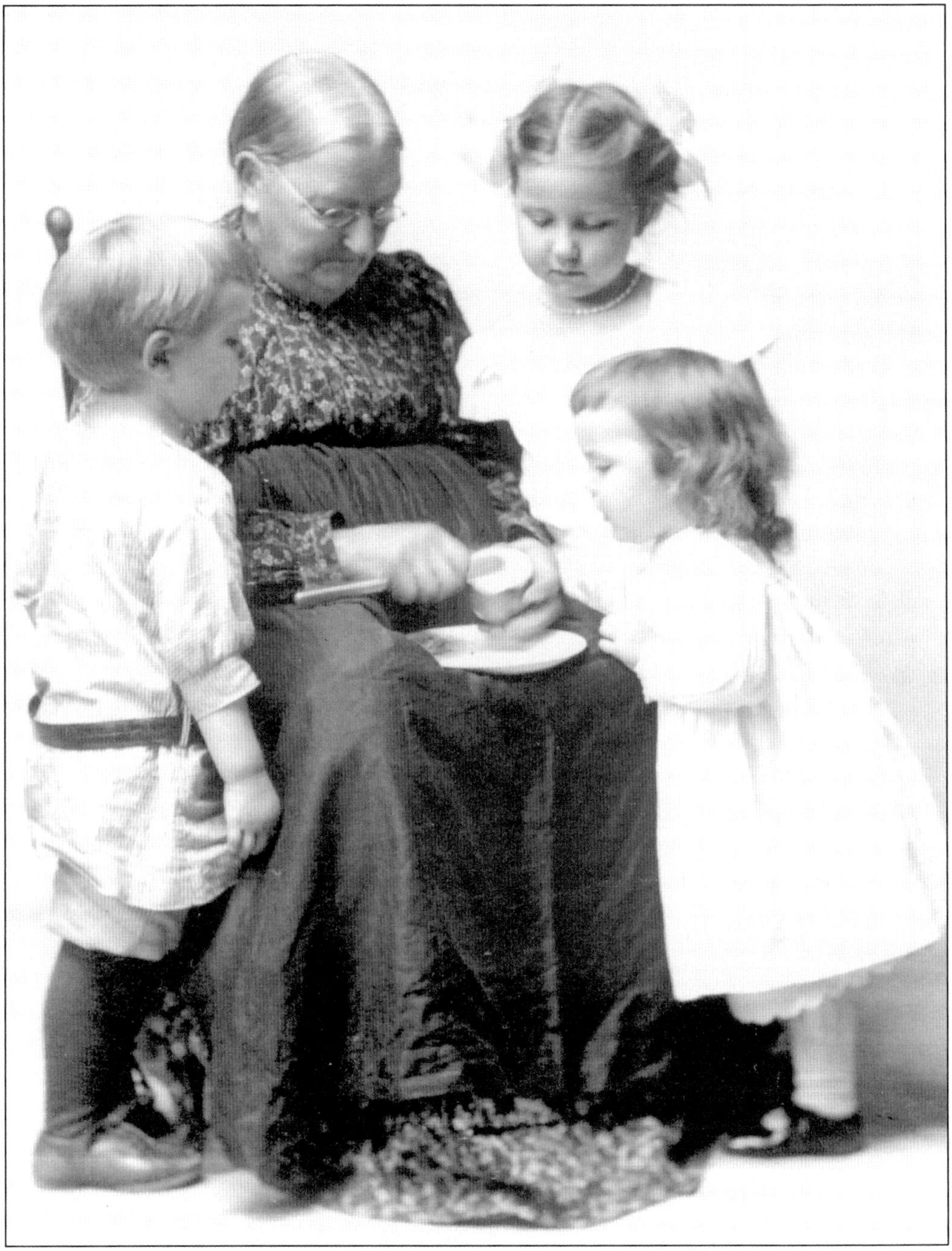

Hannah (Tilley) West, the photographer's mother, enjoyed posing for her son. Here she is with Maude's young children, shortly before her decease in 1910.

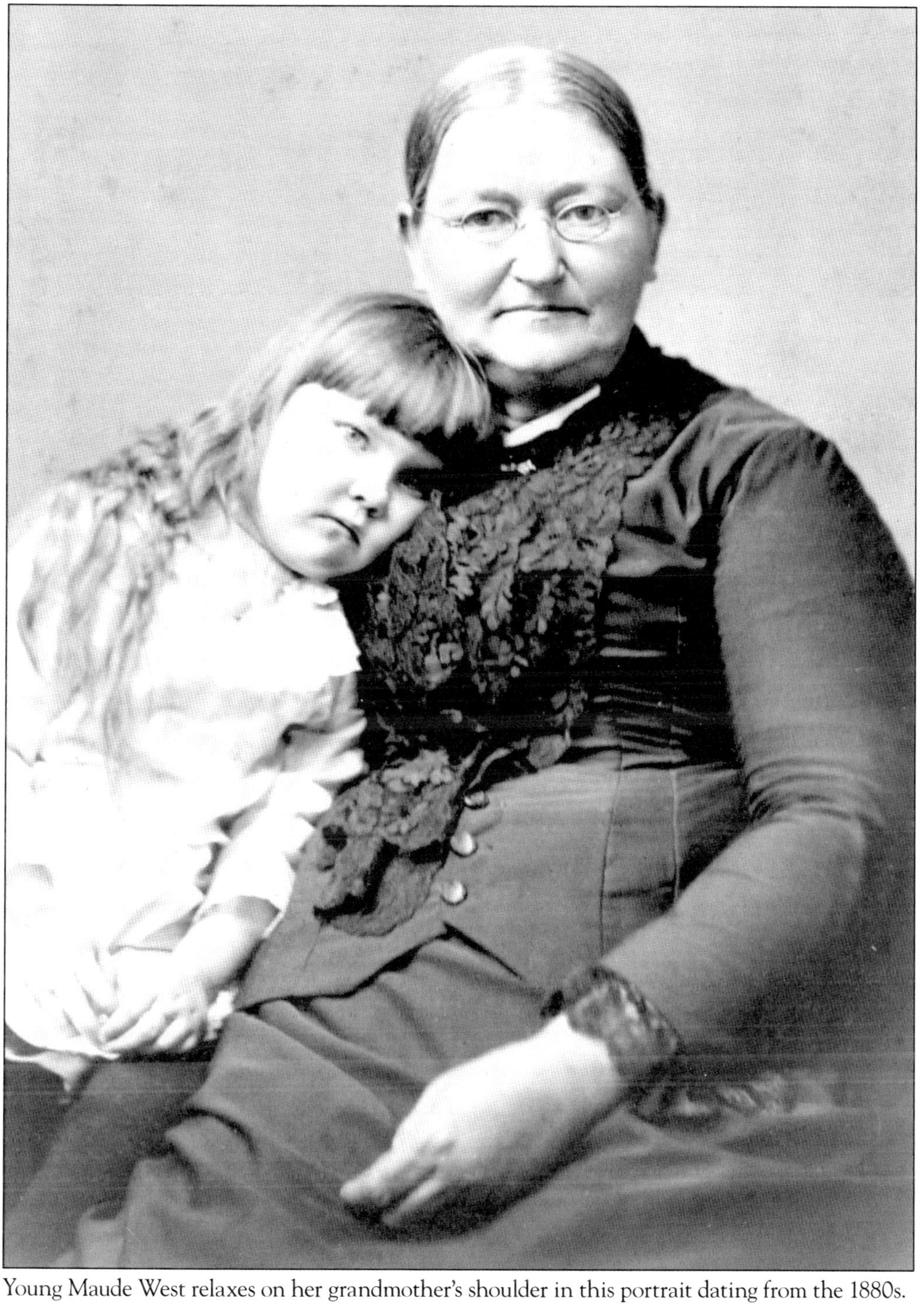

Young Maude West relaxes on her grandmother's shoulder in this portrait dating from the 1880s.

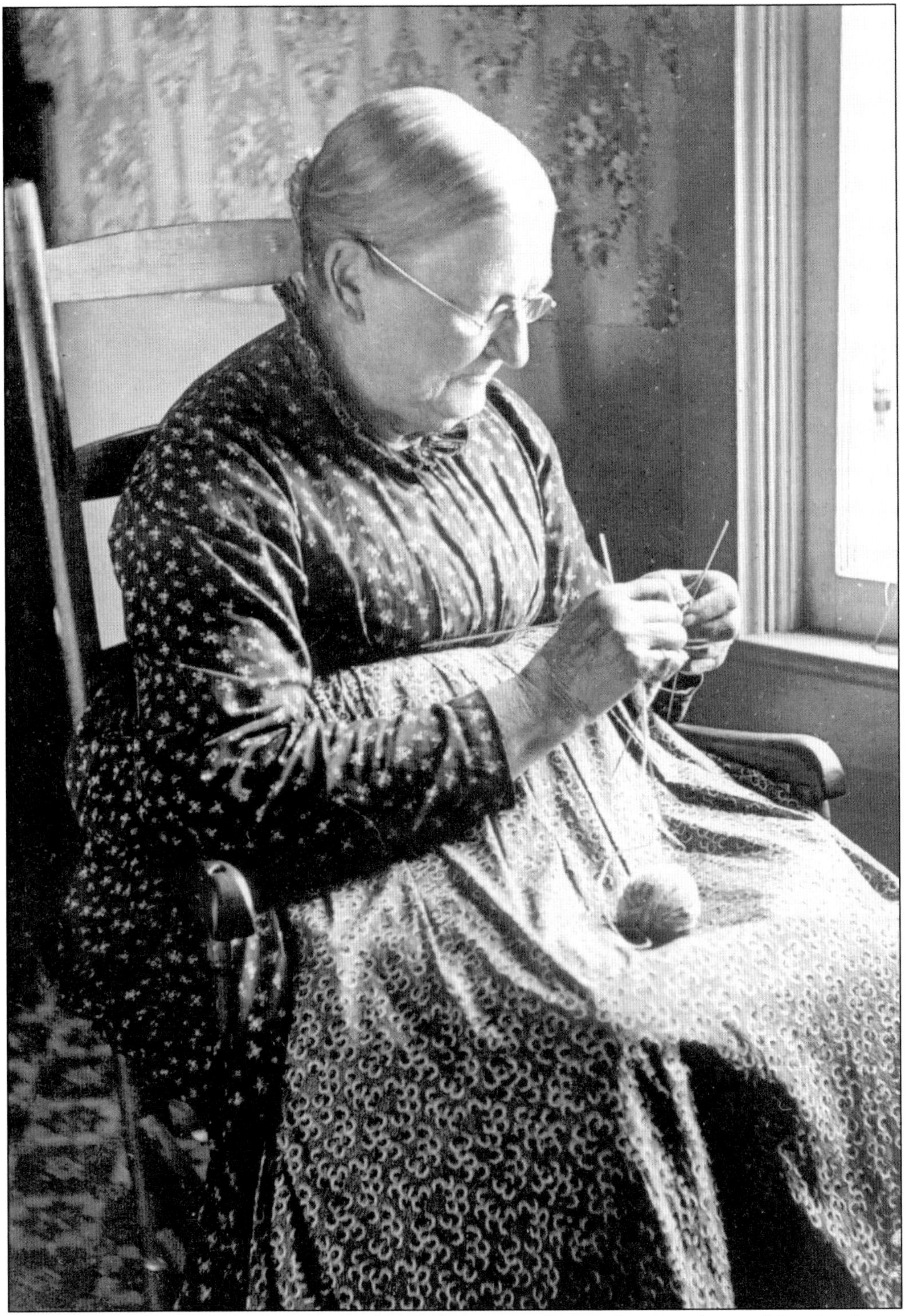
Hannah West enjoyed the final years of her life living with the photographer and his family.

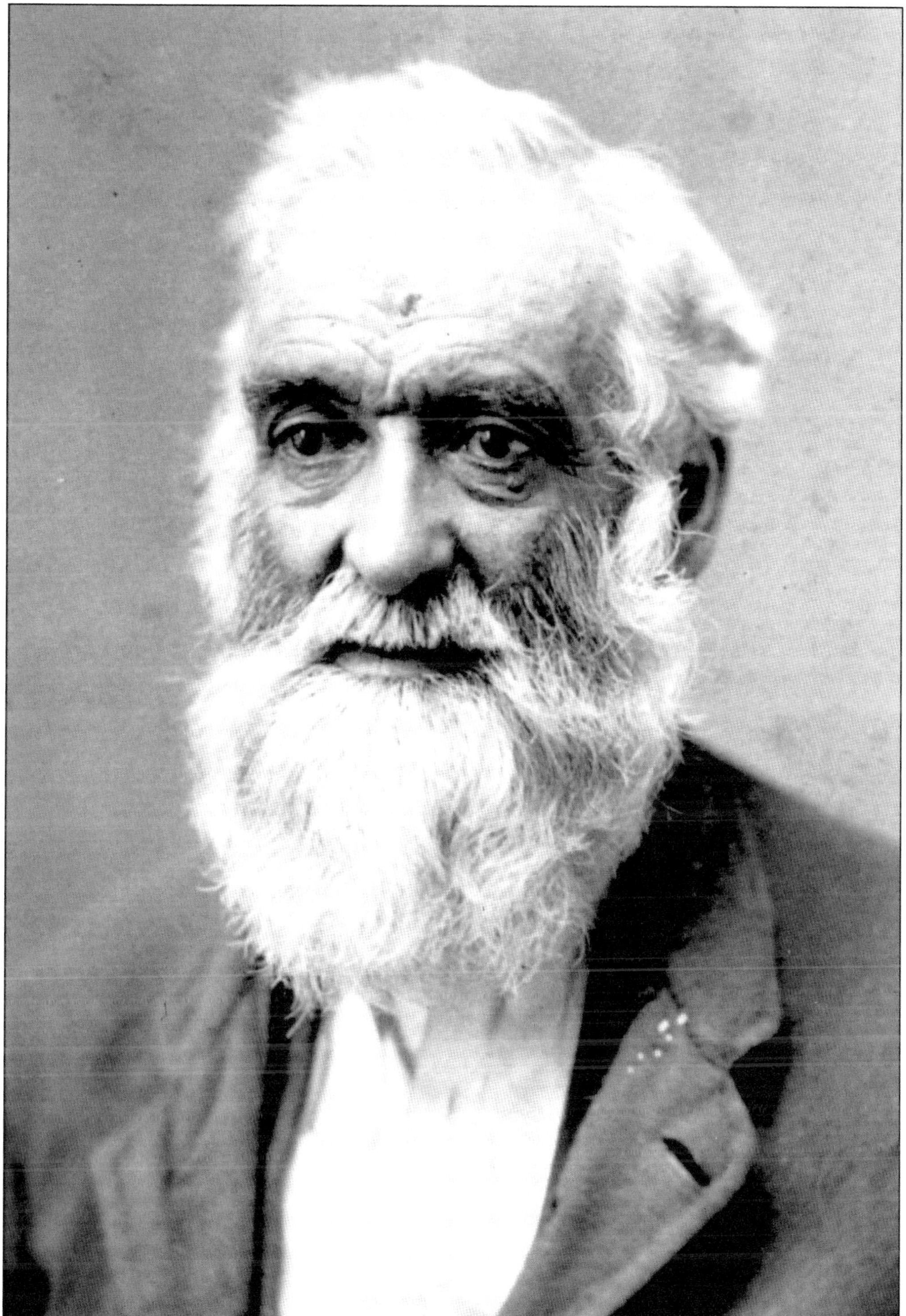

Reynolds Palmer West, the photographer's father, who had operated a general store in Grafton years before, passed away in 1897.

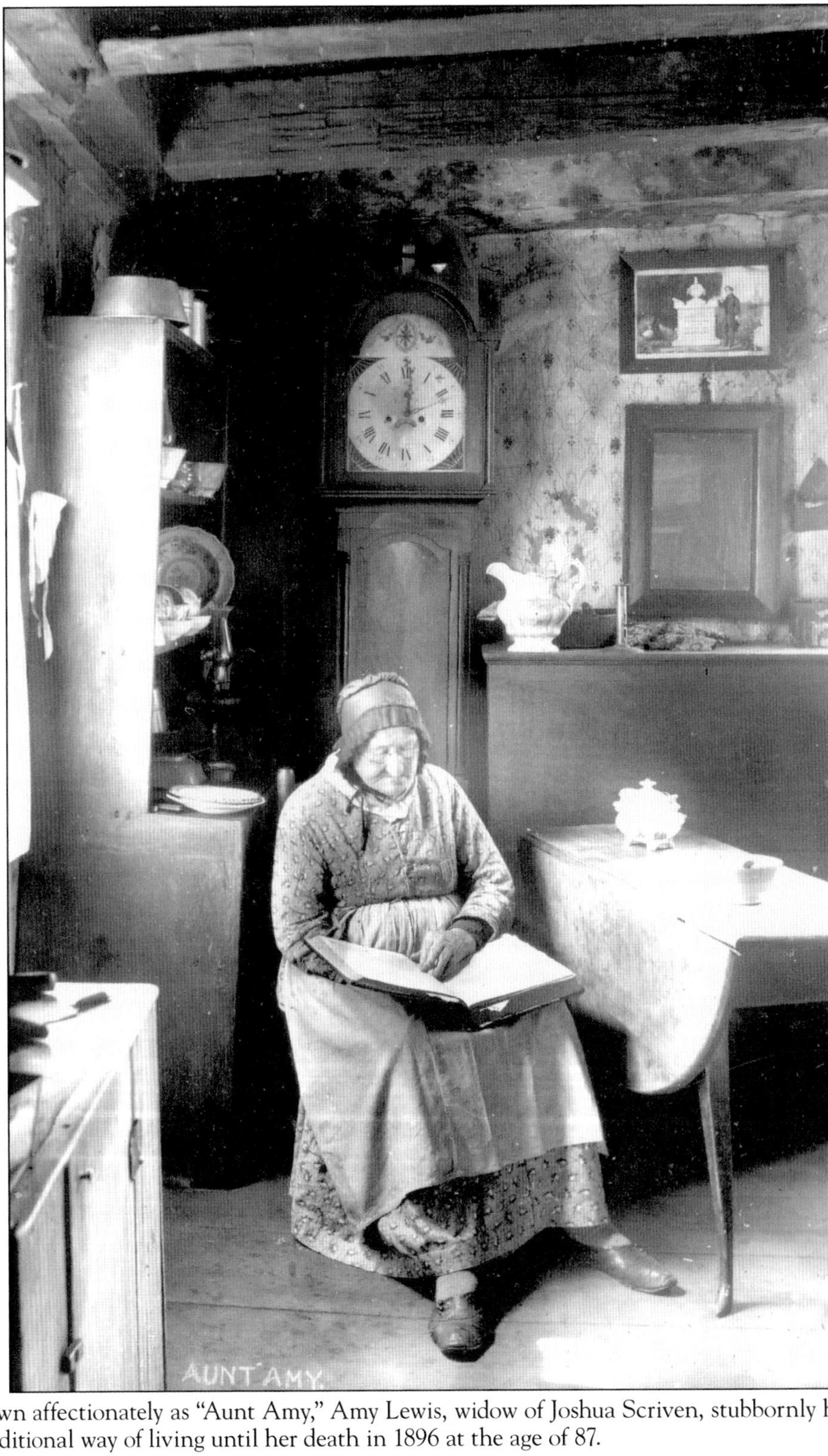

Known affectionately as "Aunt Amy," Amy Lewis, widow of Joshua Scriven, stubbornly held to a traditional way of living until her death in 1896 at the age of 87.

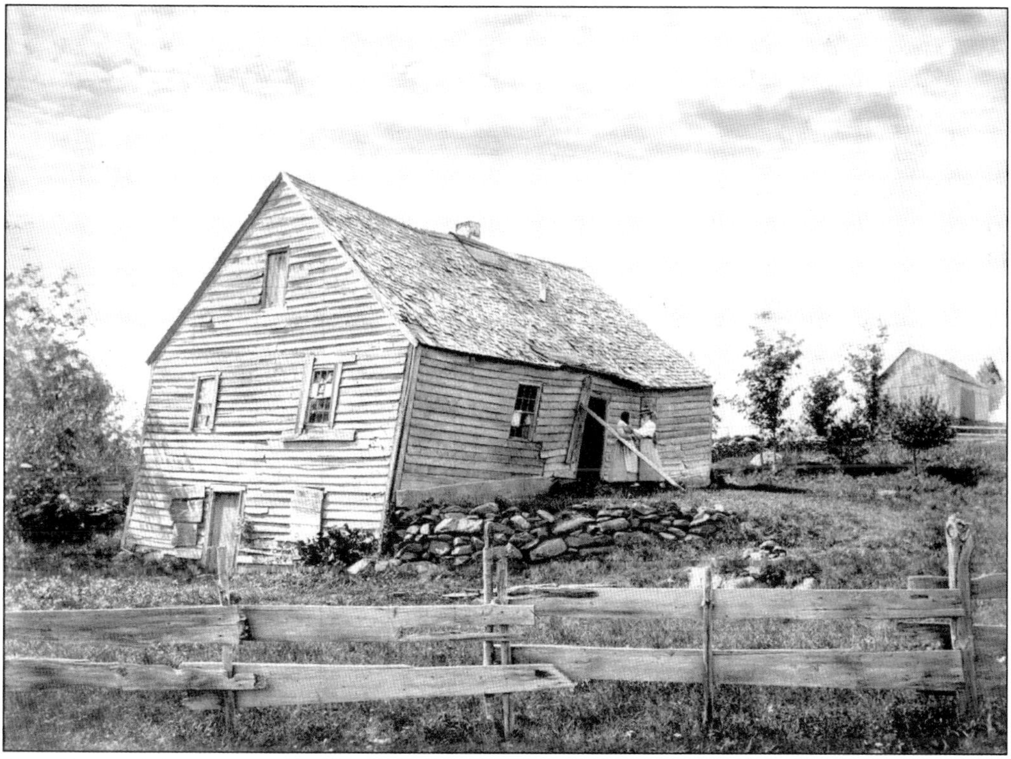

Amy Scriven's home, a relic from the late 18th century on Crandall Road, collapsed into ruin shortly following her passing.

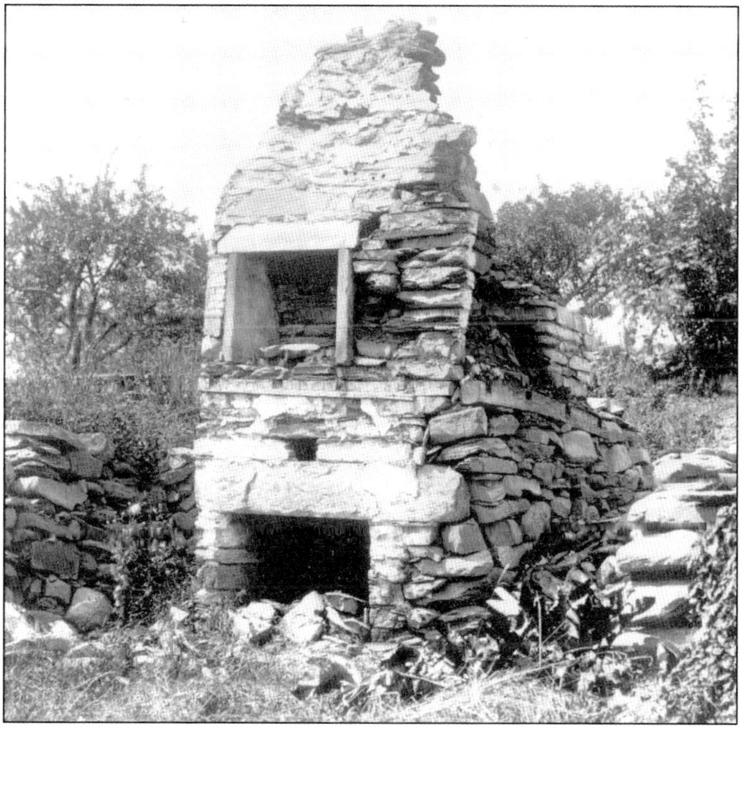

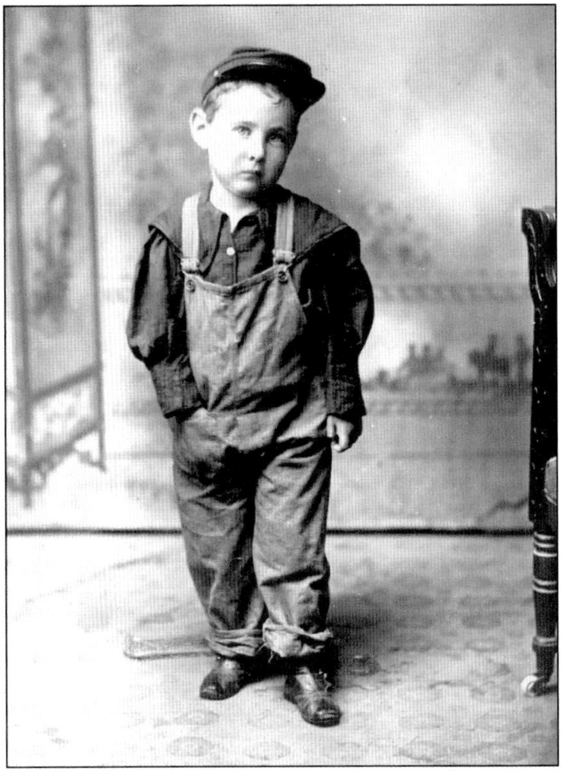

James E. West was frequently engaged to compose studio portraits of young children. The boy wearing the cap (left) is Ernest Agan, while the baby posing with his cat (below) is Millard Waite. These portraits were taken around 1883.

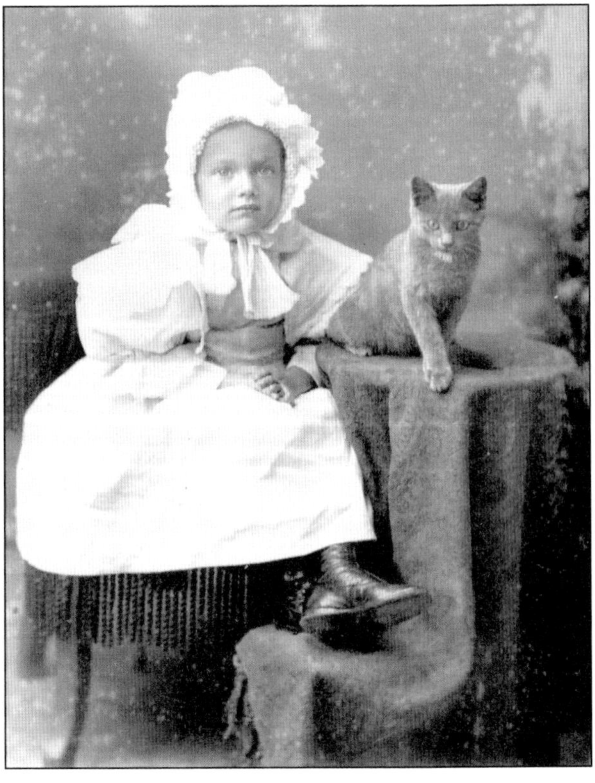

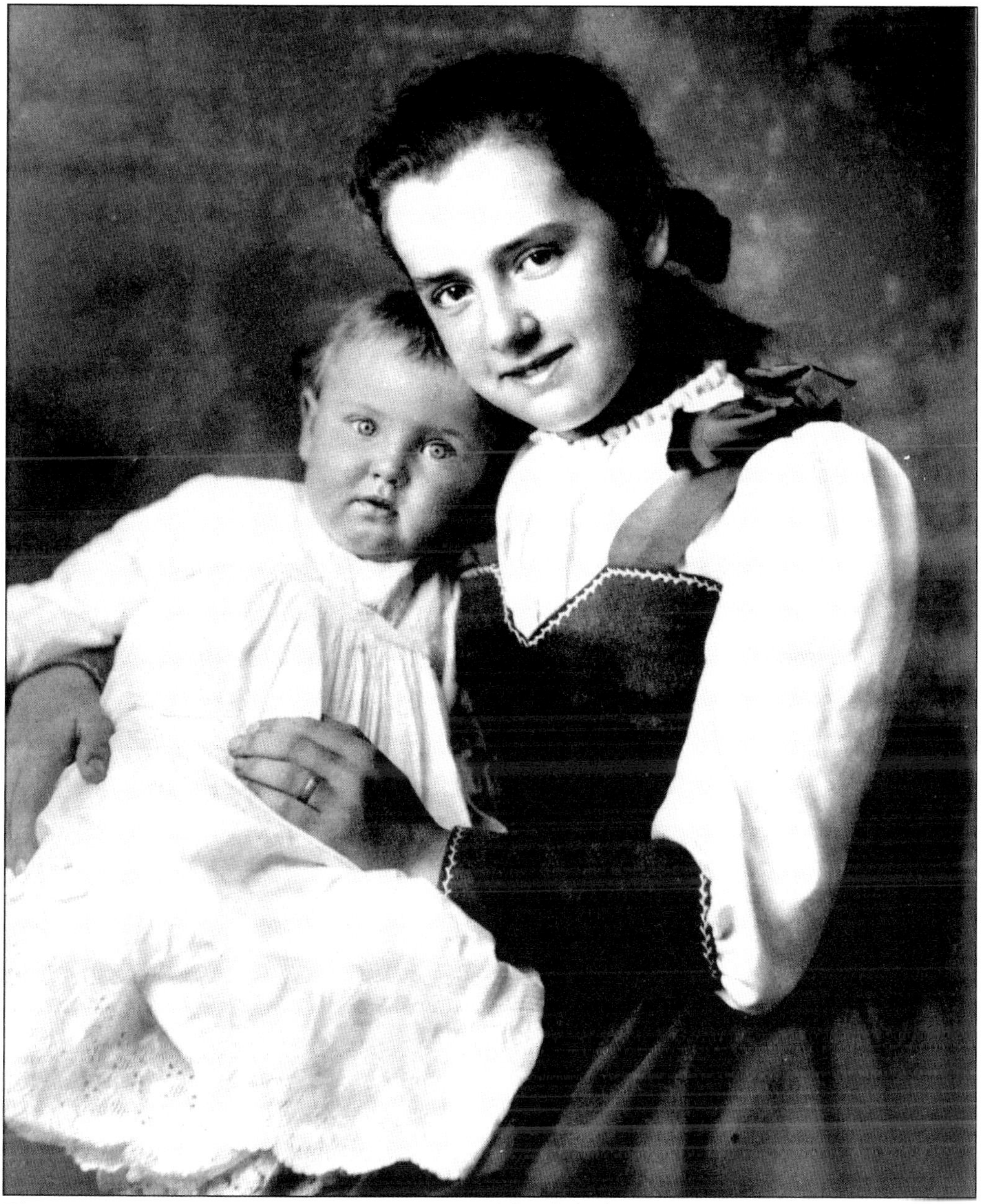

The young teenage mother who proudly posed with her baby has unfortunately not been identified.

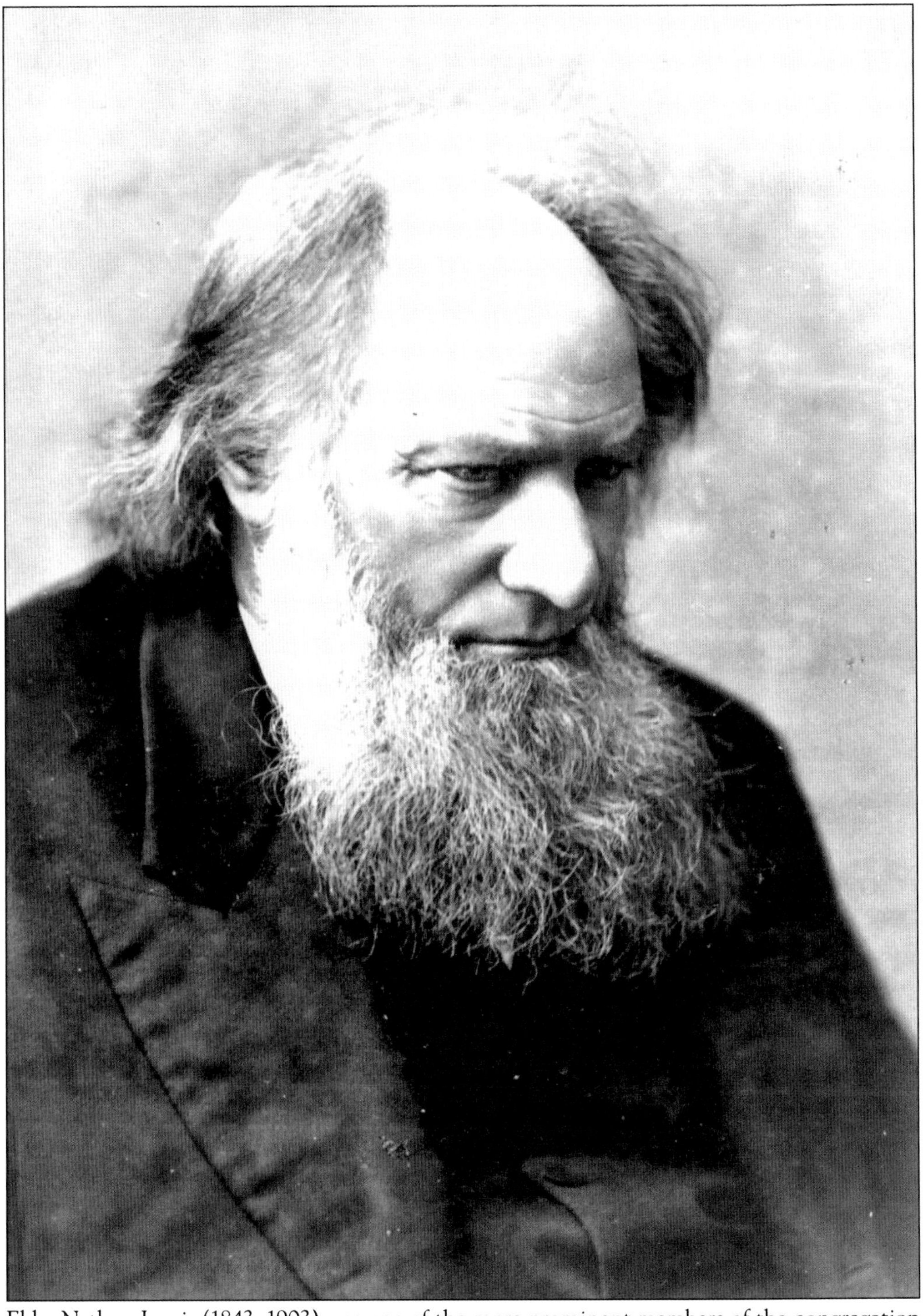

Elder Nathan Lewis (1843–1903) was one of the more prominent members of the congregation of the Grafton Baptist Church.

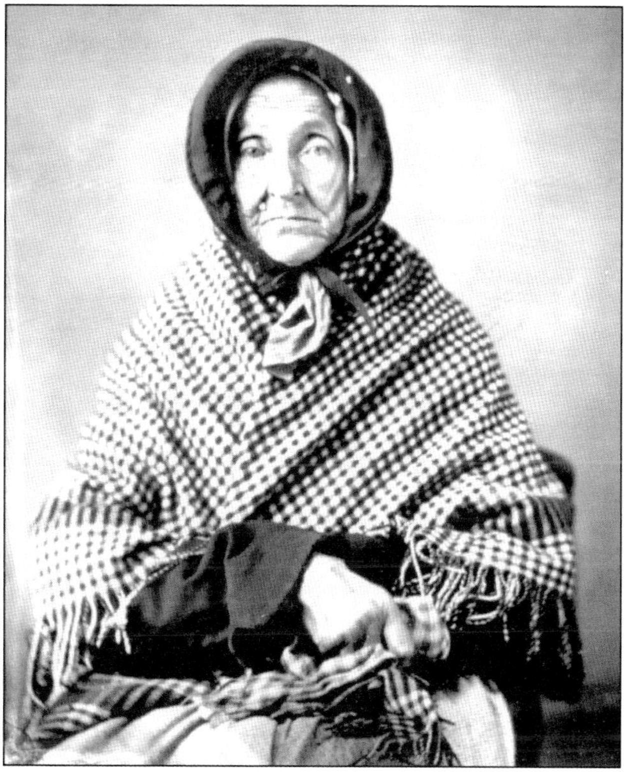

Martha (Rogers) Moon (1797–1885), known as "Aunt Patty," (right) was one of Grafton's more respected older residents. Hannah Hakes (1824–1915), the widow of Ira Ford, (below) was the mother of the photographer's sister-in-law, Maria, wife of Harrison West. The Fords operated a general store in Grafton Center.

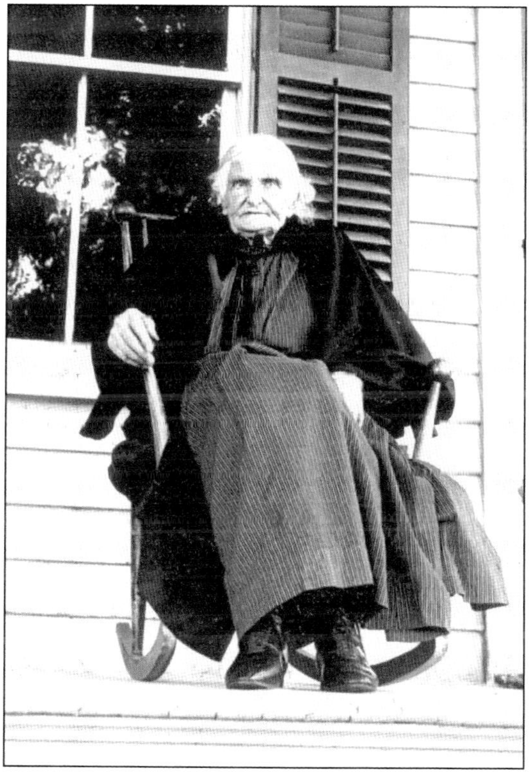

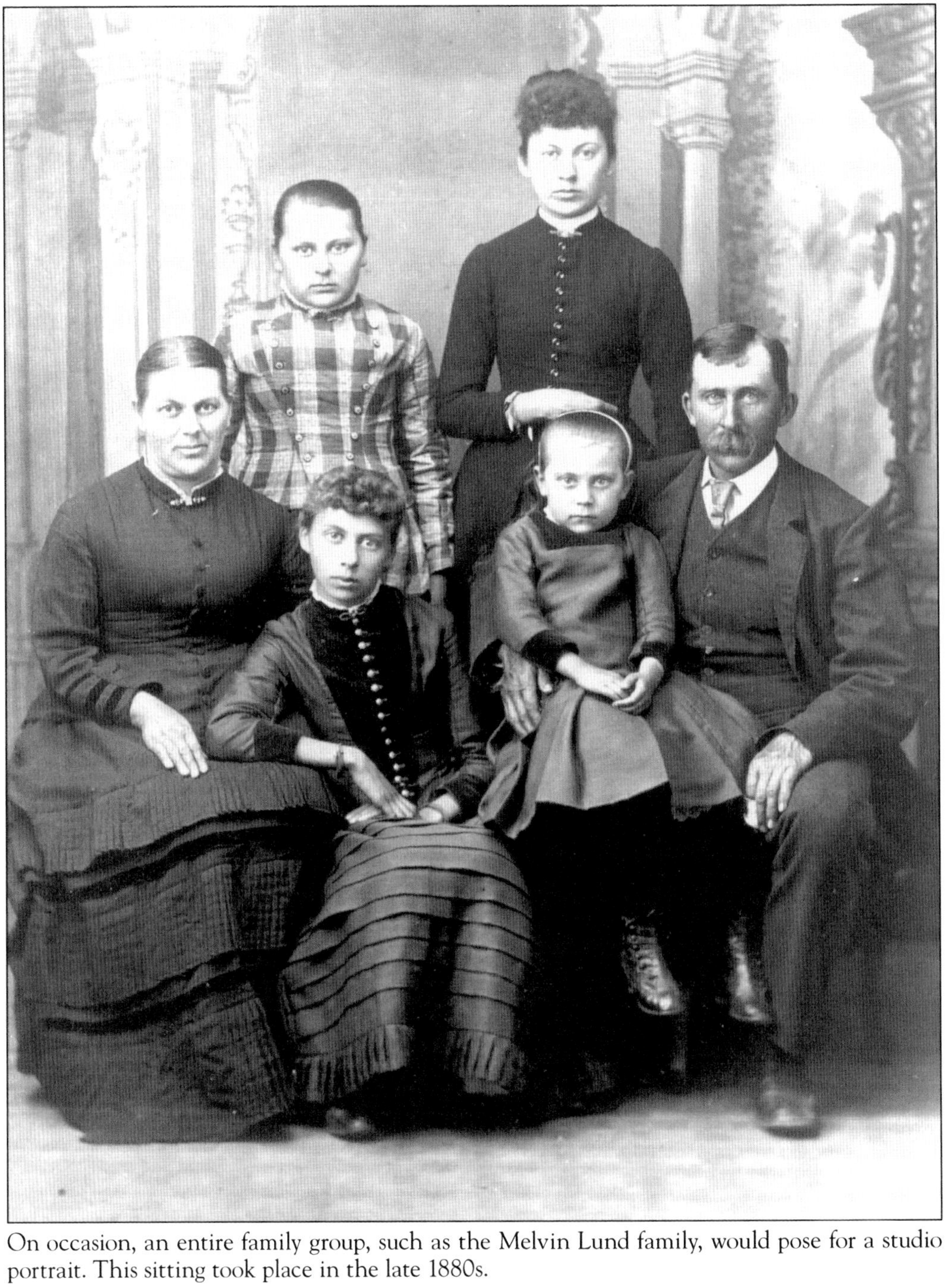

On occasion, an entire family group, such as the Melvin Lund family, would pose for a studio portrait. This sitting took place in the late 1880s.

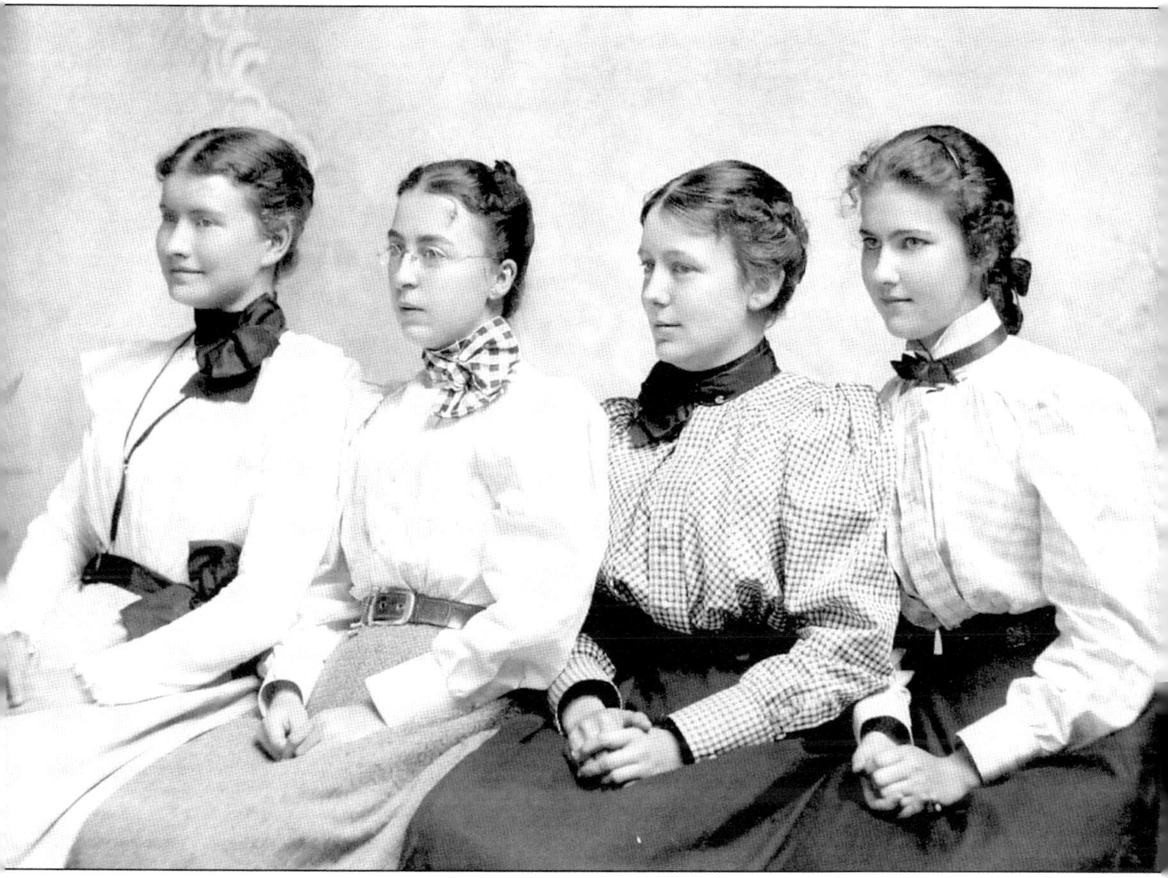

Just prior to the end of the 19th century, Maude West (the young woman on the right) posed for her father along with three of her girlfriends.

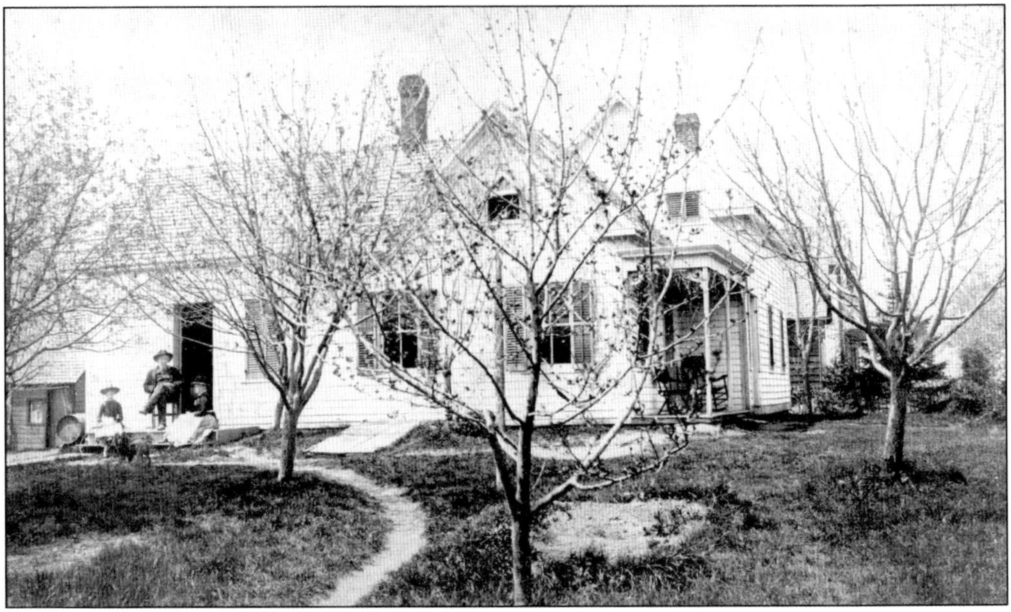

Nathan Hakes's first house (above) stood where the Grafton Community Library is now located. In 1891, he purchased the former Dr. Rufus Waite home (below) adjacent to the Grafton Baptist Church.

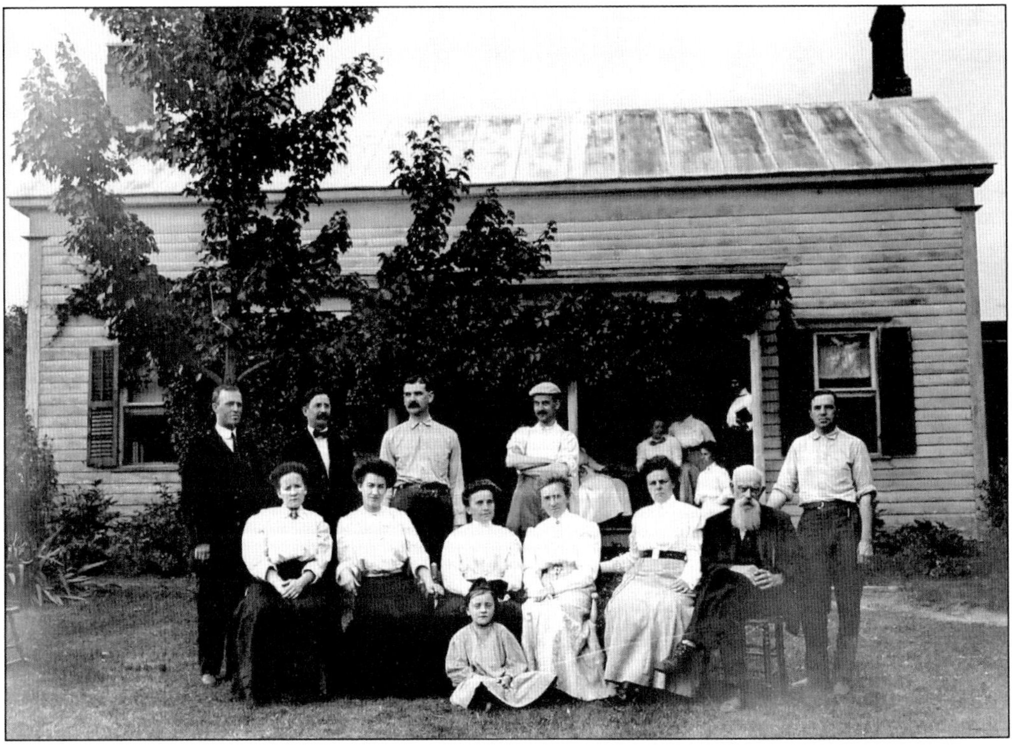

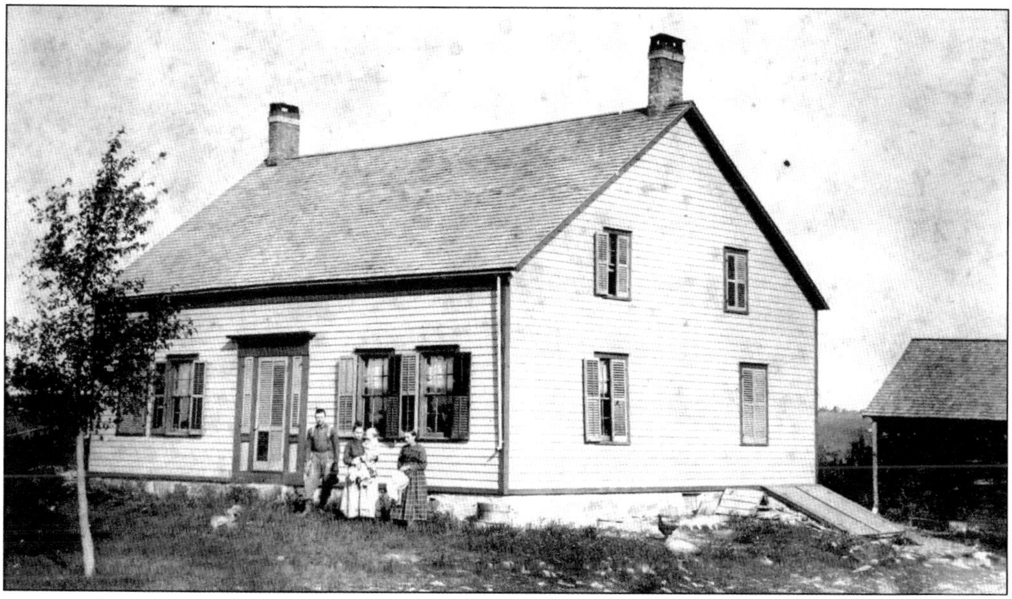

The Amos Sweet home stands today on the north side of Old Road; it was originally the home of Charles Ferry, who settled in Grafton in the 1790s and moved out of the area a few years later.

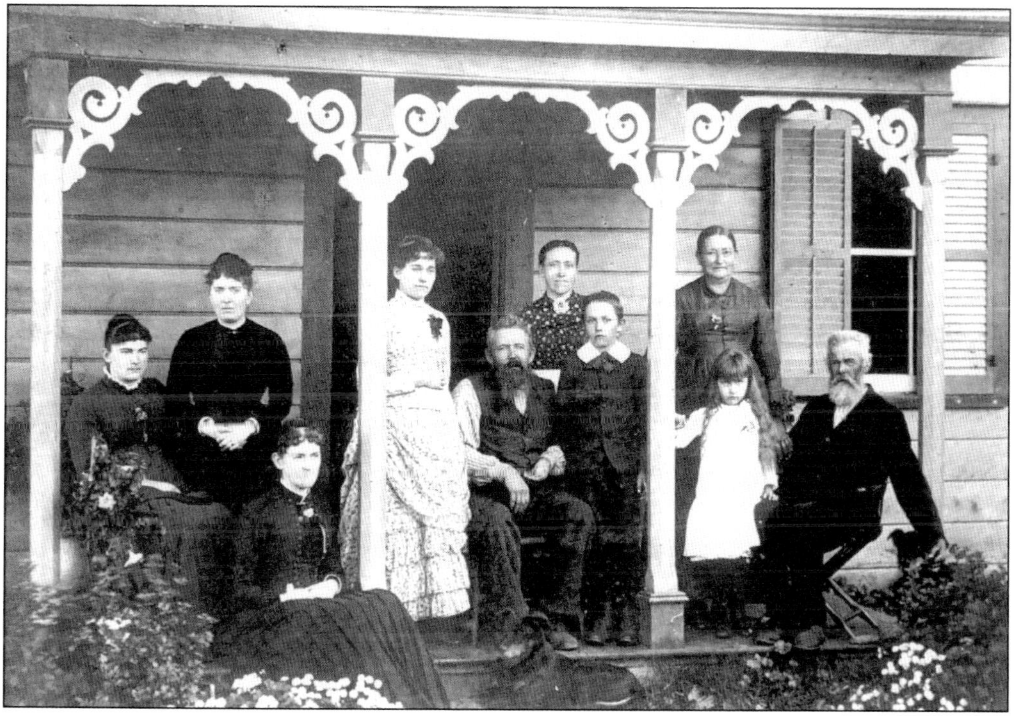

Reynolds Palmer West and his wife, Hannah, pose with the Calvin Agan family for the photographer on the porch of the Agan home, the old Francis West place, on Shaver Pond Road.

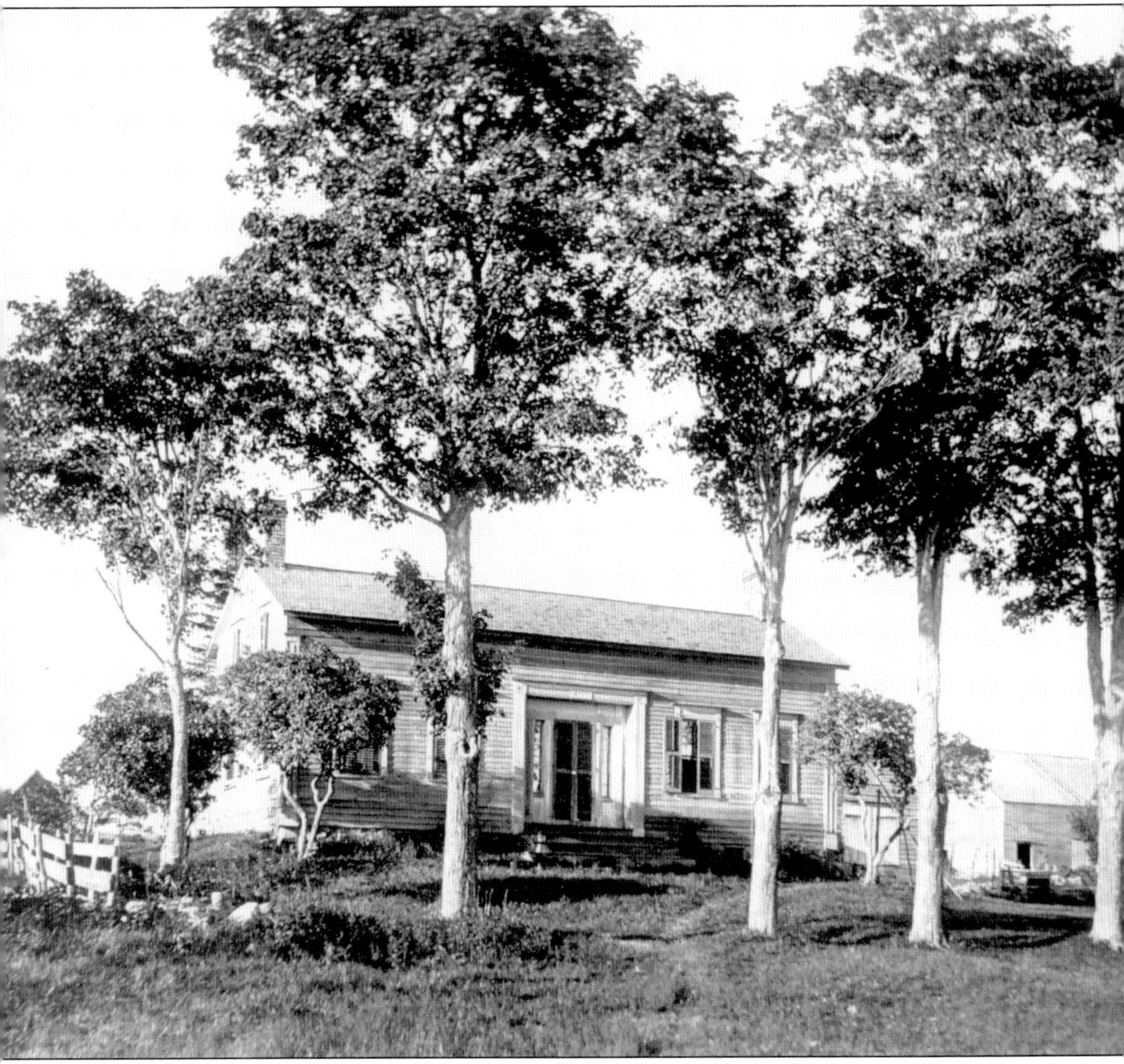

The Thomas or Church residence stands today on the north side of Dumbleton Road, formerly the main highway. Darius, Lewis, Hiram, and Lottie Thomas still farmed the traditional way here in the early 1900s.

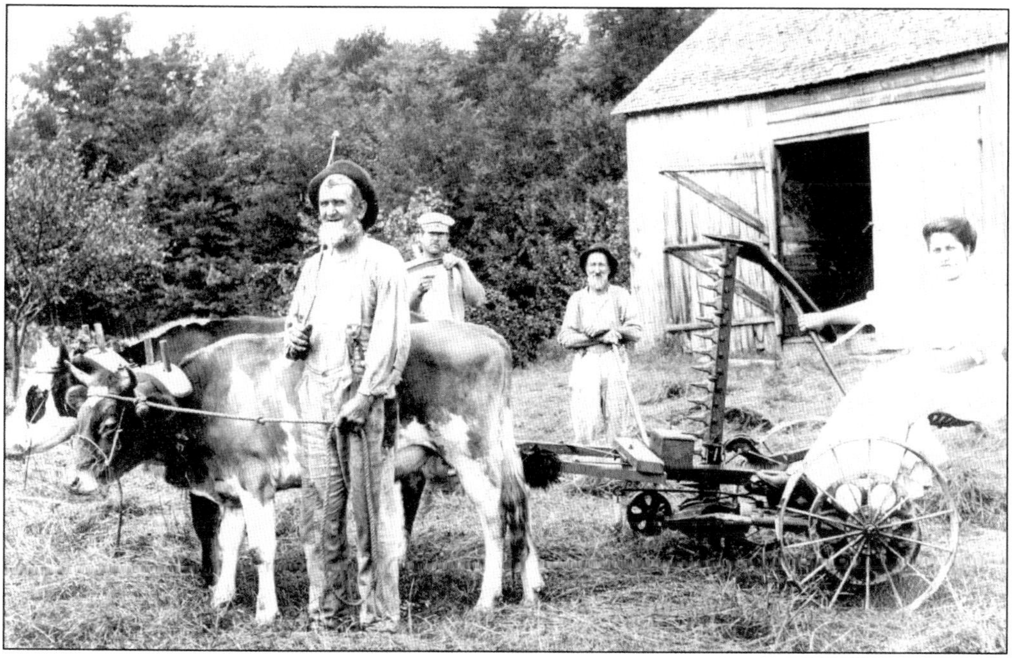

They proudly display their mowing machine drawn by oxen as well as their horses; the mower was probably manufactured by the renowned Walter A. Wood company of Hoosick Falls.

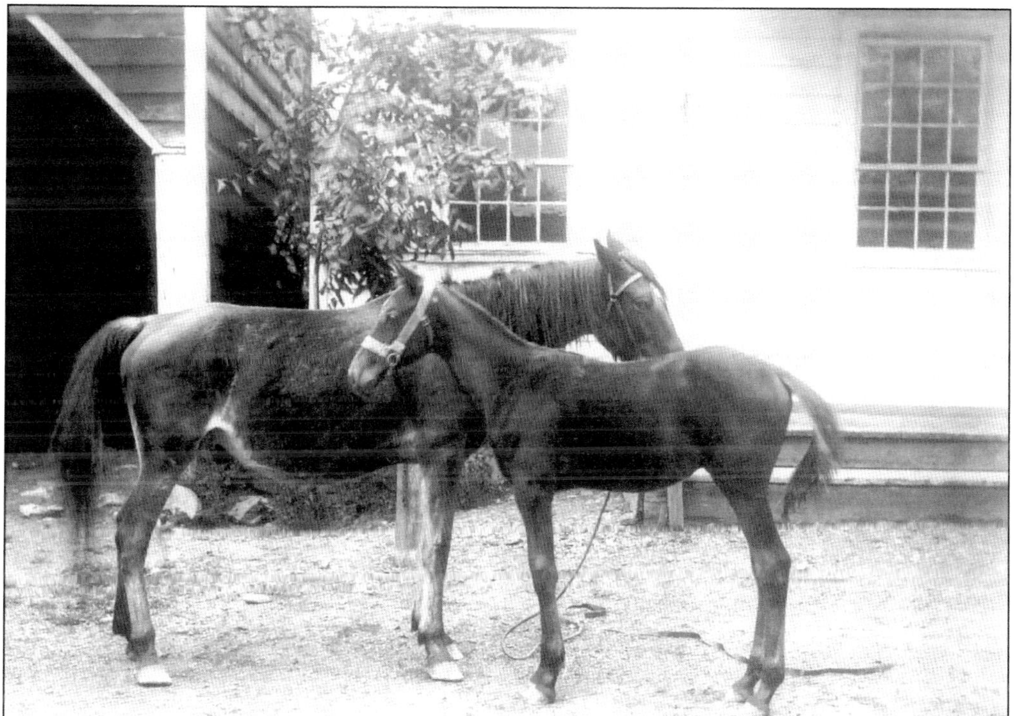

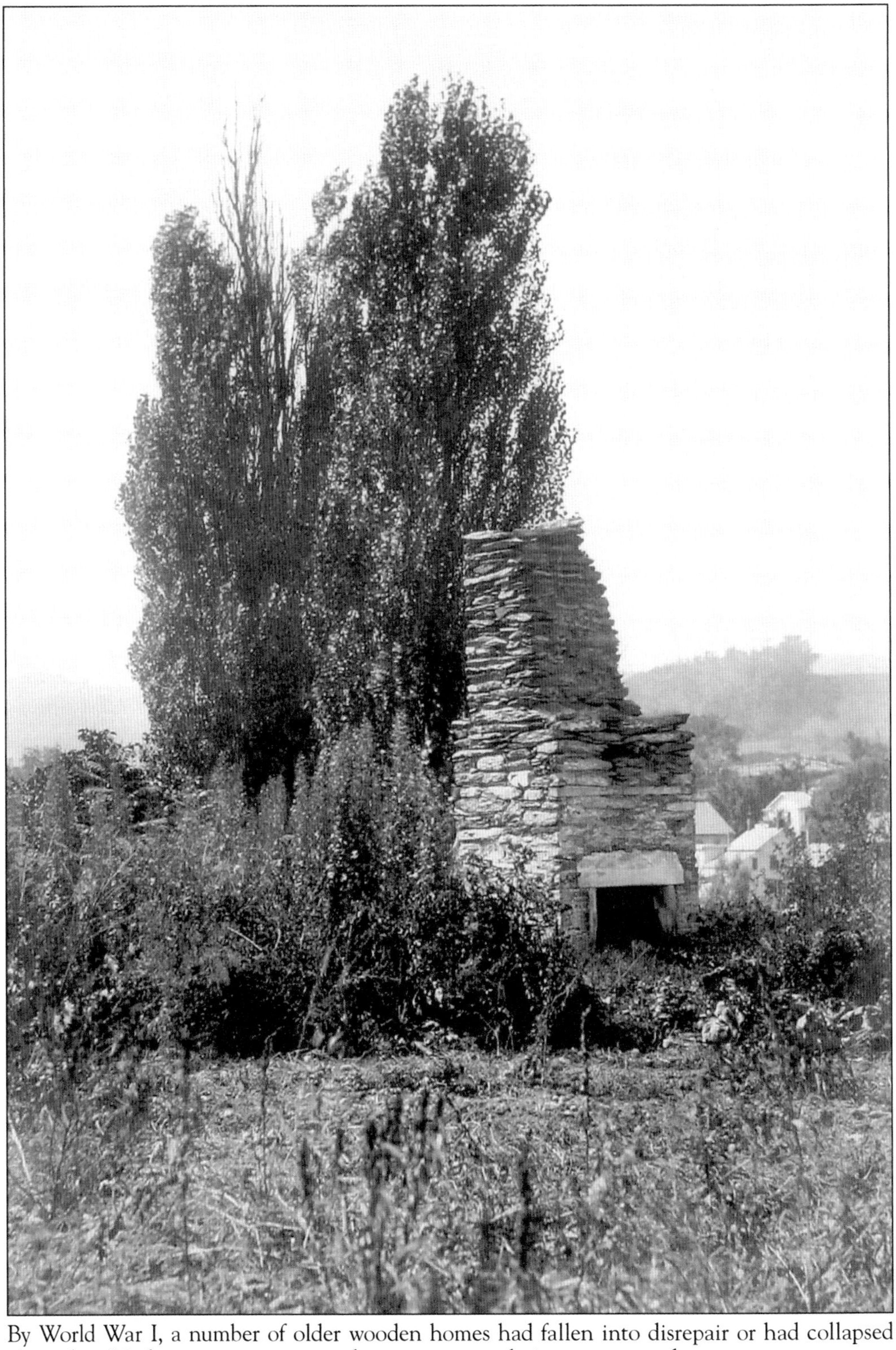

By World War I, a number of older wooden homes had fallen into disrepair or had collapsed altogether. Modern, more ornate residences were now being constructed.

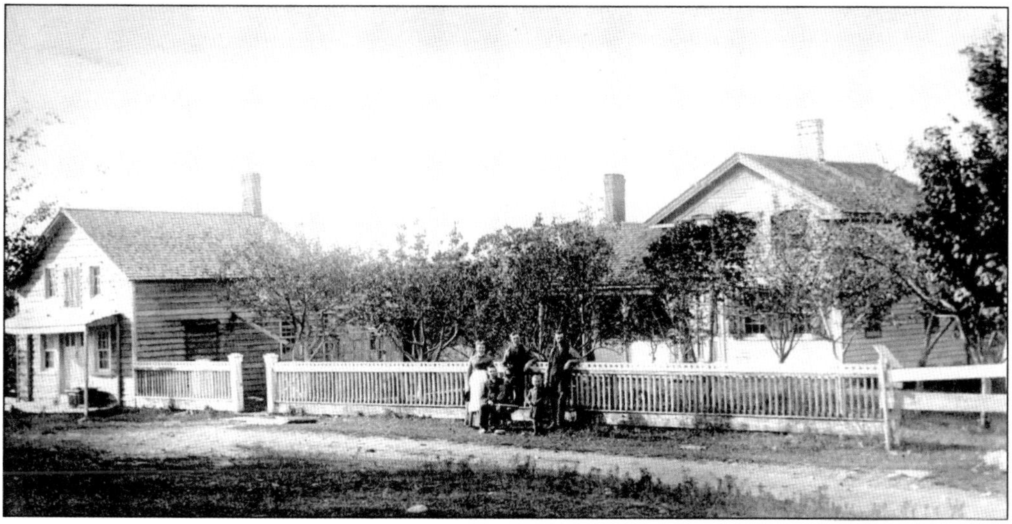

Some early homes, such as the Linus V. Snyder place on South Road known as "Point Pleasant," have survived. The house appearing in the photograph is also shown on page 92 extensively renovated, while the barns maintain their original appearance today.

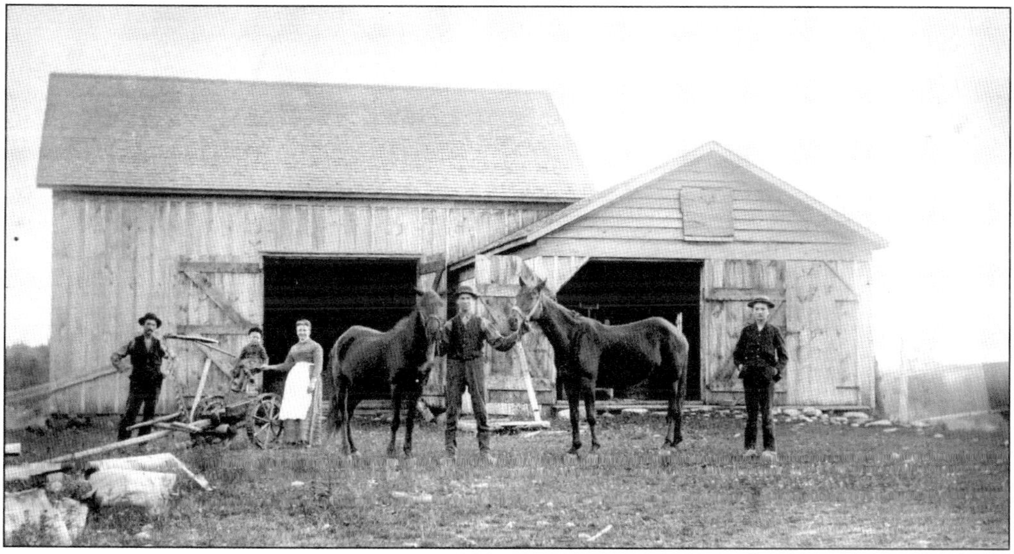

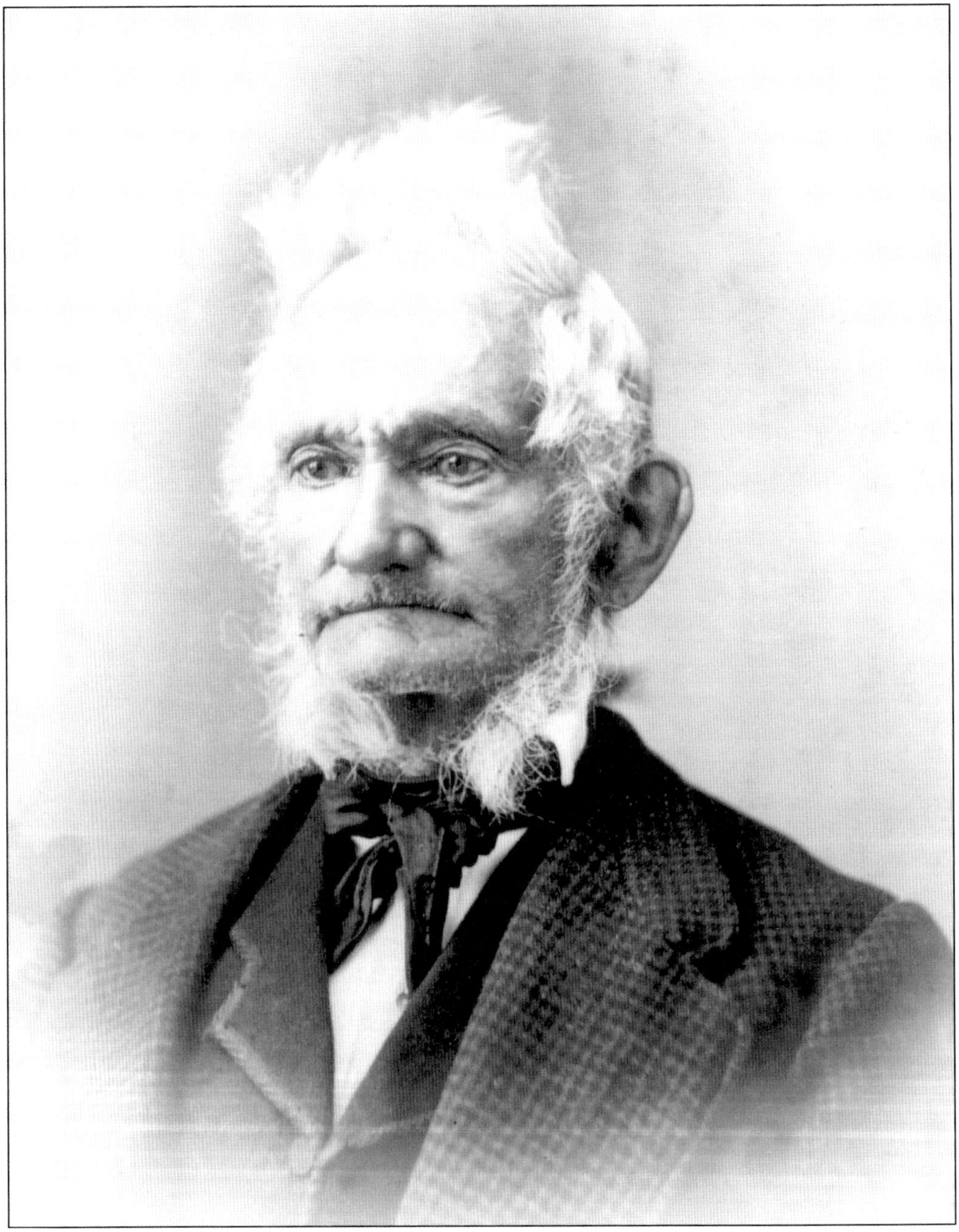

Dr. Hiram Moses of Petersburgh (1800–1885) was for many years the most respected physician in the region.

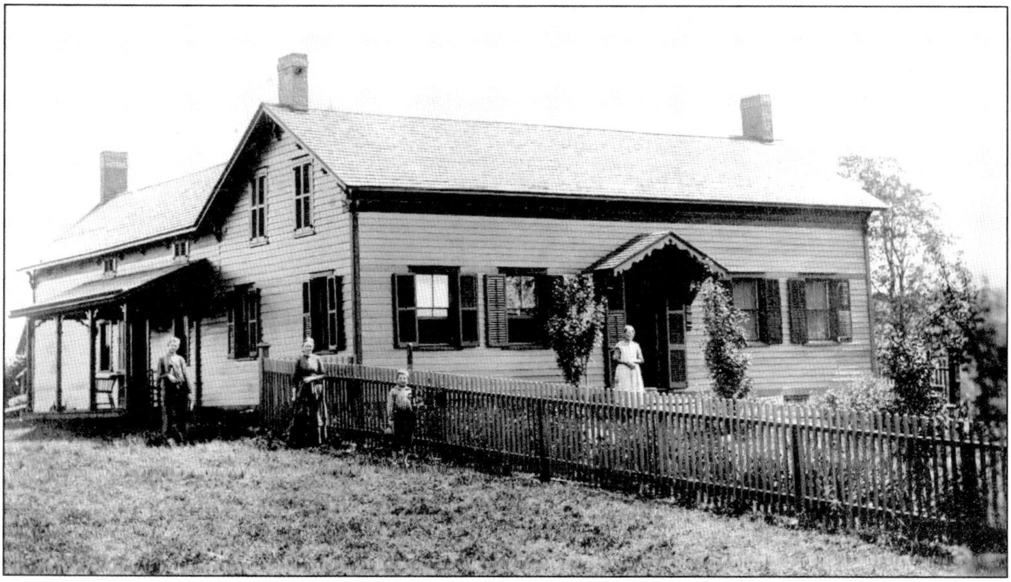

The Calvin Dunham farm stood on the west side of Dunham Reservoir Road, just south of the current State Route 2 in West Grafton, until its destruction by fire. The former Cottage Hotel is visible in the background in the photograph below.

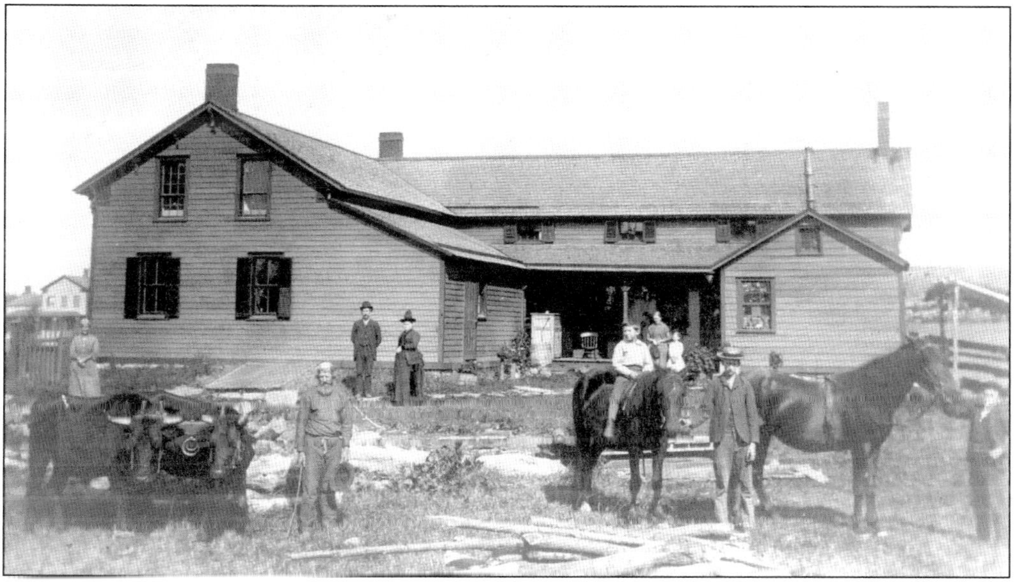

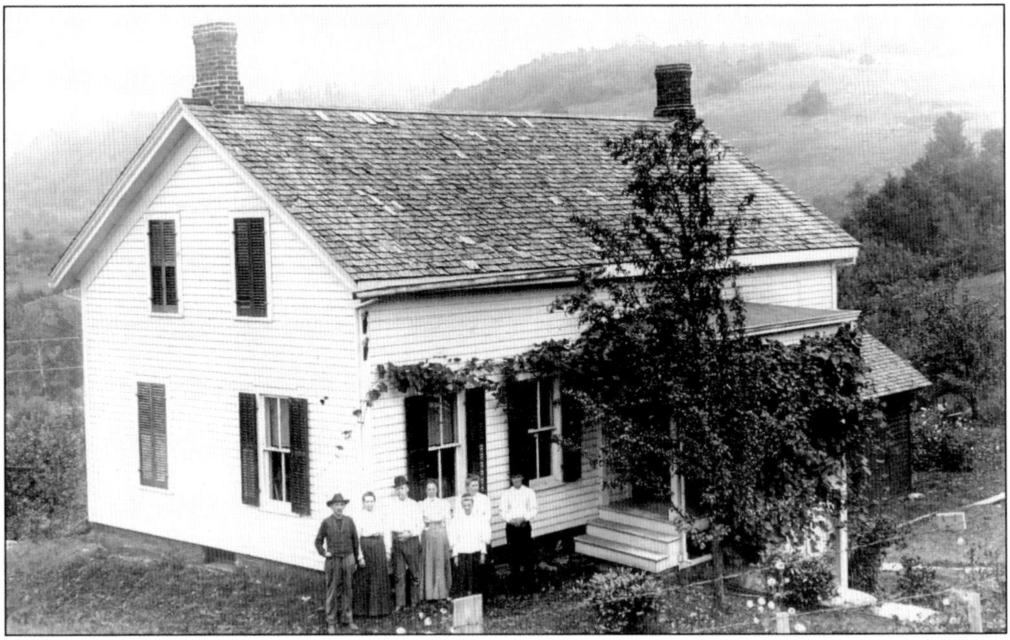

The houses shown on these two pages sadly have not been identified. The home shown above stood on a side hill overlooking a valley. Based on the terrain, this photograph was probably taken in either Berlin or Petersburgh.

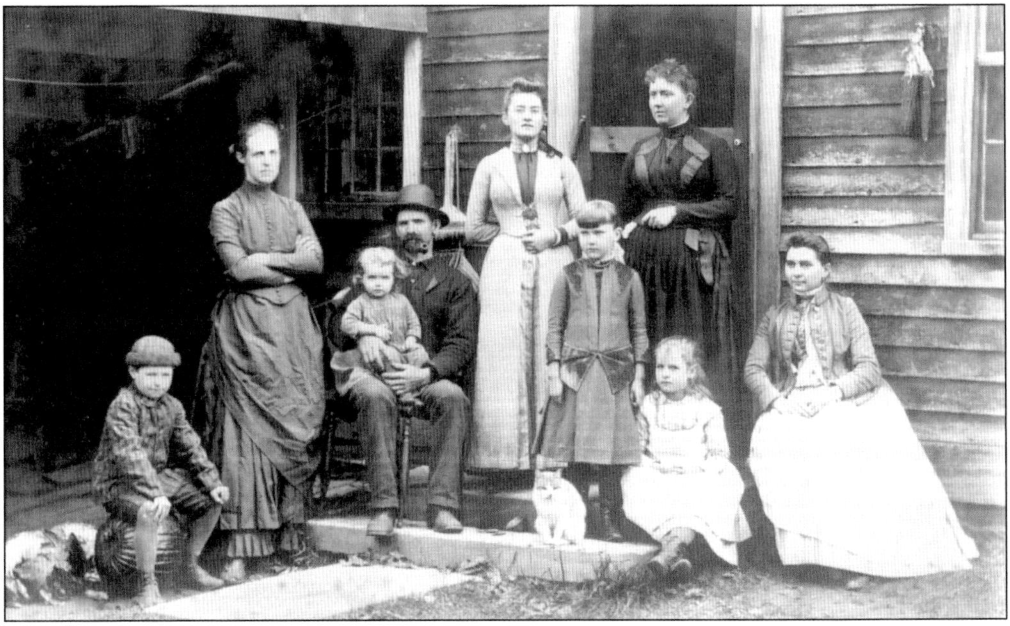

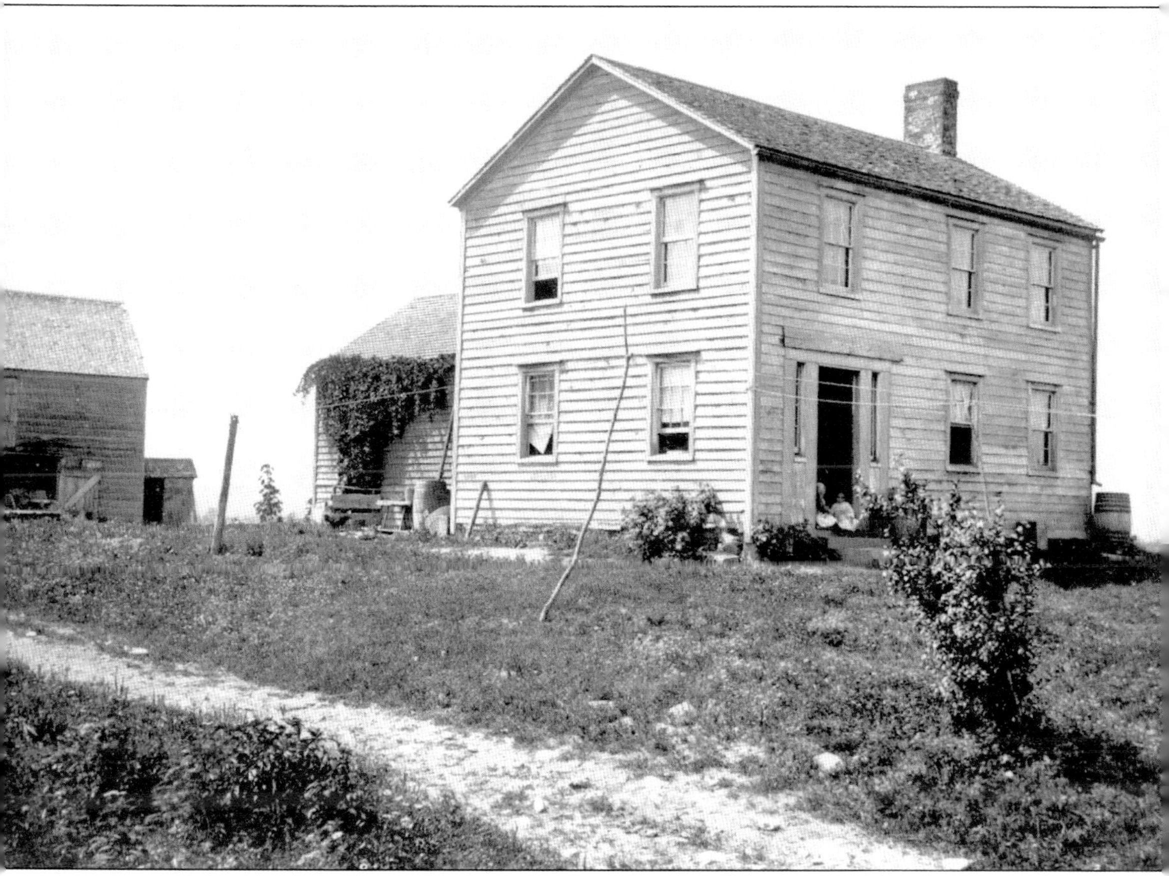

Some have speculated that this unadorned wooden house was the early Jedediah Burdick home located on South Long Pond Road in Grafton near "the Pinnacle."

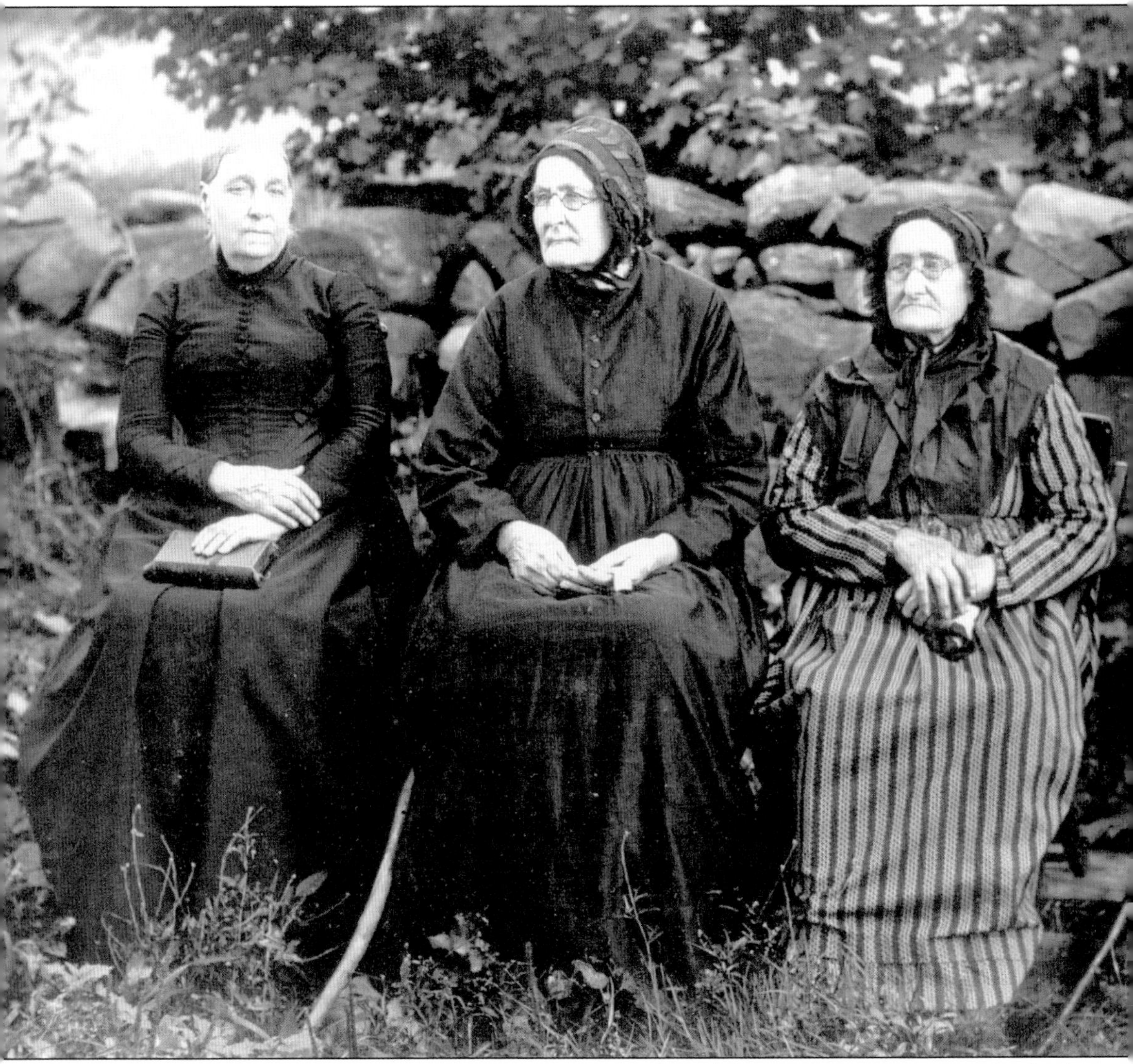

Three sisters, photographed around 1890 and listed from left to right, were among Grafton's venerable matriarchs. All three women, Betsey Ann (1811–1901), widow of Leonard C. Burdick; Hannah (1803–1893), wife of Jabez Hakes; and Amy (1809–1896), widow of Joshua Scriven, were daughters of the early town residents, Nathan Lewis and Mercy (Scriven) Lewis.

Five

At Work and Leisure

James E. West delighted in capturing people at their work, at school or religious service, or merely enjoying themselves. While these photographs were mainly created for his own enjoyment, some of the subjects doubtless purchased copies for themselves. Because of the time involved in composing and shooting photographs using a large camera mounted on a tripod and using flash powder for indoor shots to obtain optimum sharpness and the proper exposure, these photographs all required some posing. West nonetheless was able to capture the wide variety of activities that comprised daily life in the rural Northeast with remarkable spontaneity.

Ironically, West was portraying the social life of fairly small rural communities that would largely vanish after World War I. The mobility that came with the advent of the automobile, the decline of a sustainable agricultural economy, and the exodus of a younger generation to nearby cities, would leave small towns such as these each fighting for the survival of their unique identity. By capturing these varied activities with his camera for posterity, James E. West helped these communities today retain, to quote Grafton author and critic, Granville Hicks, the vital "sense of community past."

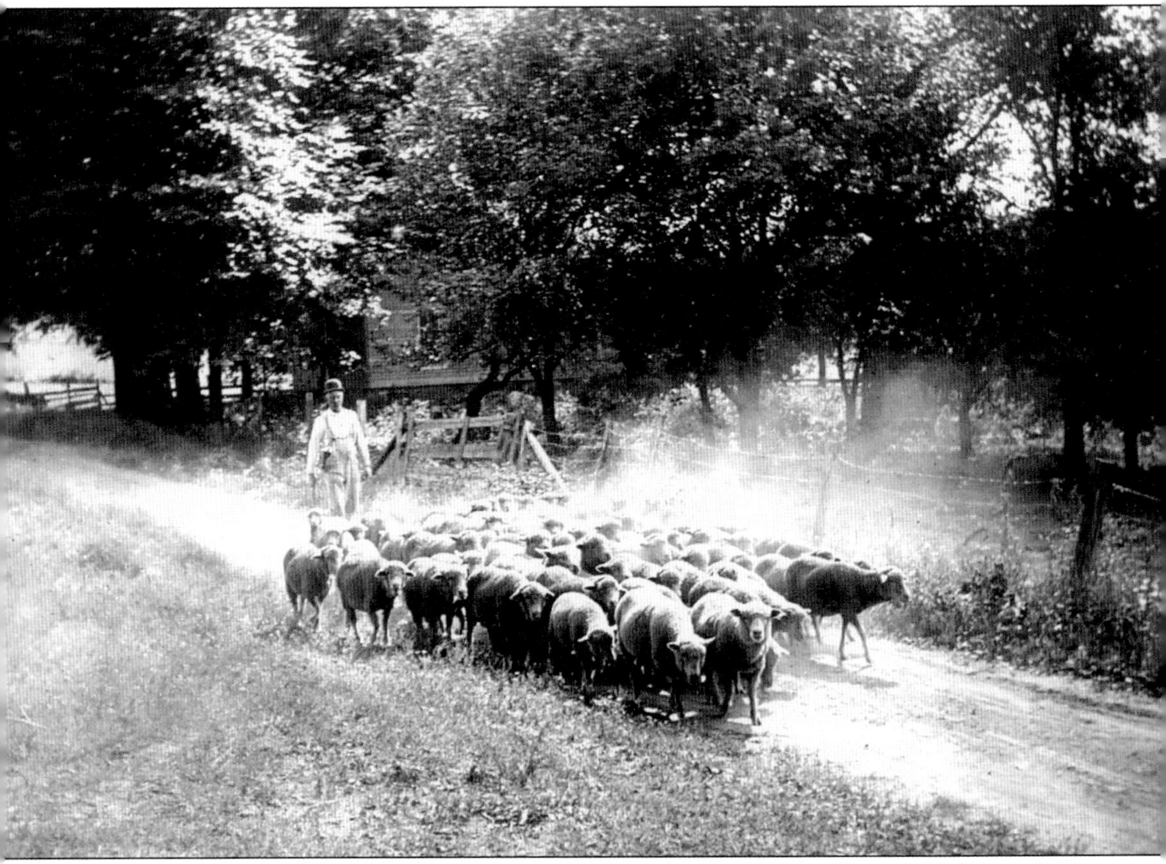

Harry L. Hull herds his sheep down a dusty back road, most likely in Brown's Hollow in Berlin.

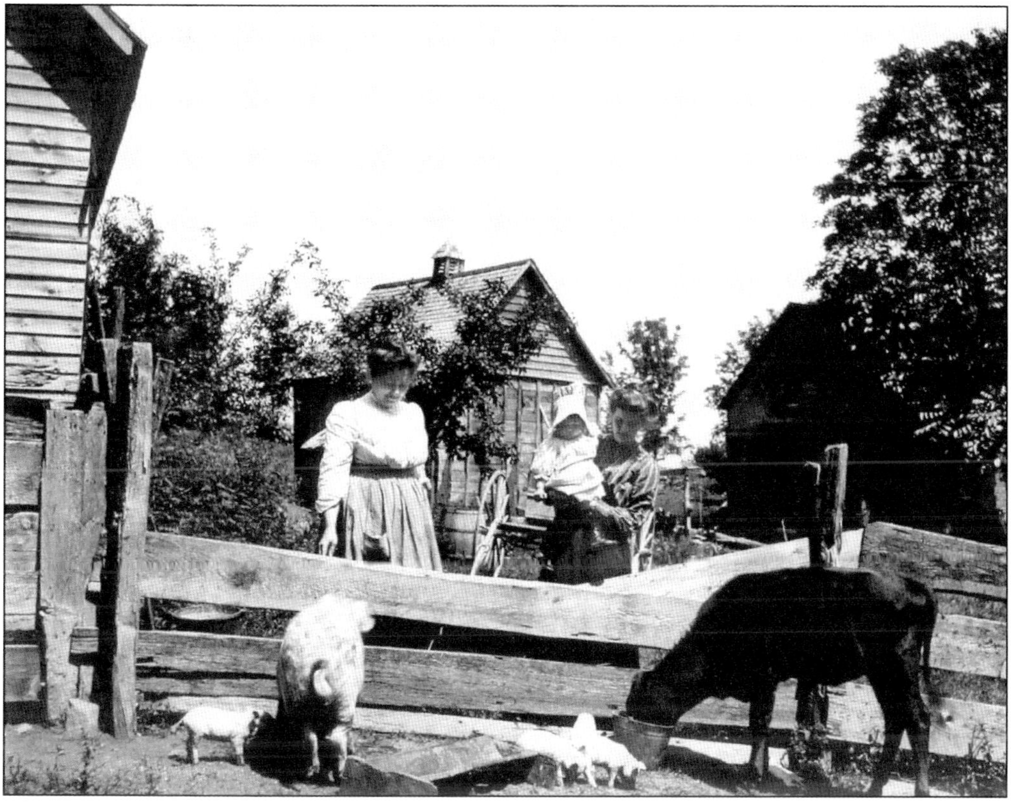

The Agan family (above) proudly admires the livestock in the barnyard of their farm on Shaver Pond Road in Grafton. Nathan Hakes (1835–1913) works at his blacksmith's trade (below) in his shop behind his Grafton Center home.

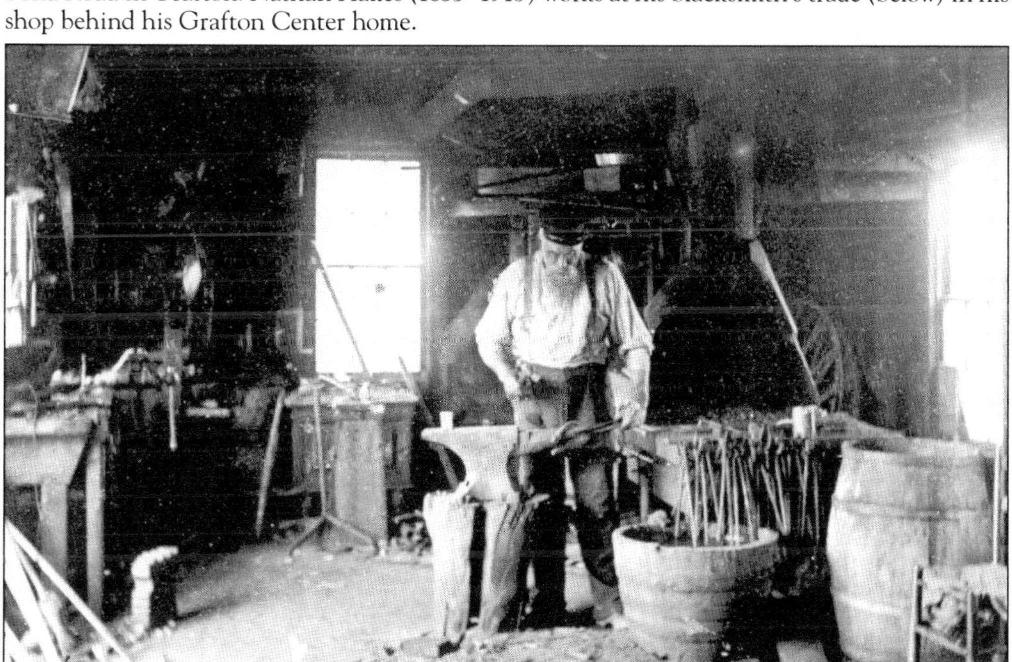

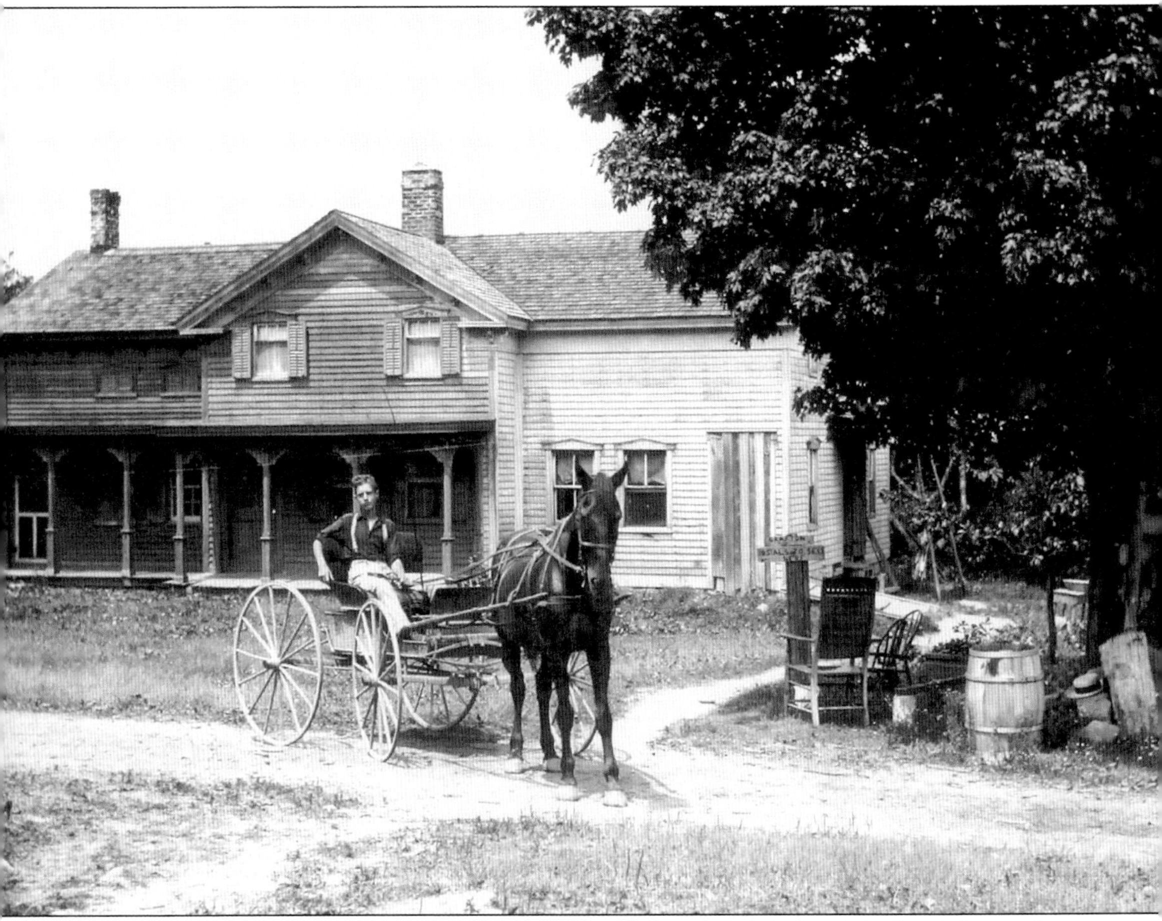

A young man in the Snyder family is captured in his wagon in front of the family home, known as "Point Pleasant," on South Road in Grafton. The Snyders apparently marketed James E. West's "real photo" postal cards, as indicated by a sign on the post which reads "Grafton Postals for Sale."

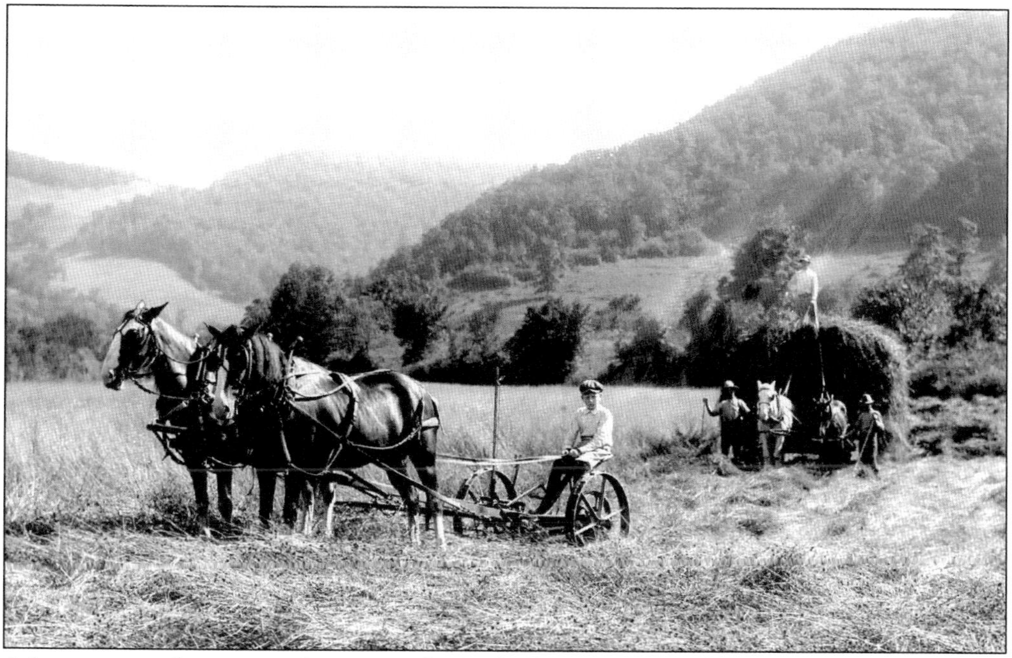

A late summer day is spent haying in the Little Hoosic River valley in Petersburgh; this view looks south toward the "Double Road Crossing" and Prosser Hollow.

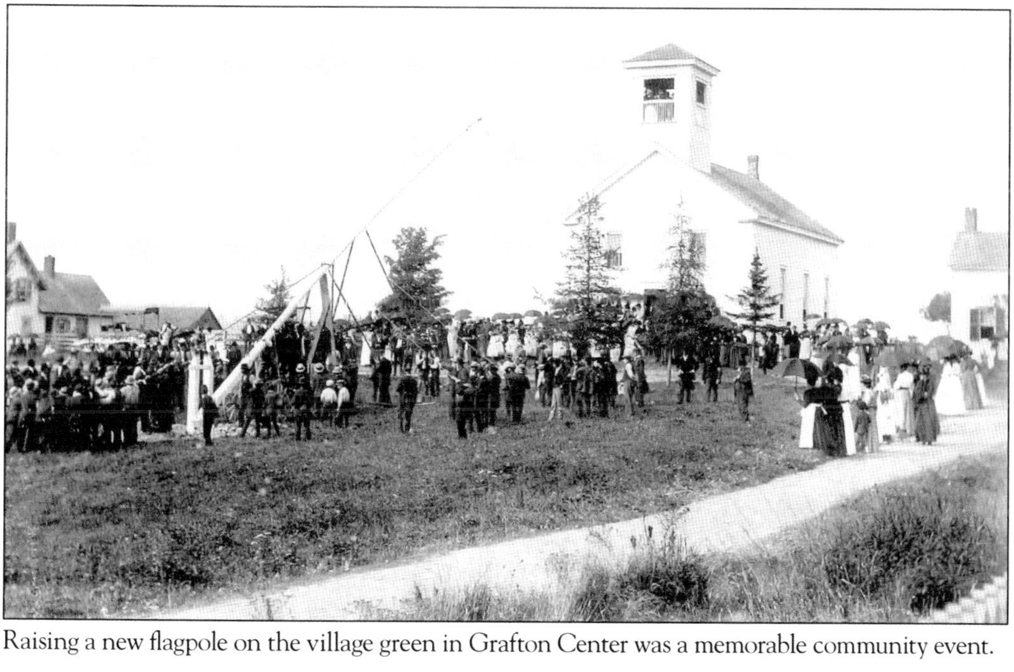

Raising a new flagpole on the village green in Grafton Center was a memorable community event.

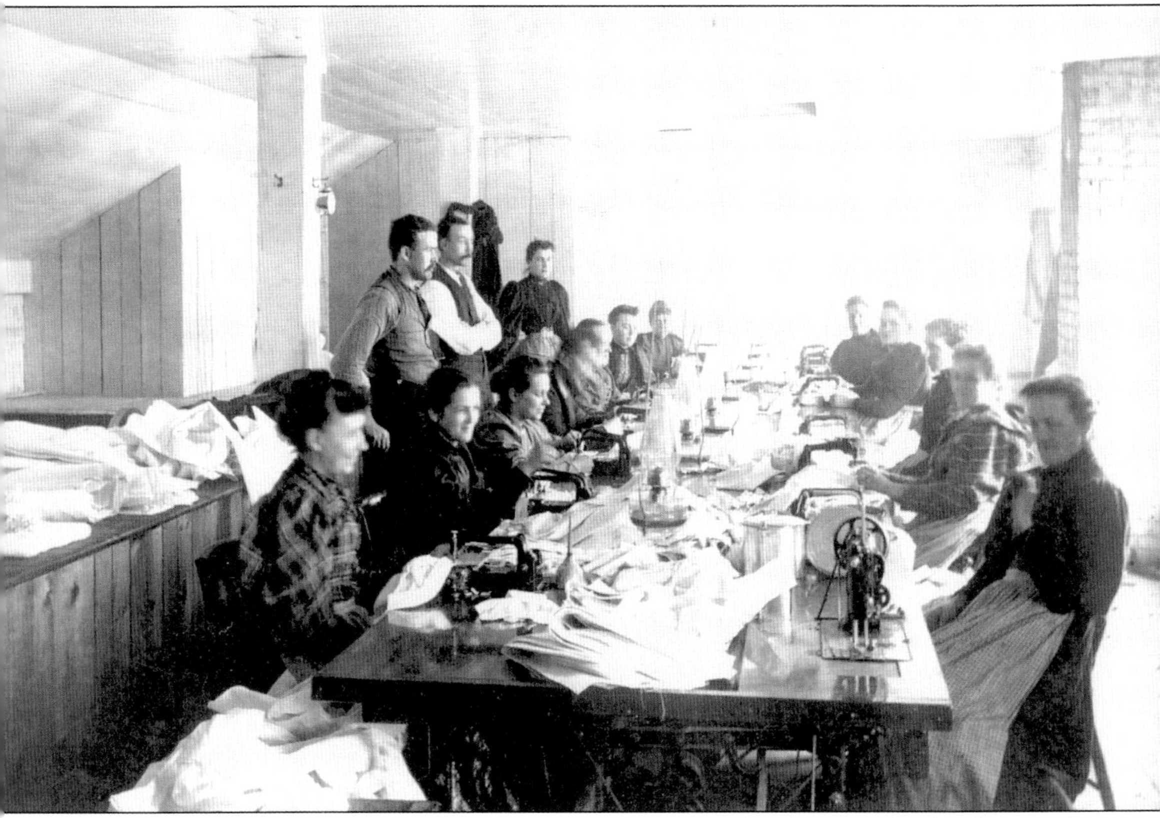

Workers at the Scriven shirt factory in Grafton Center take a break to pose for the photographer.

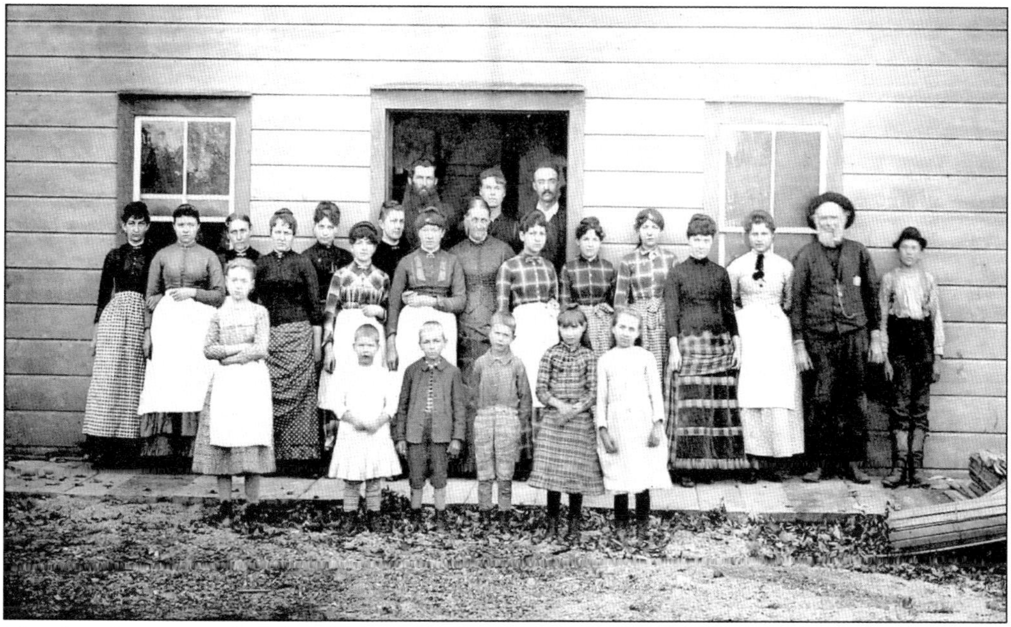

The shirt factory employed a number of workers (above) of various ages, in spite of the fact that the owners told census takers in 1880 that no "children or youth" were employed there. Some members of the well-dressed group of Grafton men (below) are seated on folding carpet stools manufactured at Saunders's folding carpet chair once located factory on North Road.

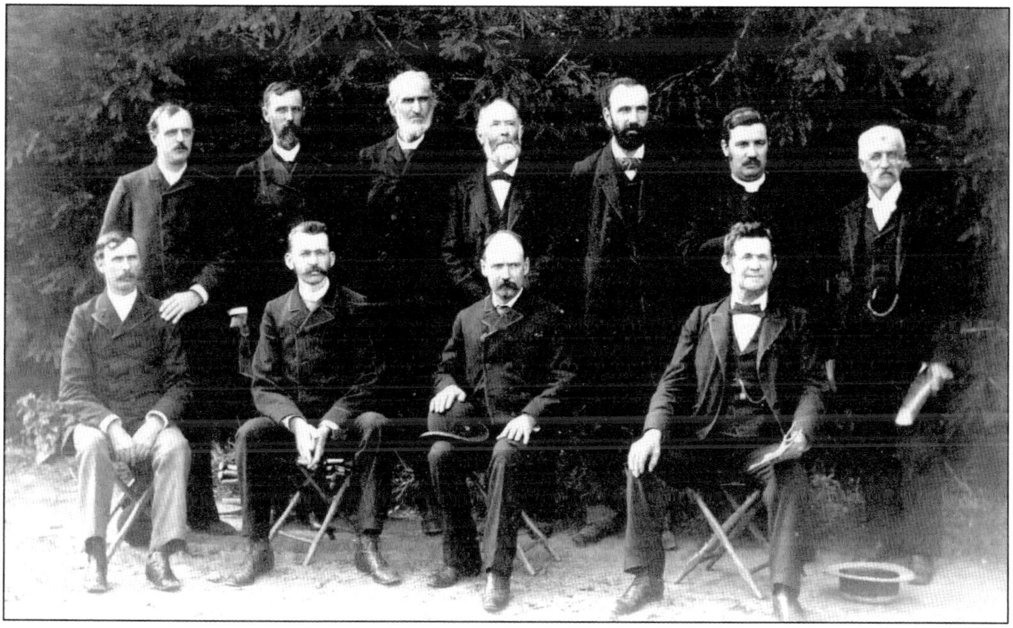

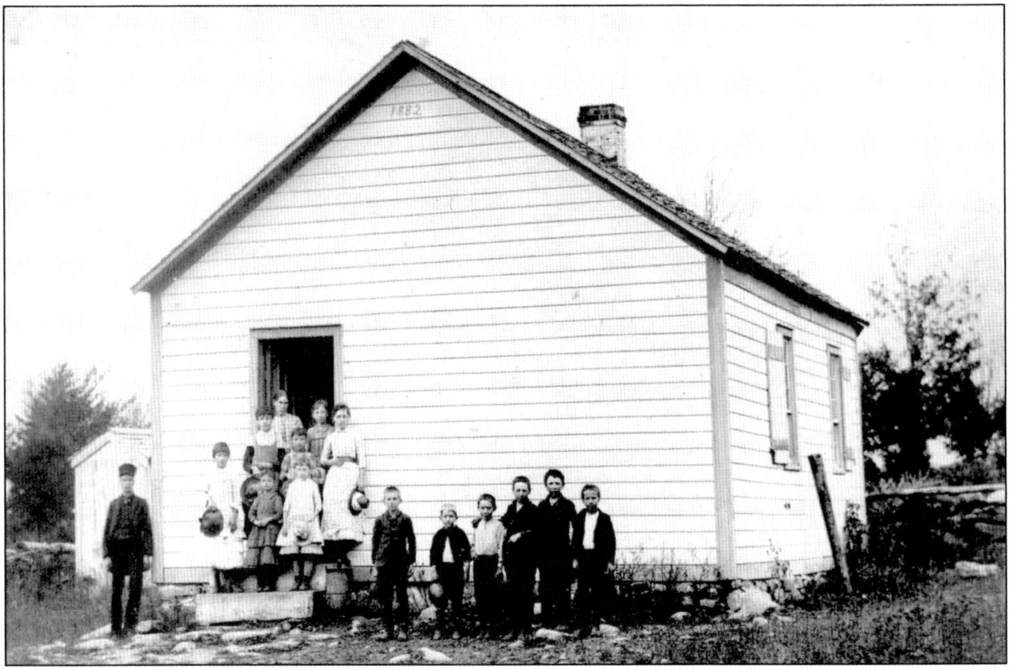

School No. 1 (above), constructed in 1882 on Cranberry Pond Road, was one of Grafton's more isolated rural schools. The District No. 3 schoolhouse in East Grafton (below), photographed in 1893 or 1894, has been converted into a residence.

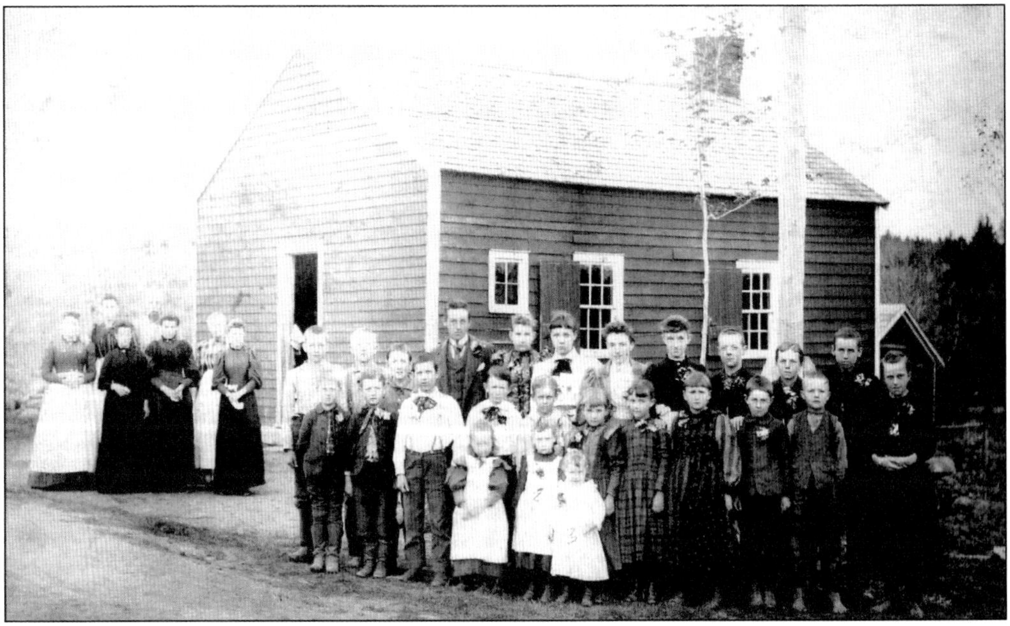

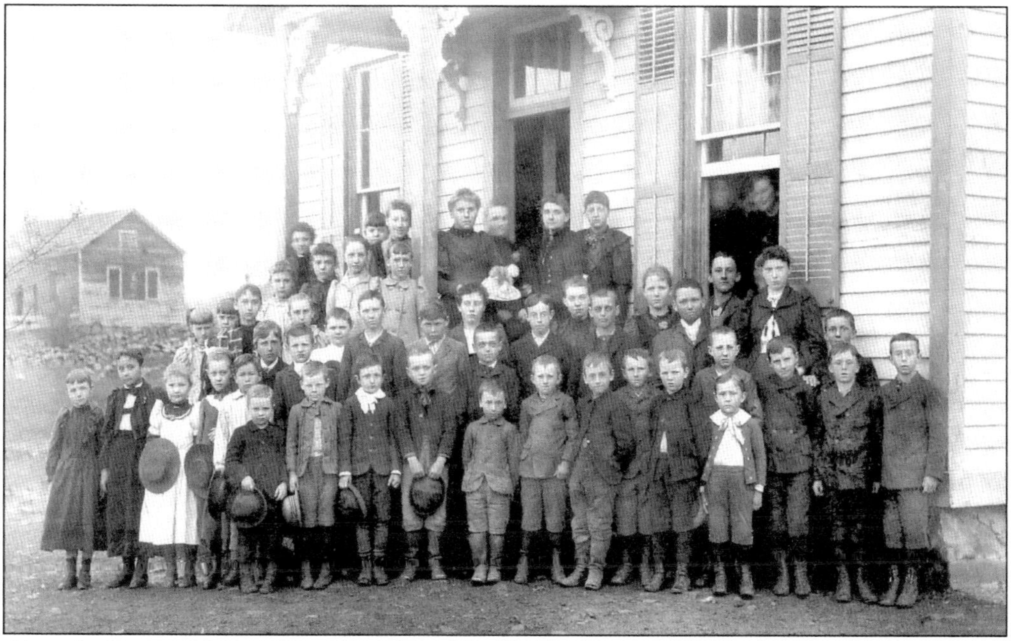

Alice Corbin was the teacher when this view of the substantial District No. 9 or West Grafton schoolhouse (above) was taken shortly after its construction in 1889; the old "red" schoolhouse appears in the background. The Snyder School in District No. 6 (below) is a private residence today, but its appearance has been greatly altered.

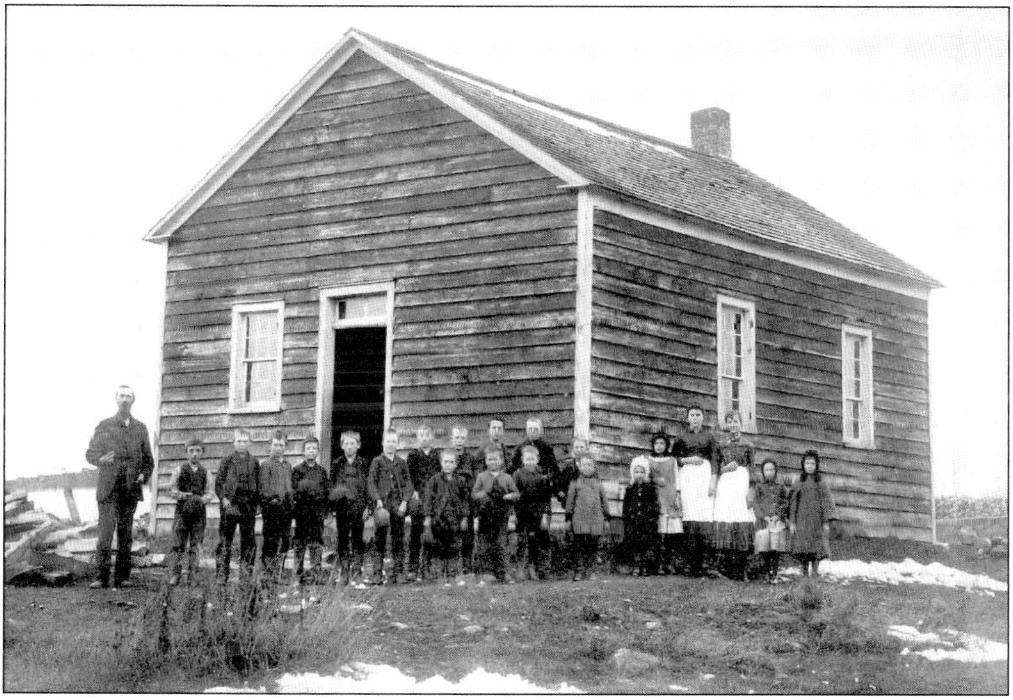

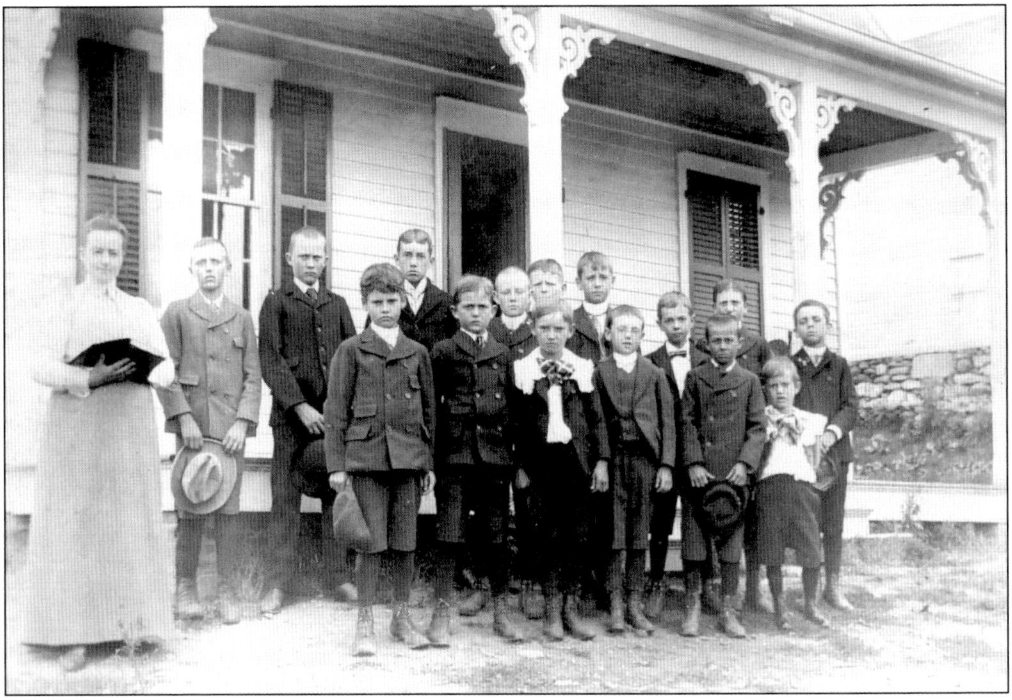

Religion played a major role in small-town life in this era. The photograph above shows a Grafton Methodist Church Sunday school class posed in front of the former parsonage. The boys shown below attended Grafton Baptist Church Sunday school in 1890.

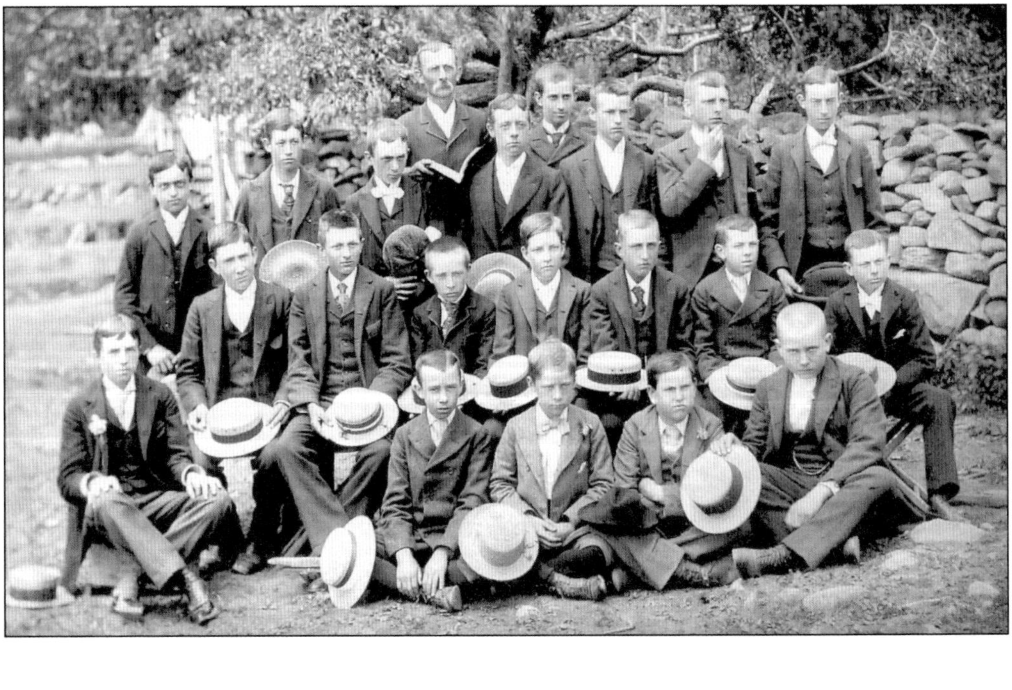

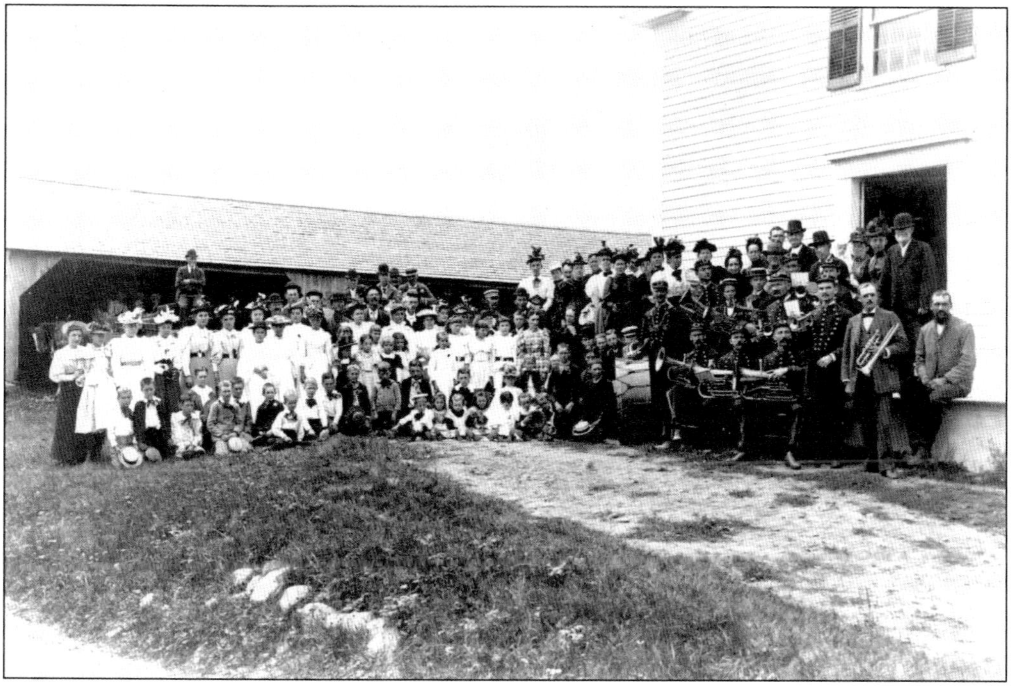

The congregation of the Grafton Baptist Church poses with the Grafton Coronet Band alongside the church, with the carriage sheds visible in the background.

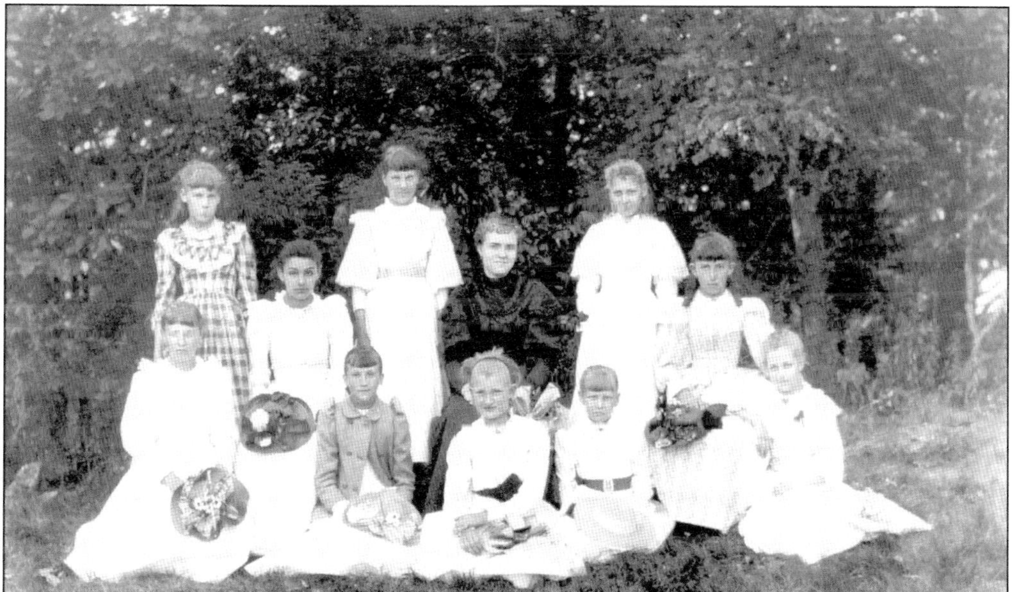

The girls in Della Whitley's Sunday school class wore their finest dresses for a Sunday church service.

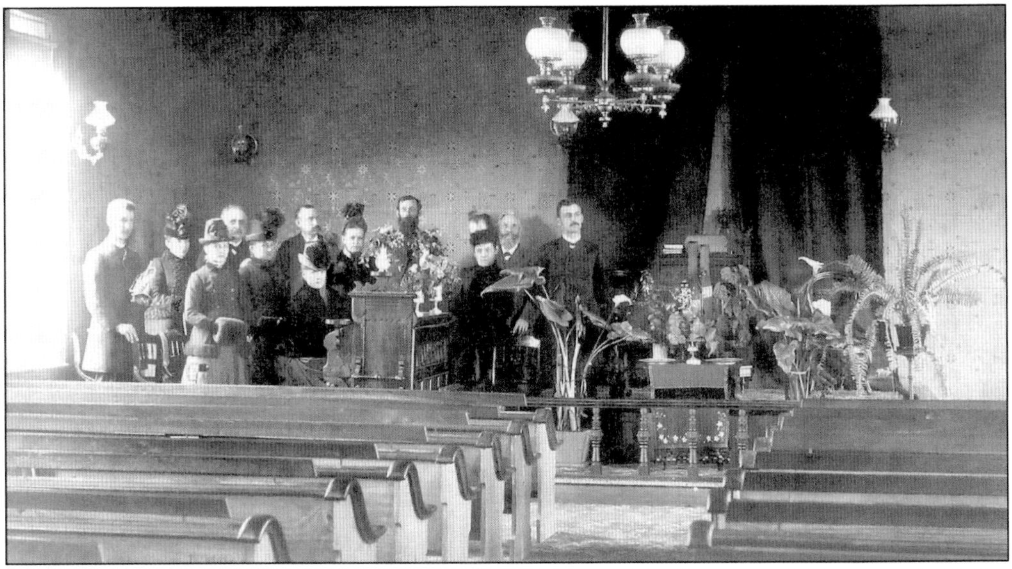

The Berlin Methodist Church (above) was finely decorated for Easter in 1888; Rev. J. P. Haller was the minister at that time. The minister stands before his pulpit (below) at the Grafton Baptist Church in the early 1900s. (Above, courtesy of the Berlin Free Town Library.)

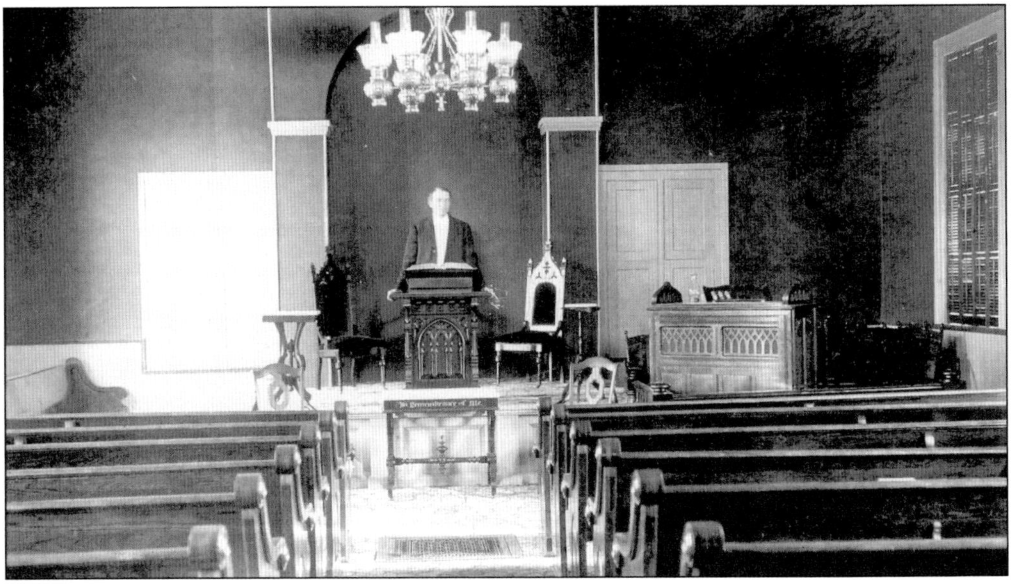

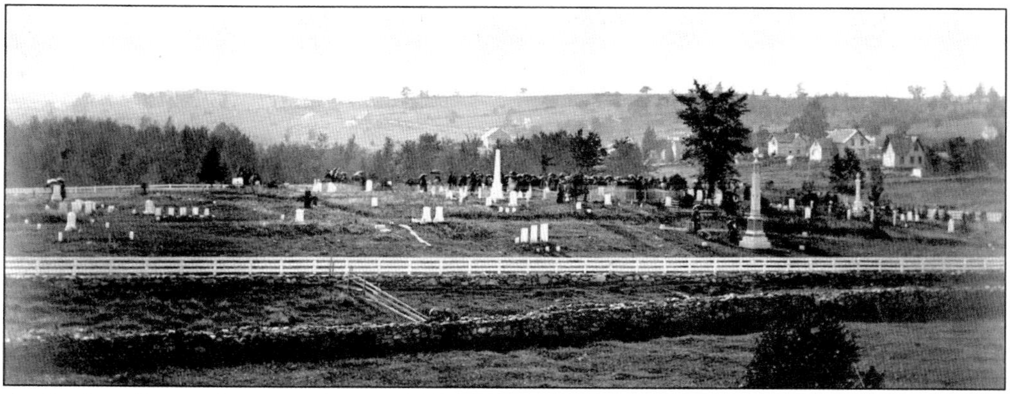

At Grafton Center Cemetery, James E. West took these photographs of the funeral of John H. Scriven, who departed on August 19, 1886, at the age of 45 years.

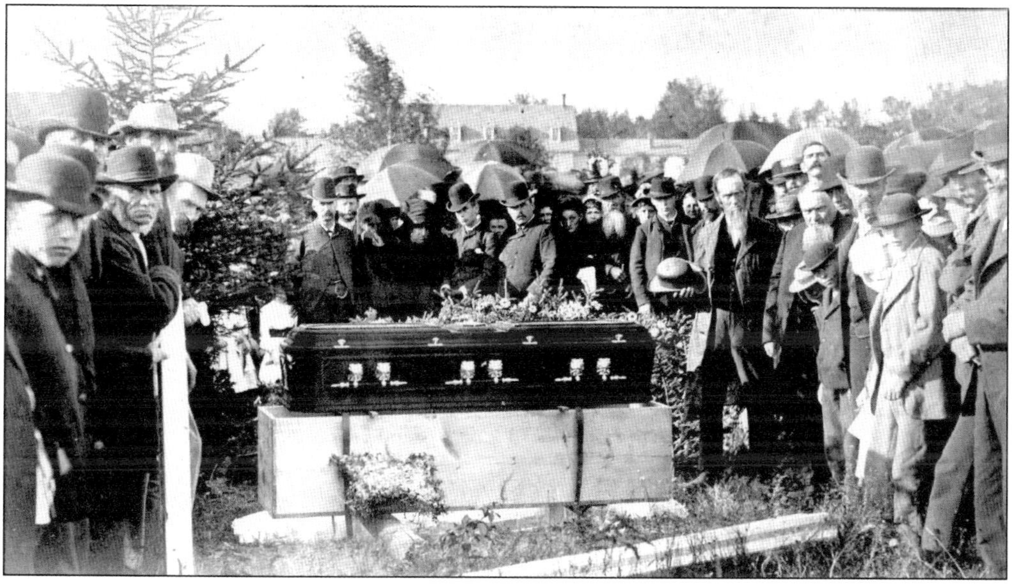

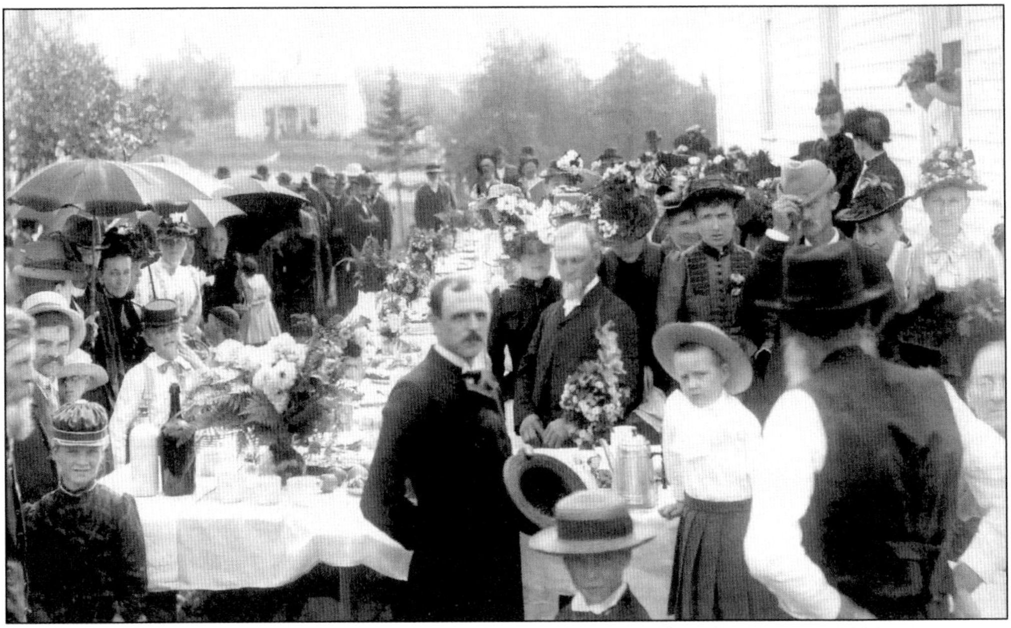

James E. West captured the townsfolk of Grafton at a Baptist church picnic in 1890.

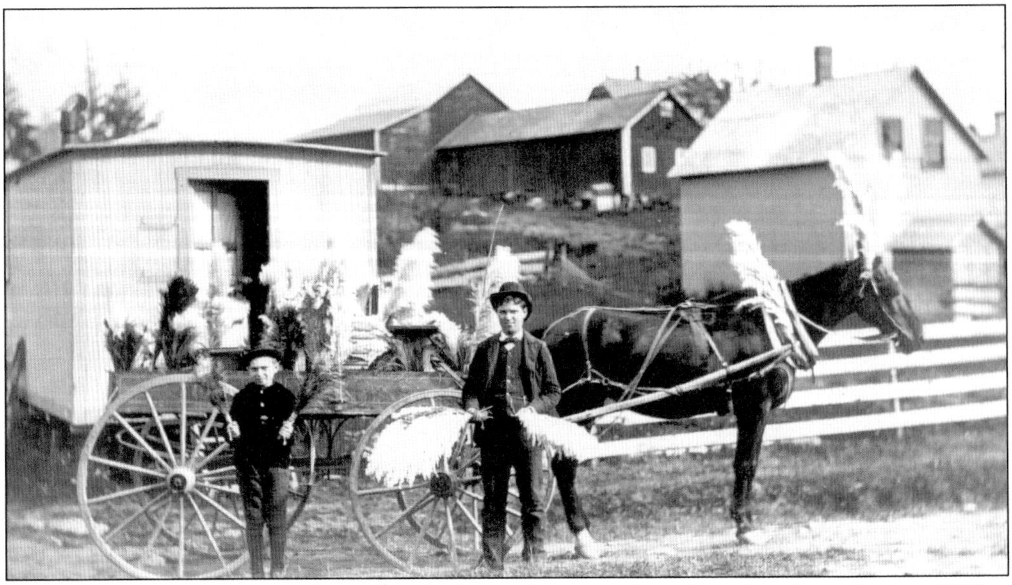

This horse and wagon were adorned with plumes for a parade in Petersburgh in the late 1880s.

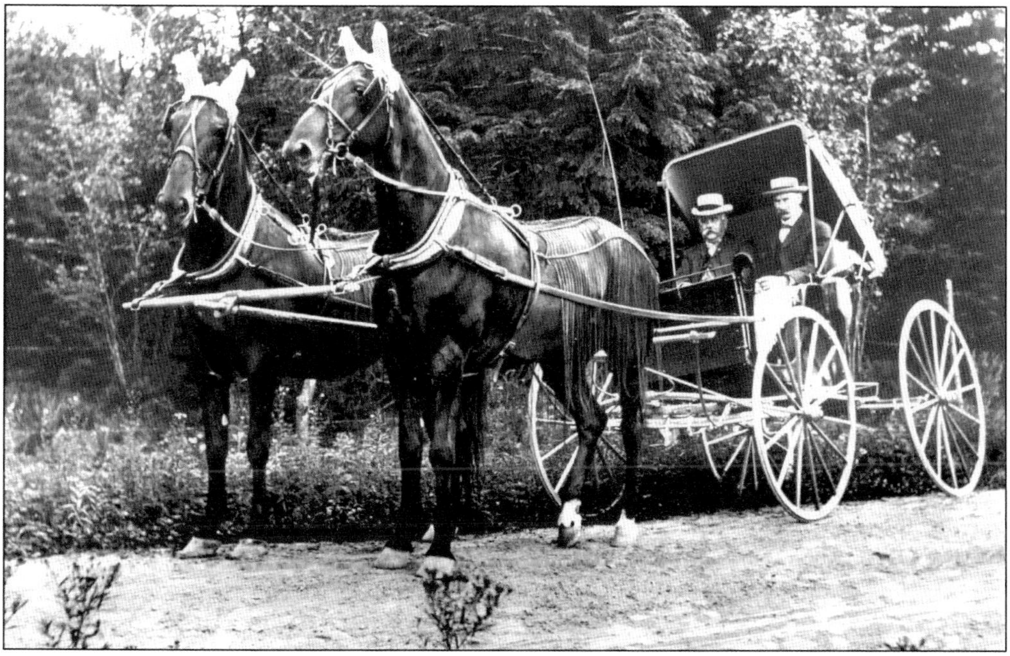

John S. Tilley and Chester Waite prepare to join a parade in Grafton to welcome the advent of the 20th century.

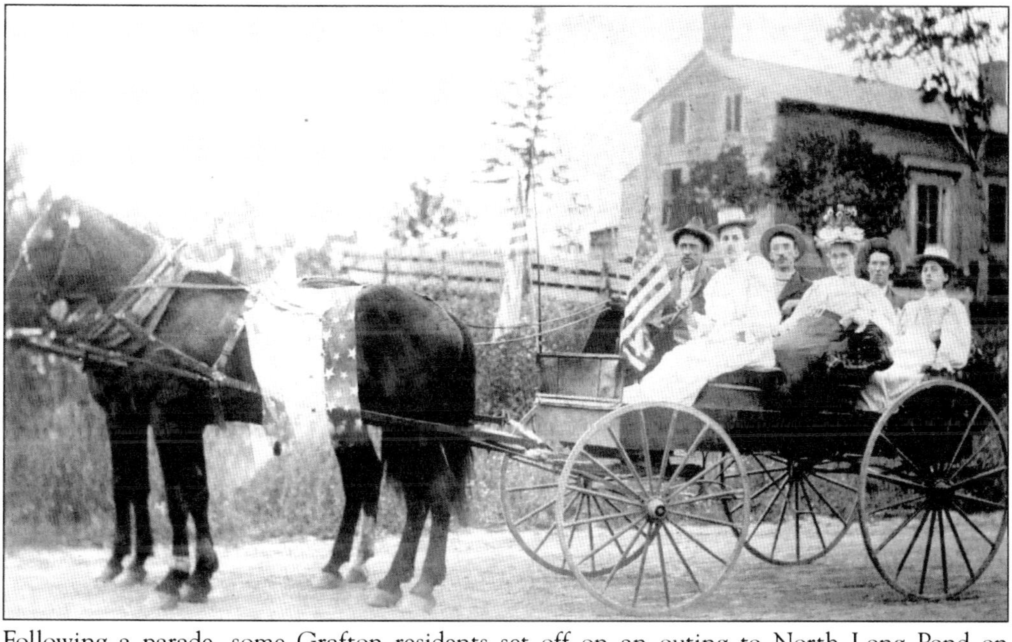

Following a parade, some Grafton residents set off on an outing to North Long Pond on July 7, 1896.

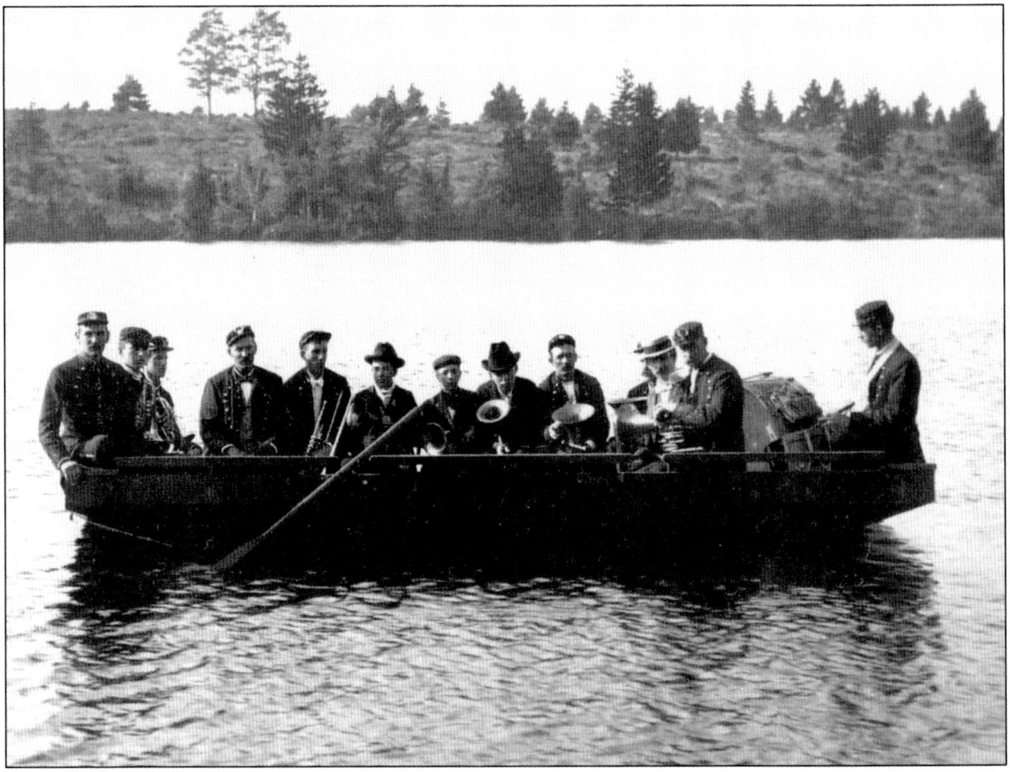

The Grafton Coronet Band posed for the photographer in a boat on Mill Pond (above) and at a picnic held in nearby Poestenkill (below) in 1897.

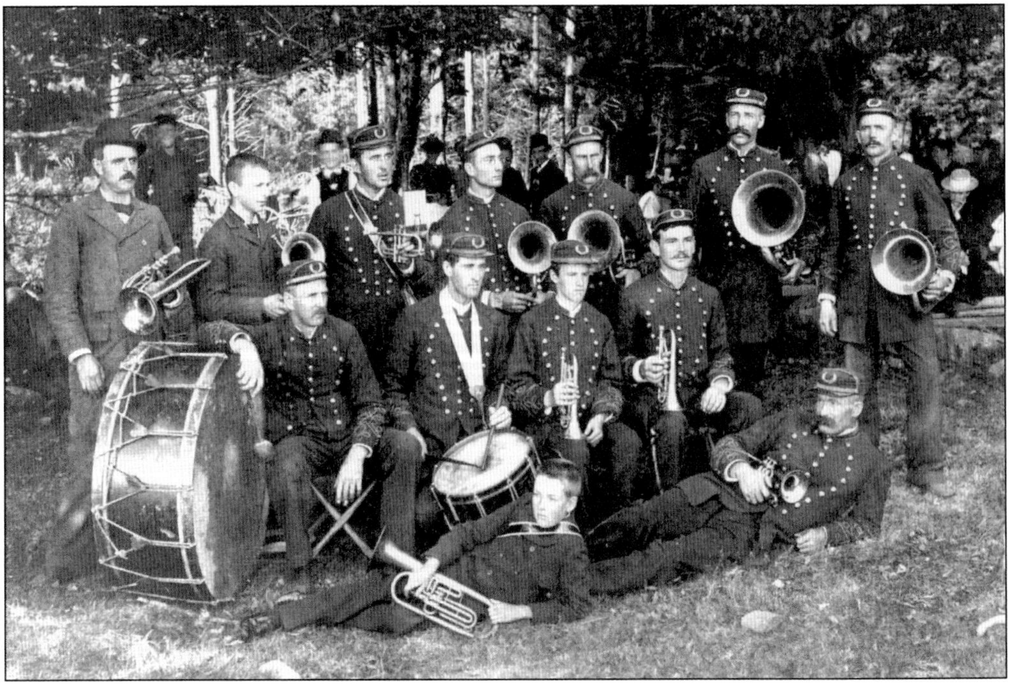

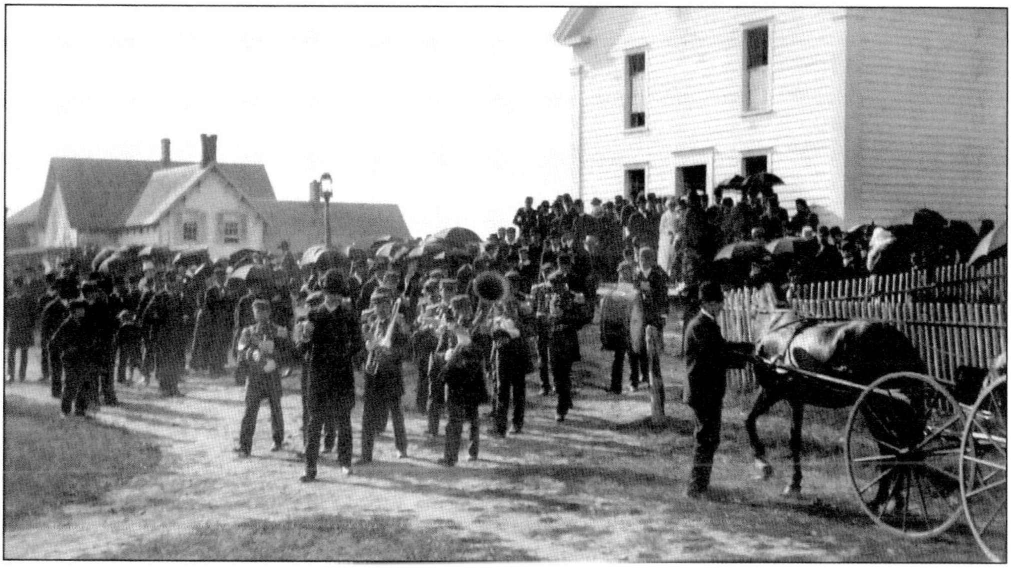

The band leads a procession out of the Grafton Baptist Church (above). The unidentified horn player (right) belonged to some band that visited Grafton to present a concert.

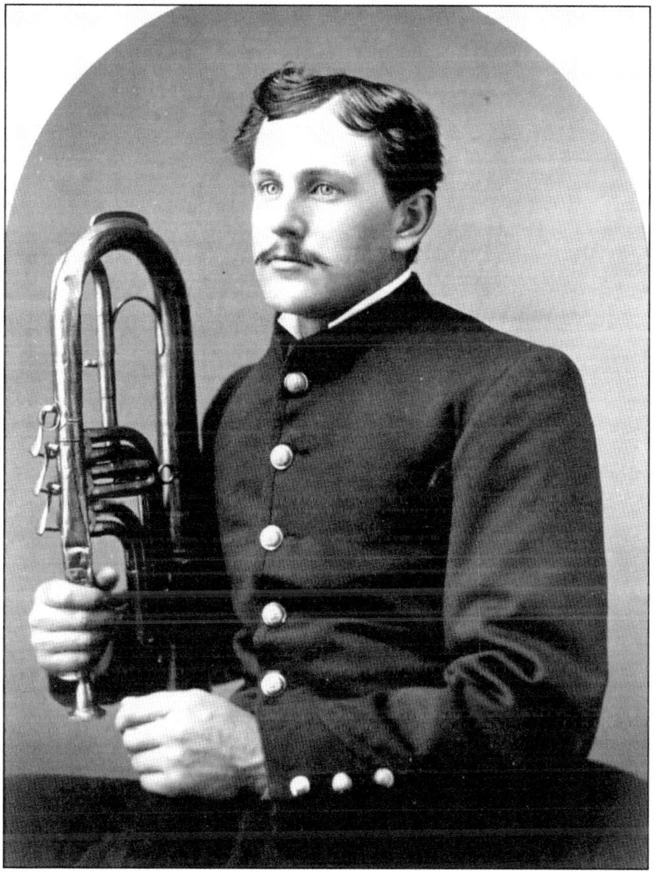

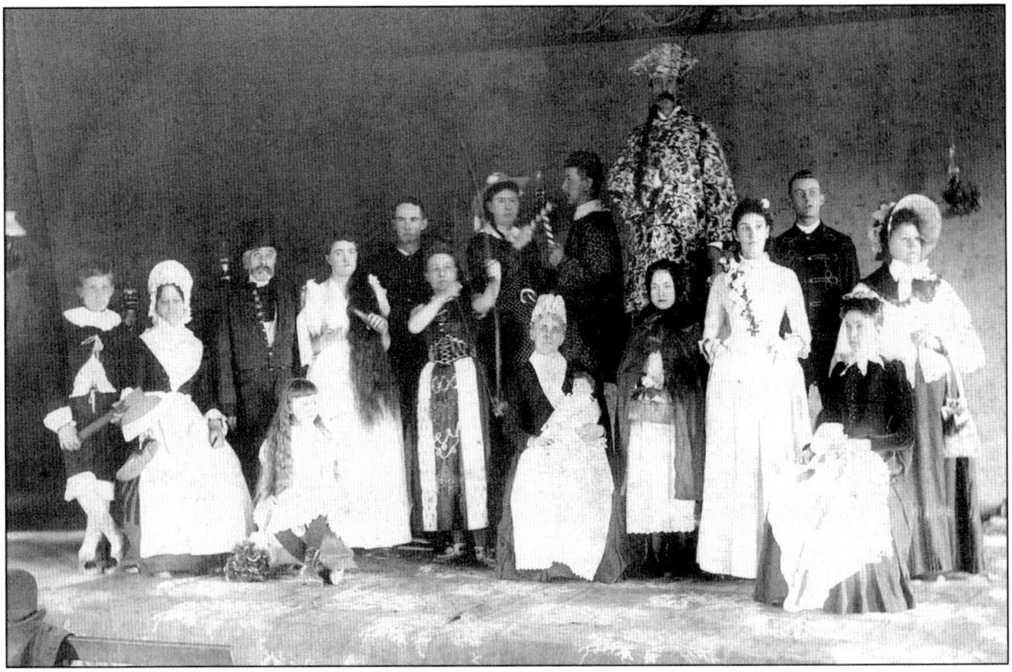

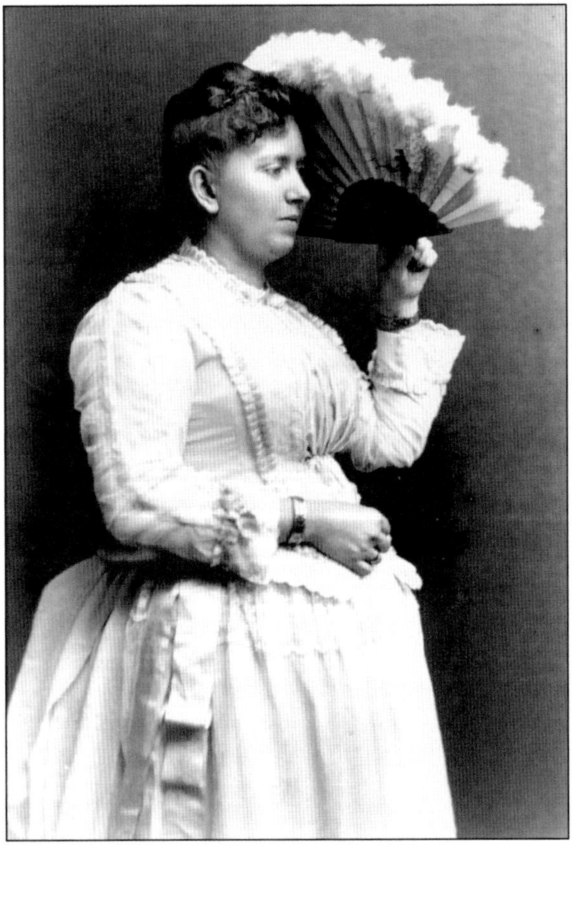

Mrs. Jarley's Wax Figures, performed by Berlin residents around 1890 (above), was a decidedly oddball play where characters dressed as figures in the famous London wax museum. The actors were carried about the stage by assistants and performed with clumsy motions as if they were wound-up automatons upon being summoned by Mrs. Jarley. Kate West (left) and her daughter, Maude, enjoyed dressing in costume and appearing in local productions. (Above, courtesy of the Taconic Valley Historical Society.)

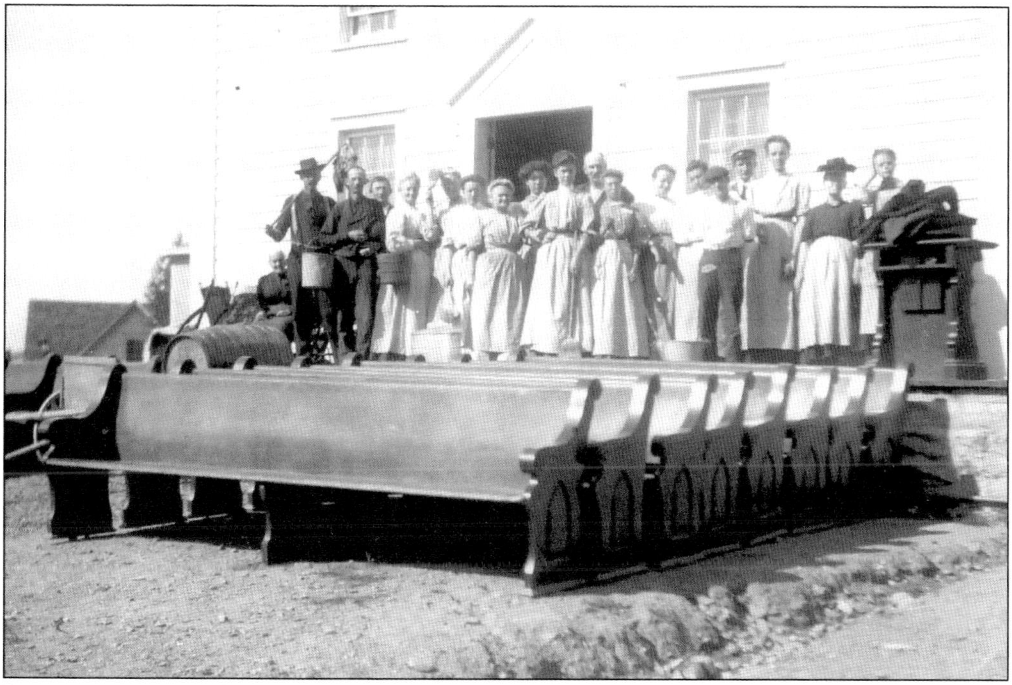

Pews were removed from the Grafton Baptist Church to accommodate a theatrical production with a frontier theme.

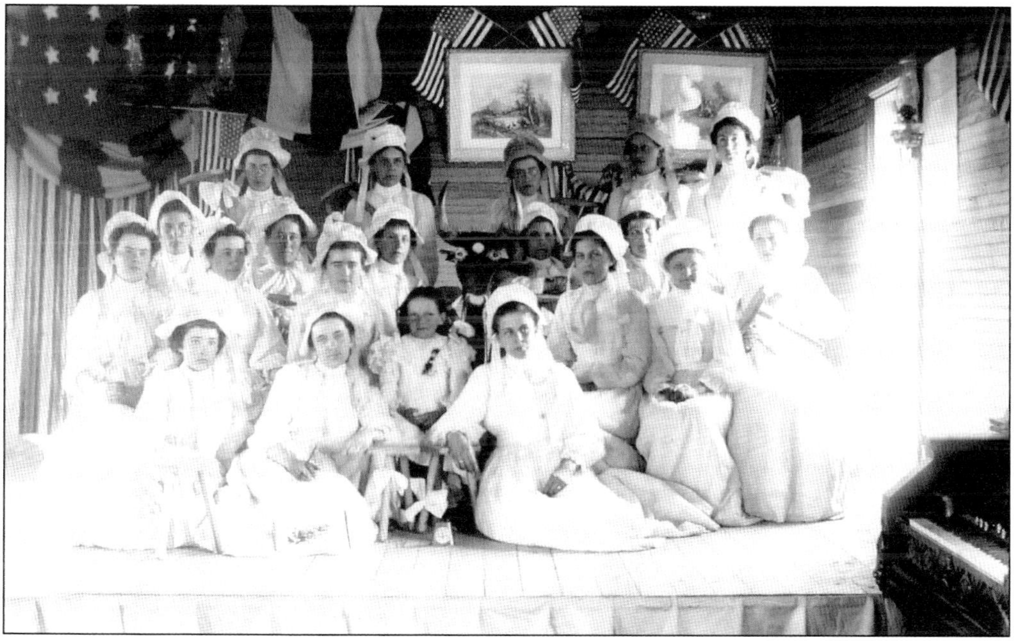

Grafton girls and women employed a cow figure in an amateur stage production known as the *Milk Maids' Drill.*

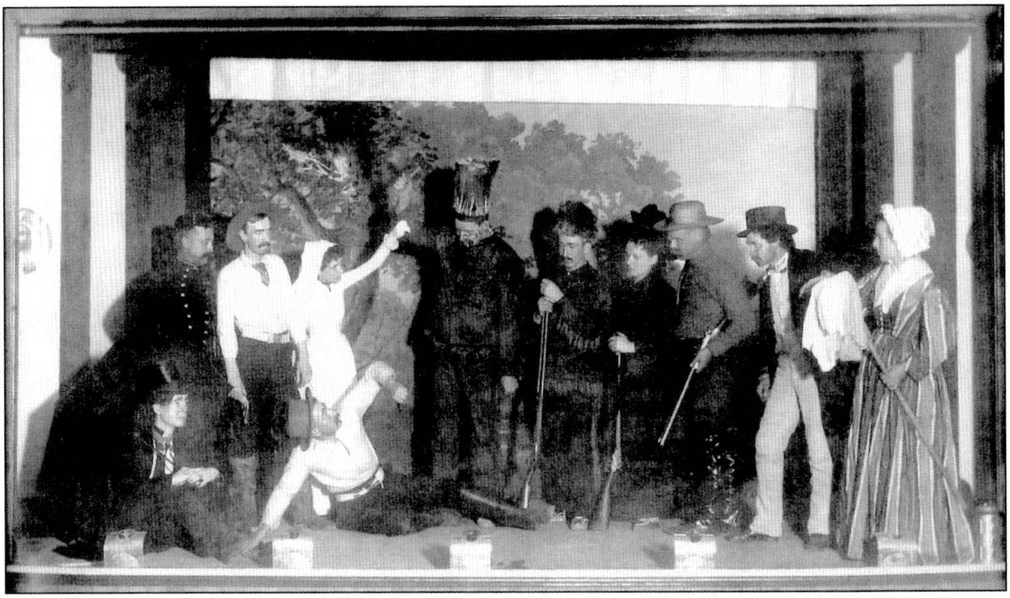

The Forty-niners, or, the Pioneer's Daughter, a popular Western melodrama written in 1879 by Thomas W. Hanshew, was performed on stage at Jones Hall on Elm Street in Berlin.

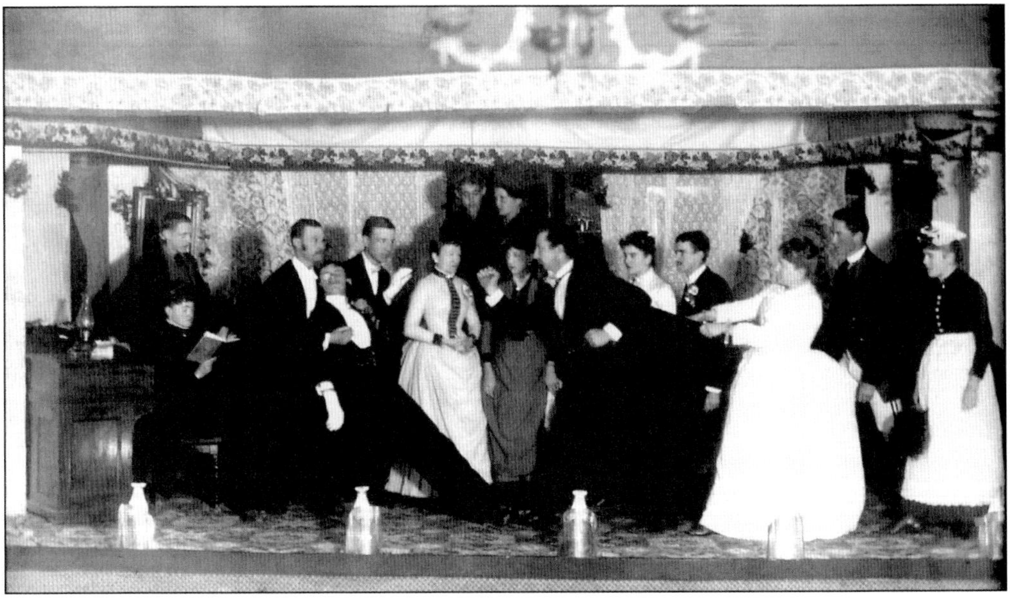

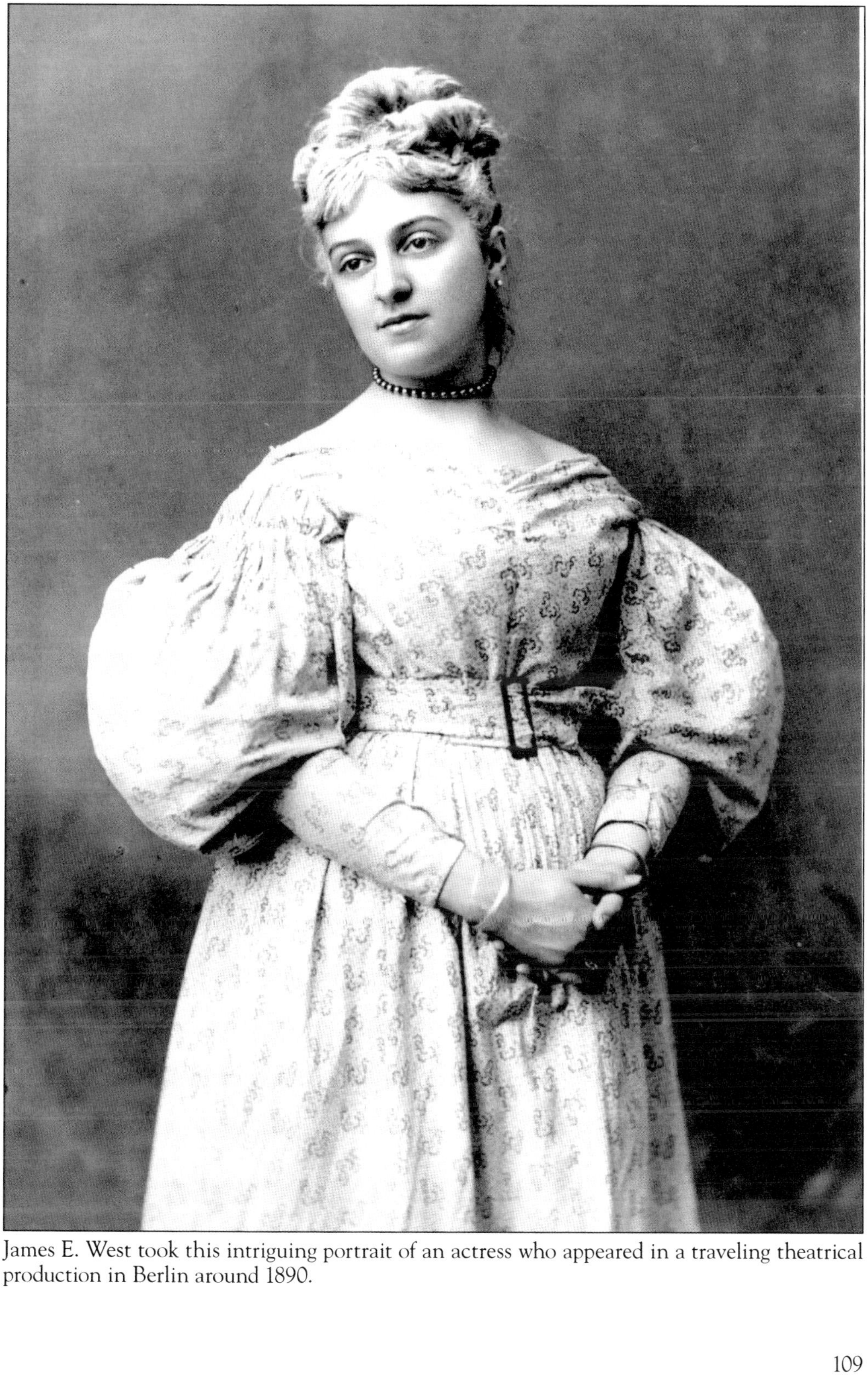

James E. West took this intriguing portrait of an actress who appeared in a traveling theatrical production in Berlin around 1890.

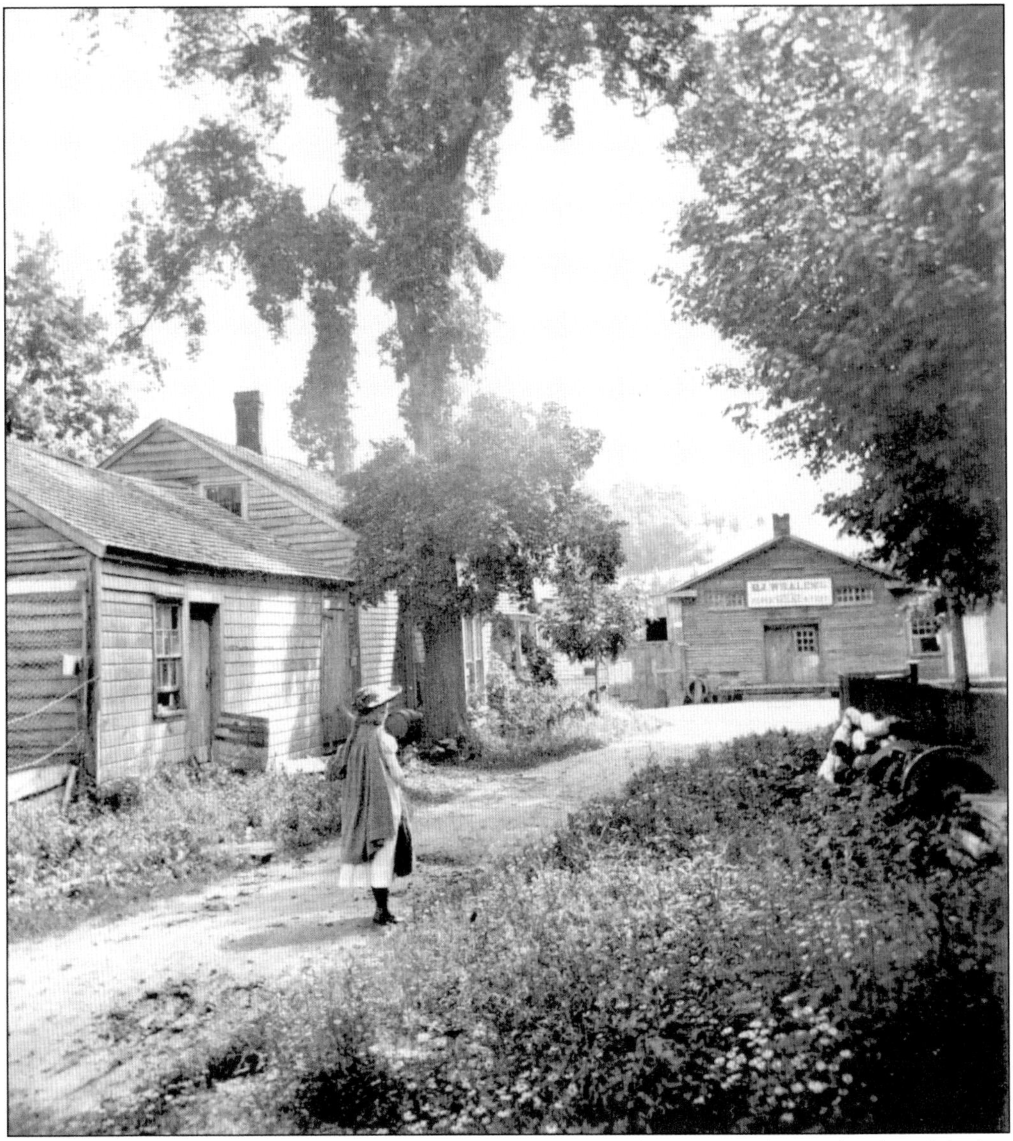

The photographer captured this idyllic image of a young girl returning from school on Maiden Lane in Berlin. Looking east toward North Main Street, H. J. Whalen's "Flour Meal and Feed" store appears in the background.

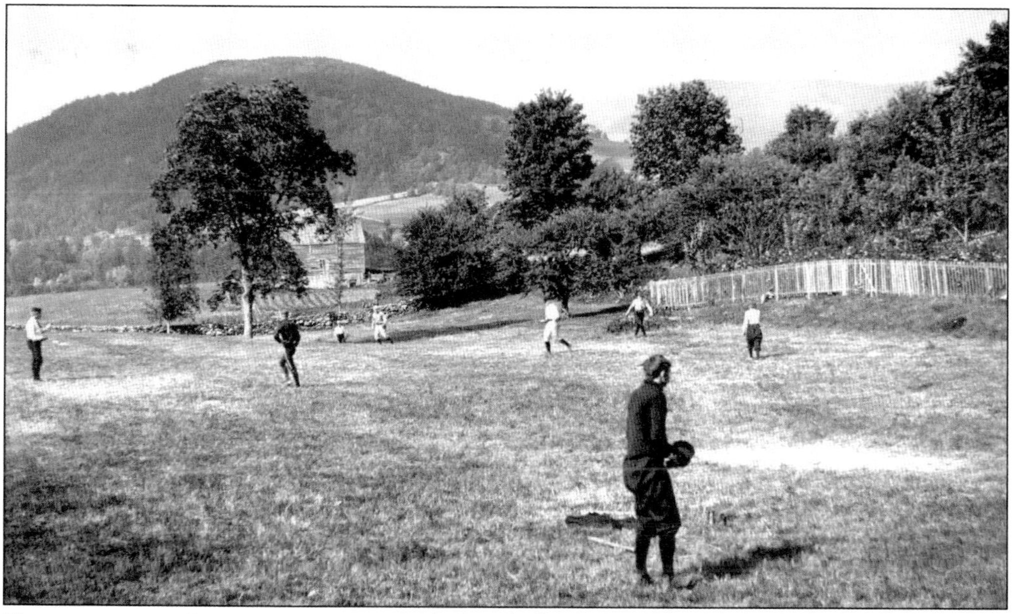

Young men in each community organized a baseball team. The game in Petersburgh (above) was played in a field near the site of the current town hall. The baseball team in Berlin (below) was photographed in 1888. (Courtesy of the Taconic Valley Historical Society.)

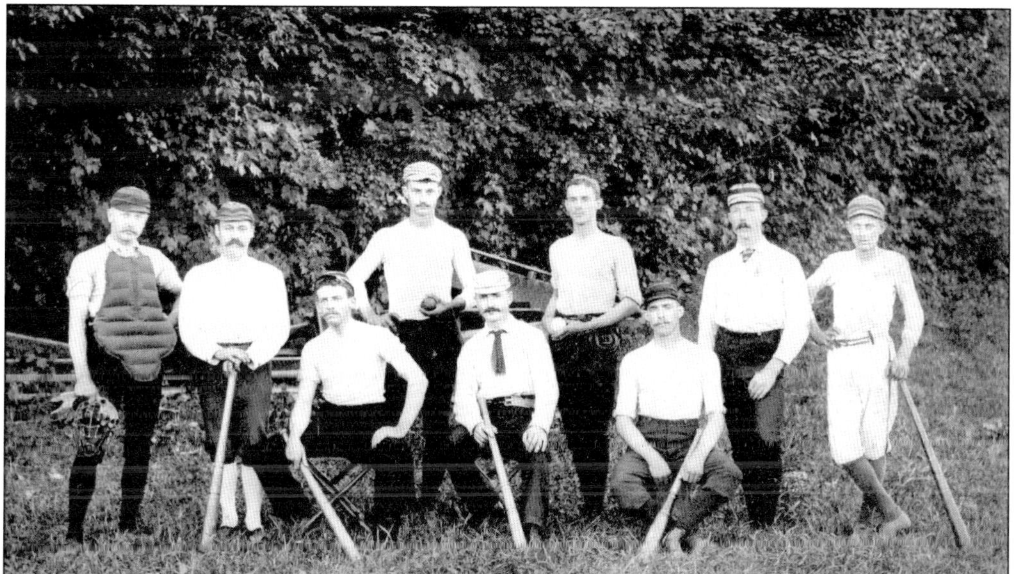

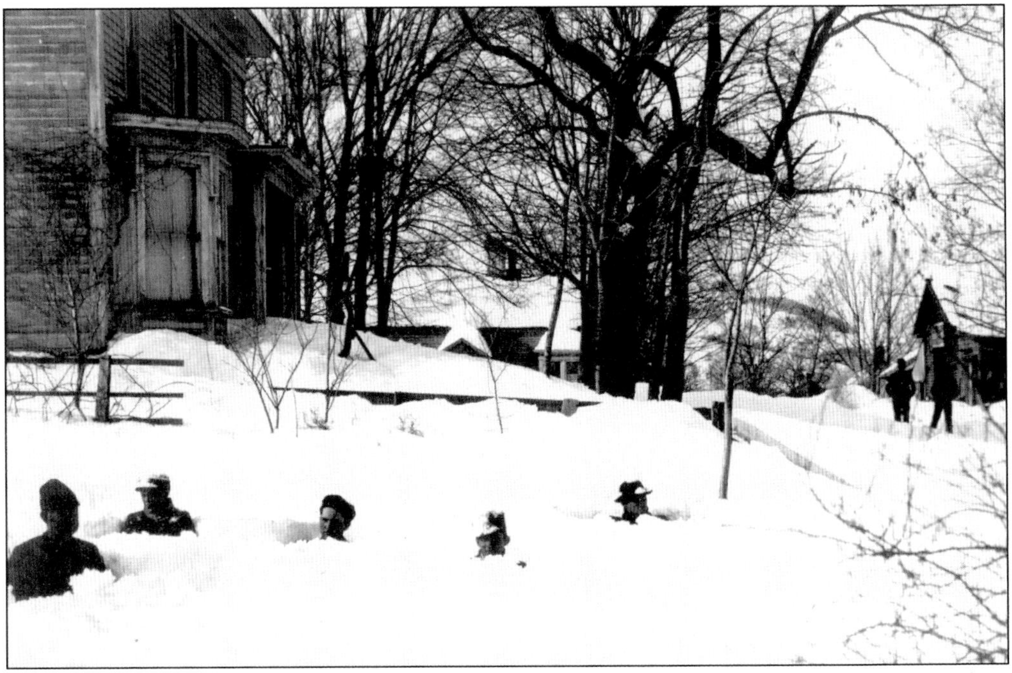

This scene showing the famous March "Blizzard of 1888" was taken looking north on Berlin's North Main Street.

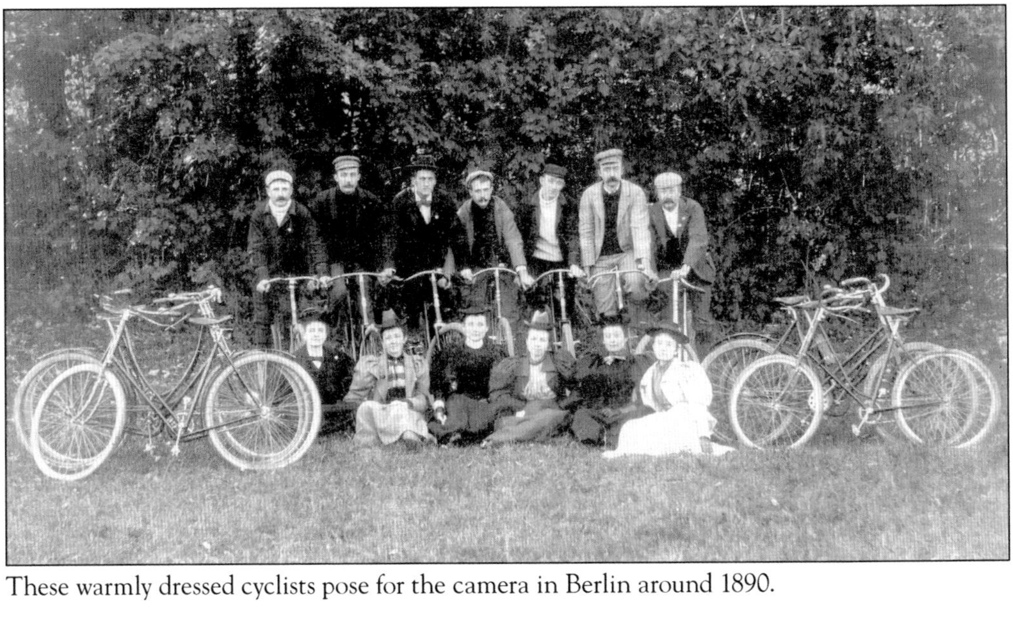

These warmly dressed cyclists pose for the camera in Berlin around 1890.

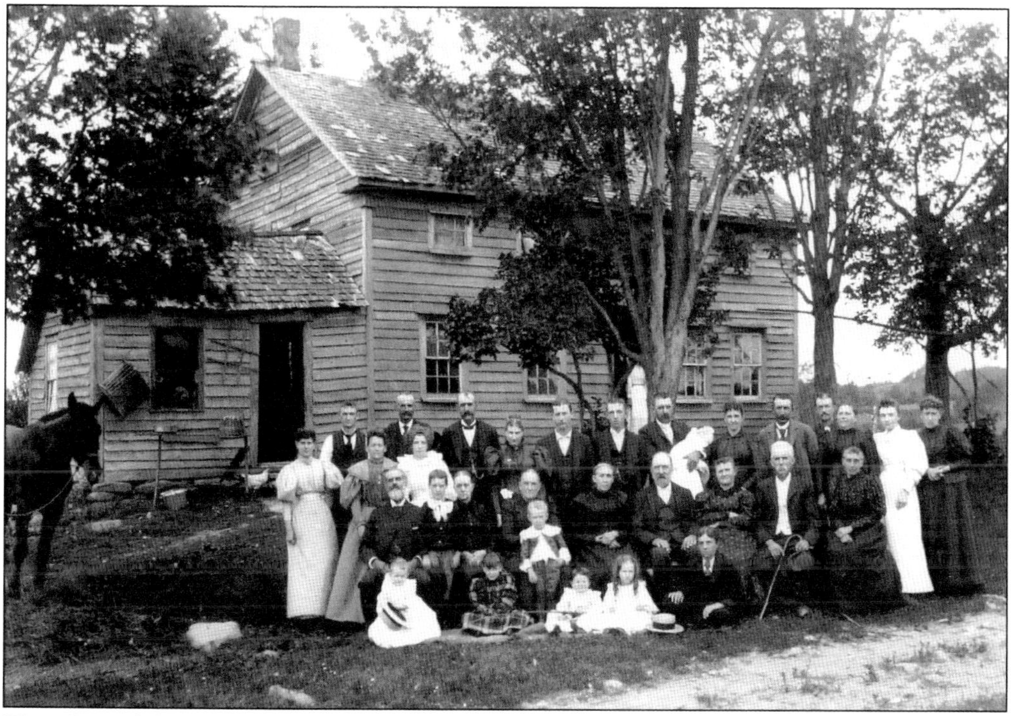

The Howard family held its reunion (above) at the long-gone homestead on Taconic Lake Road in Grafton. The group (below) poses in front of a house on Dumbleton Road in Grafton following a Methodist church picnic held on August 21, 1895.

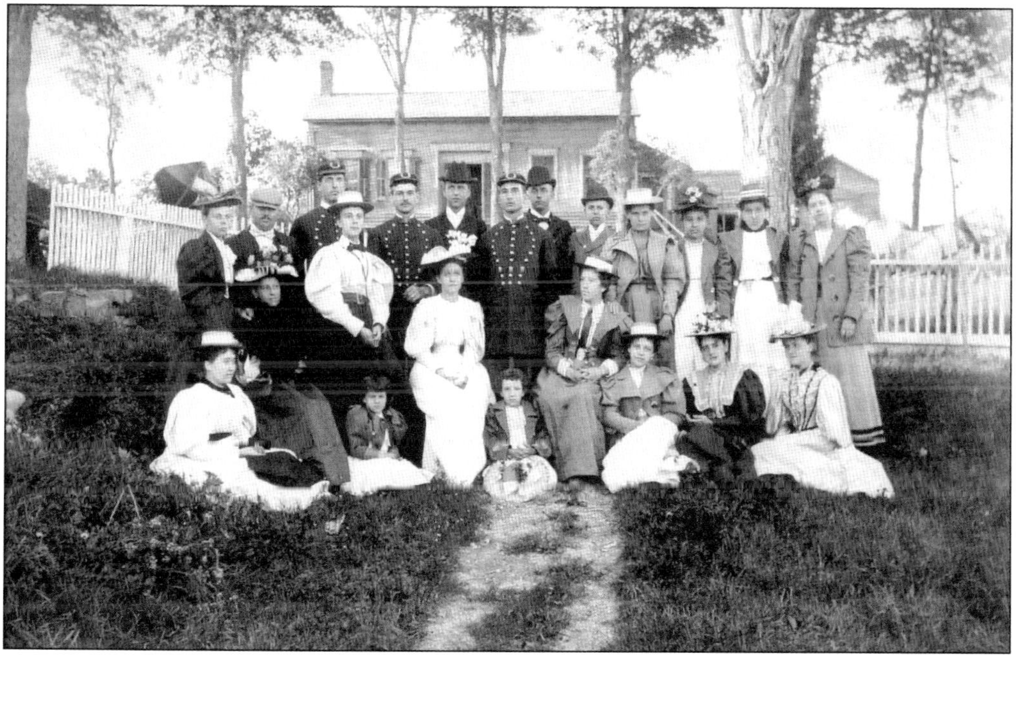

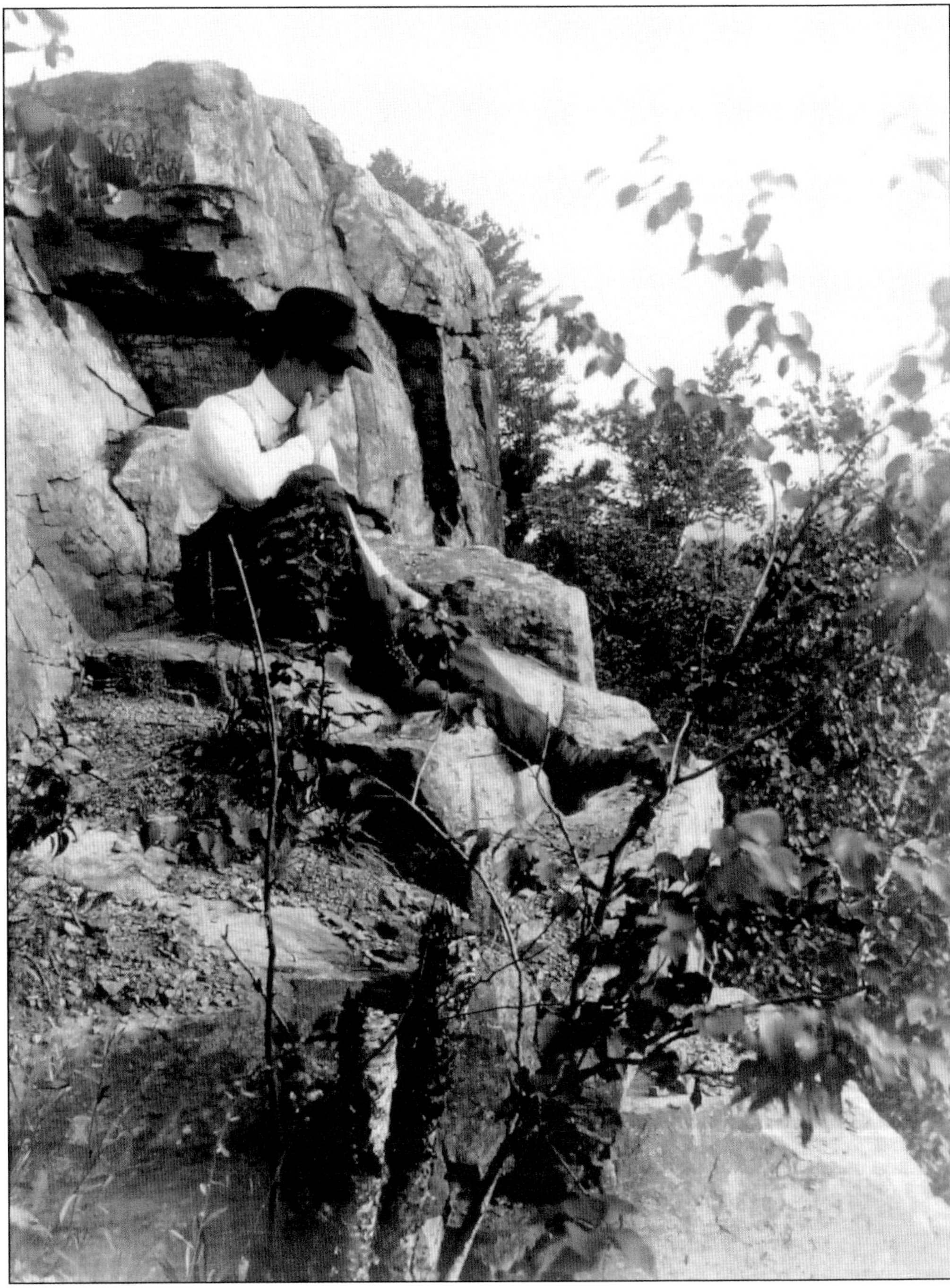

A hiker pauses to appreciate the spectacular view to the west from escapement of Slide Mountain in Grafton, near a disappearing waterfall, and high above another local landmark known as the "Cold Spring."

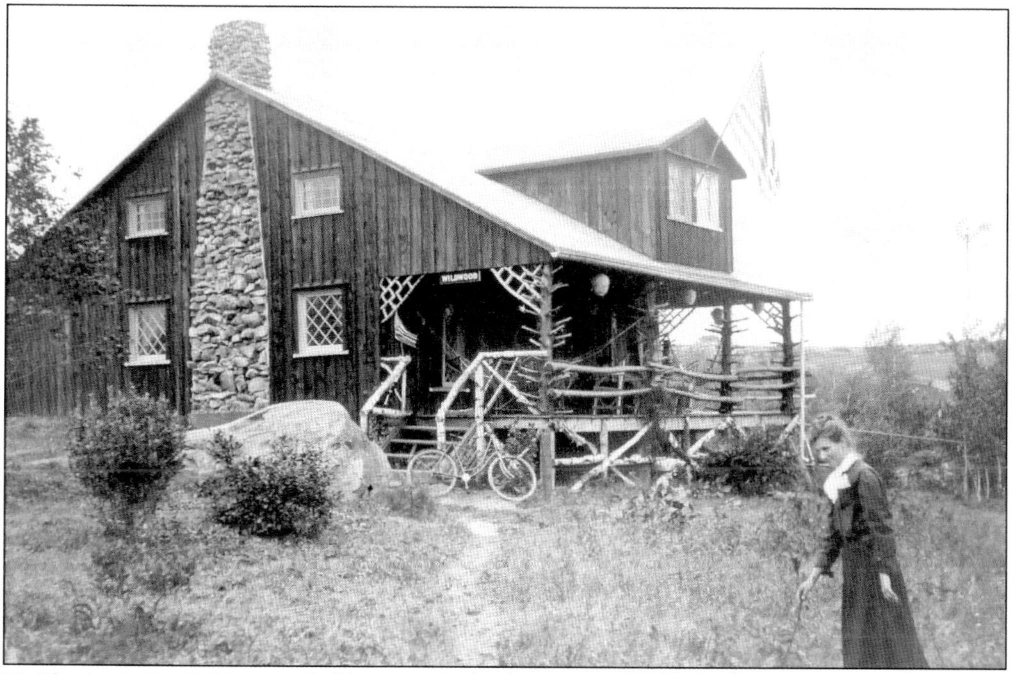

H. Elizabeth Burdick's remarkable rustic lodge known as "Wildwood," near Second Pond, was demolished when Grafton Lakes State Park was created in the late 1960s.

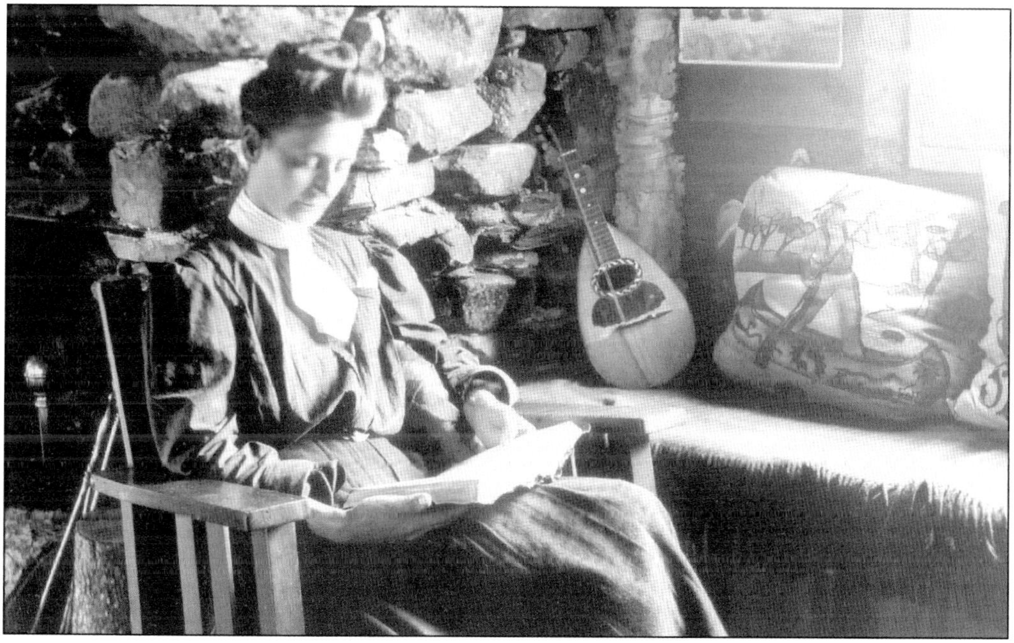

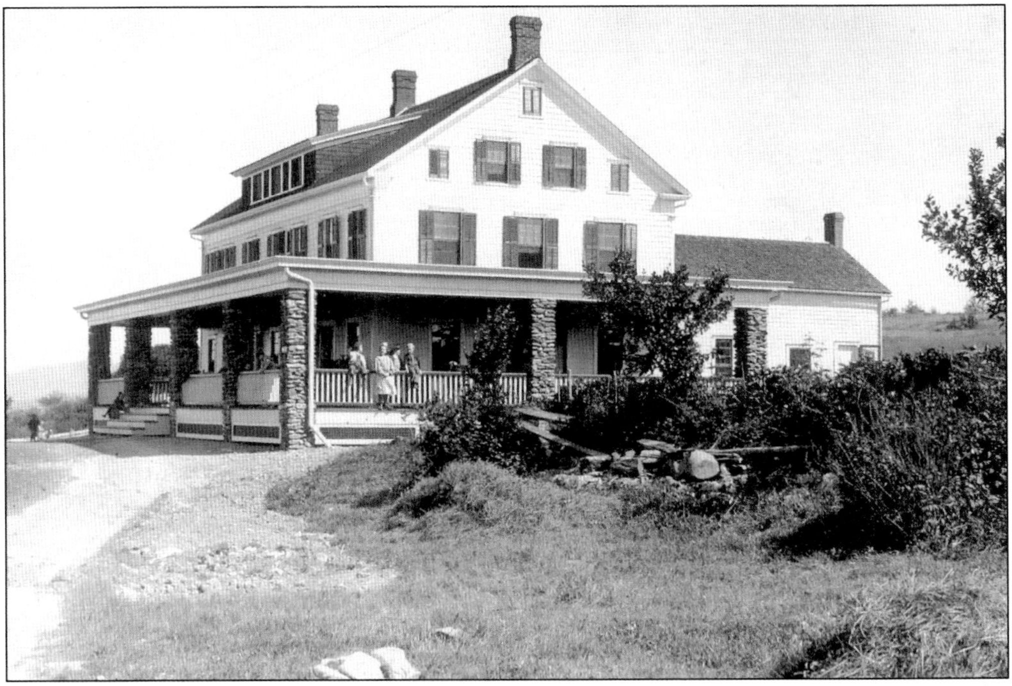

The Fresh Air Home in Grafton, still standing on State Route 2 a couple miles east of the town center, originally served as a residence and cooperage of the Tilley family. The *Troy Times* newspaper converted the building into a summer day camp for use by needy city children.

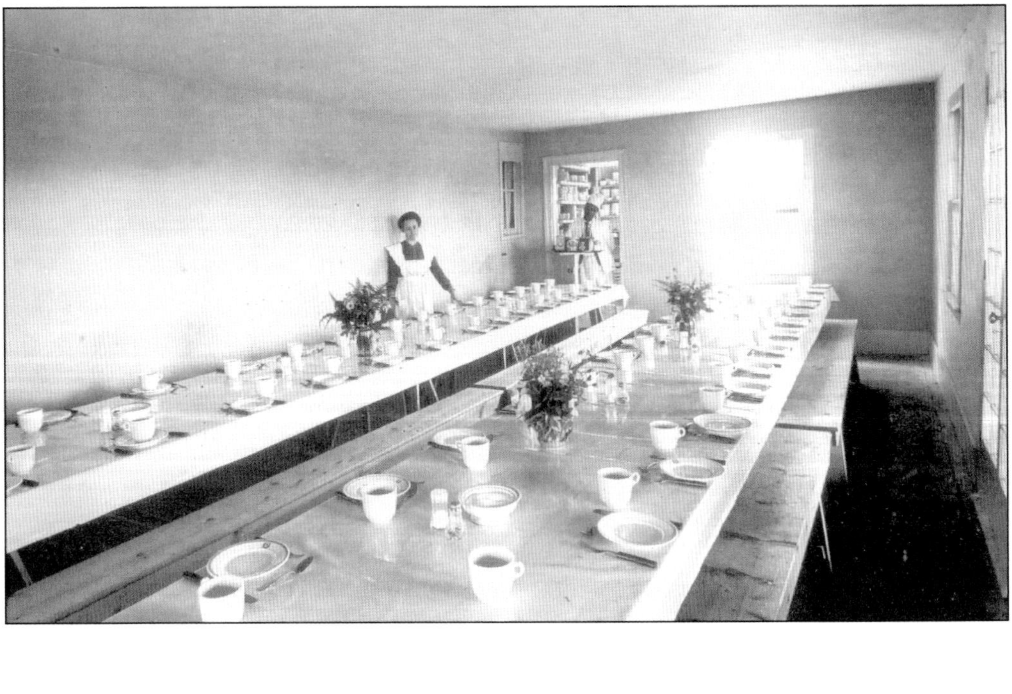

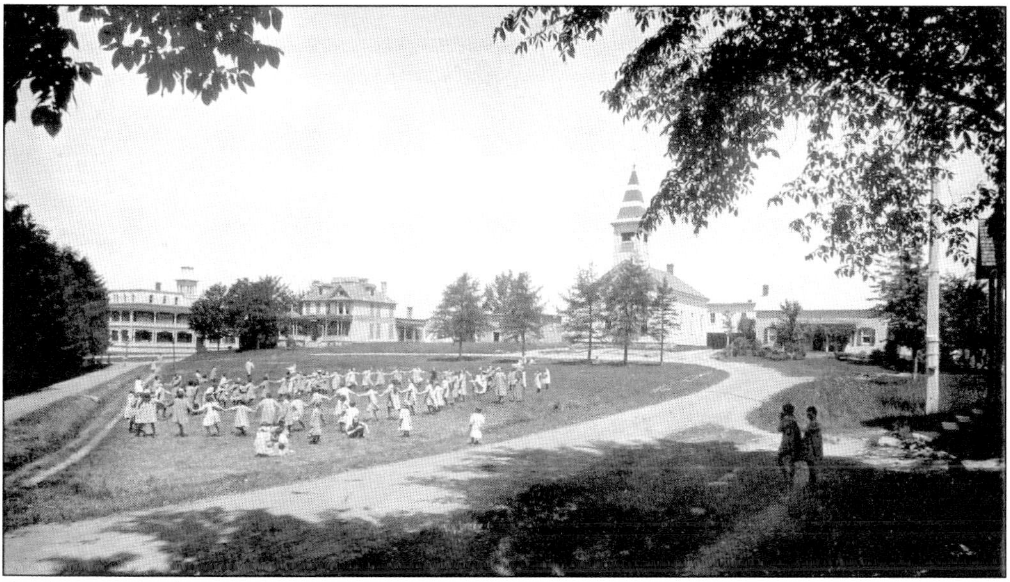

Orphans and other needy city children enjoyed relaxing summer days spent in Grafton, on the village green (above) and at the Fresh Air Home (below).

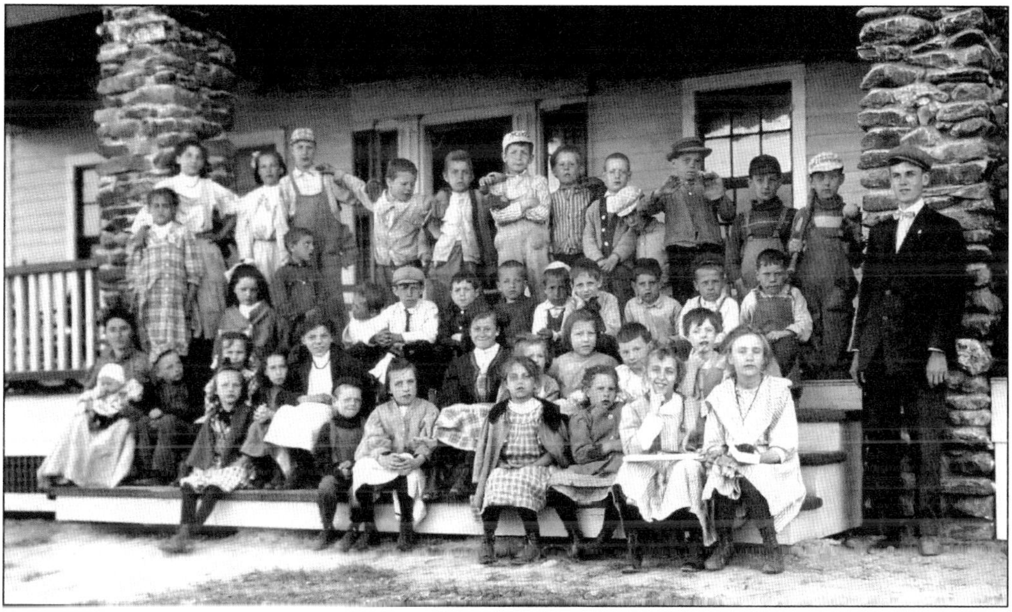

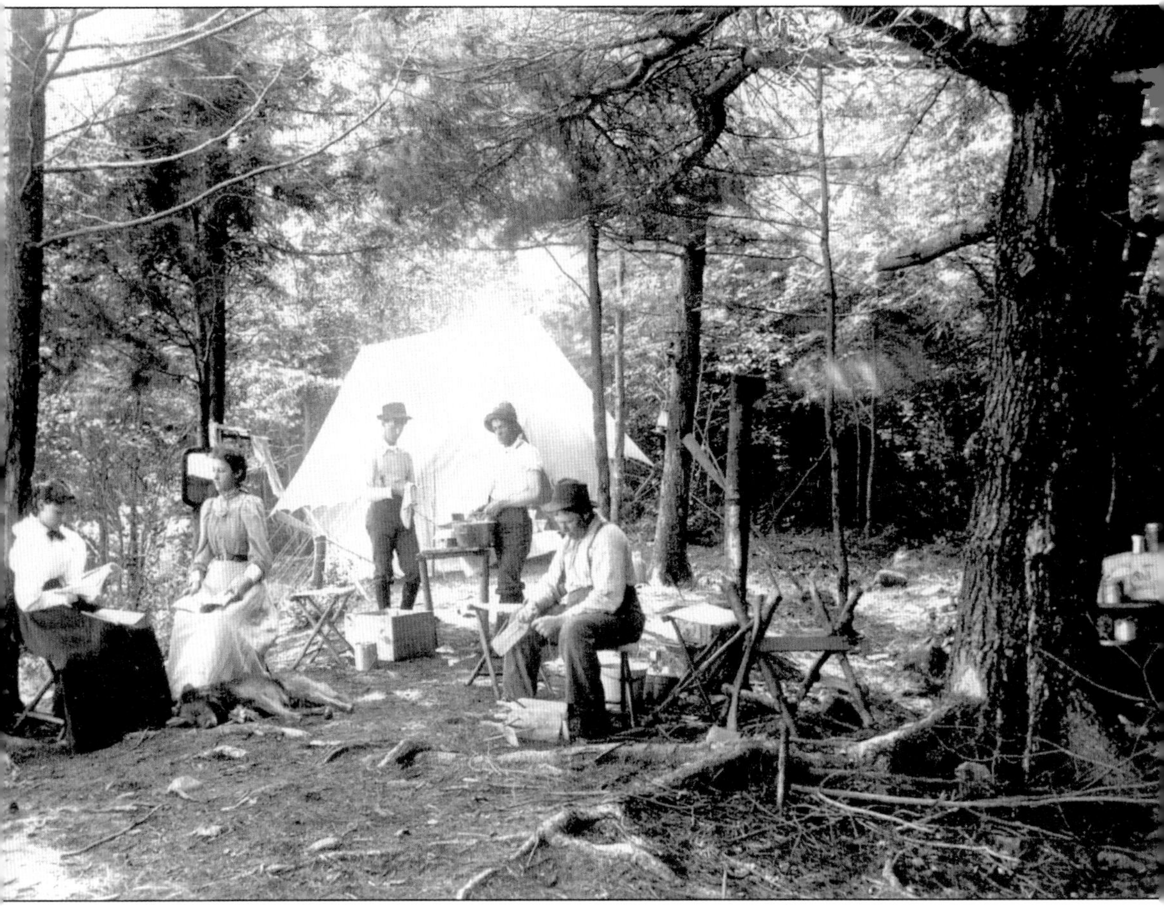

Campers enjoy a day in the woods near Shaver Pond in Grafton.

Six

THE GREAT FLOOD OF 1891

During the latter part of August 1891, the area had already been saturated by a week of heavy rain, when cloudbursts struck on the Rensselaer Plateau on the evening of Thursday the 27. The deluge continued into the night, with rain falling at the rate of two to three inches per hour. Small streams that feed the Little Hoosic River turned into raging torrents, severely damaging houses and farms along the way. Many roads and bridges in Berlin and Petersburgh were washed out along with long sections of the Lebanon Springs (later the Rutland) Railroad tracks when the Little Hoosic rose more than 20 feet above flood stage. There were three fatalities in Berlin, and damage in the area was estimated in the hundreds of thousands of dollars. Crops were ruined, and it would be months before the infrastructure would be completely restored.

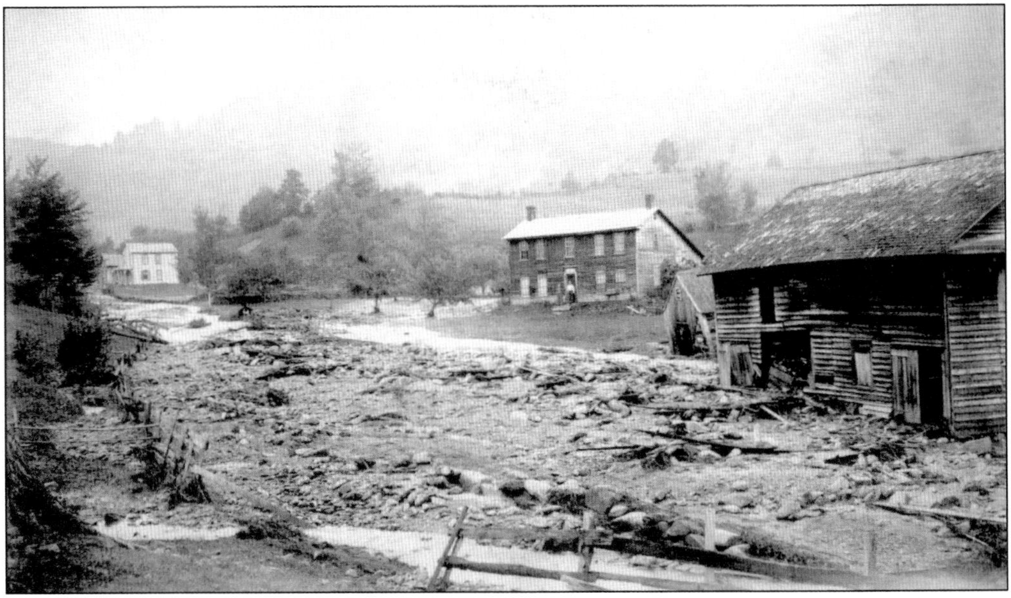

The small stream below Kendall Pond flowed in a torrent down the mountain toward Berlin. (Courtesy of the Berlin Town Historian.)

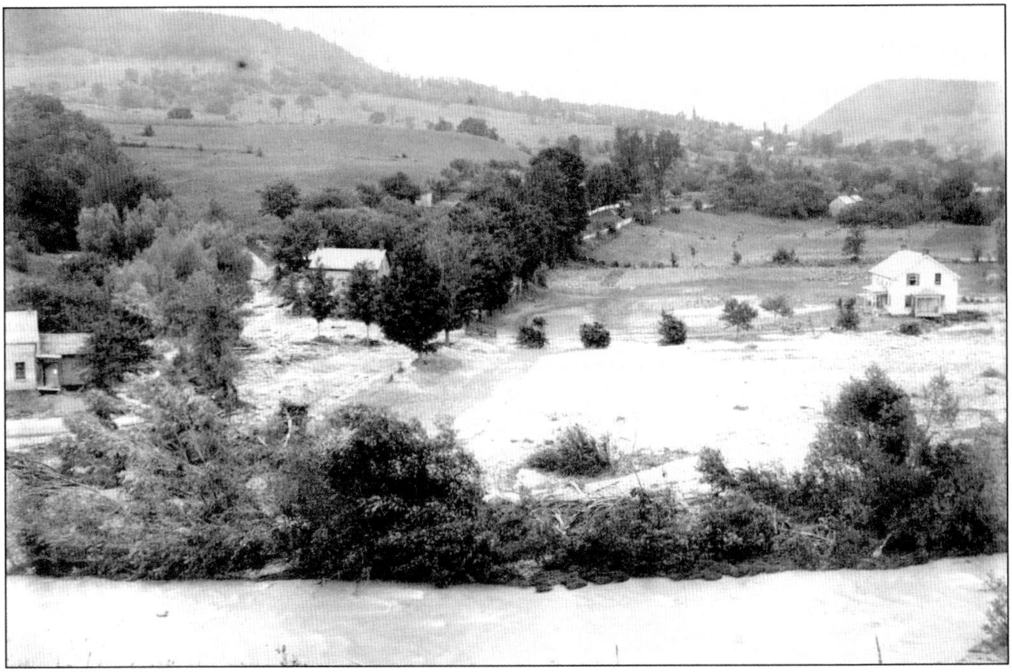

This view looking east into Jones Hollow in Petersburgh gives an indication of how high the flood waters of the Little Hoosic River had risen.

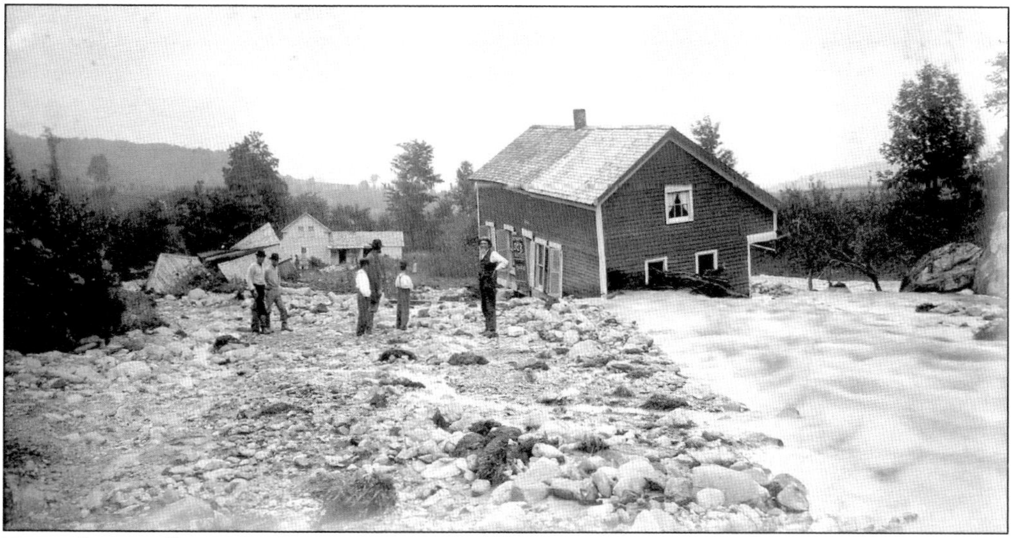

Normally a small stream, the Kendall Pond Brook caused major destruction at the intersection of Plank and Old Post Roads in Berlin. This is where John McGann was killed by the raging waters.

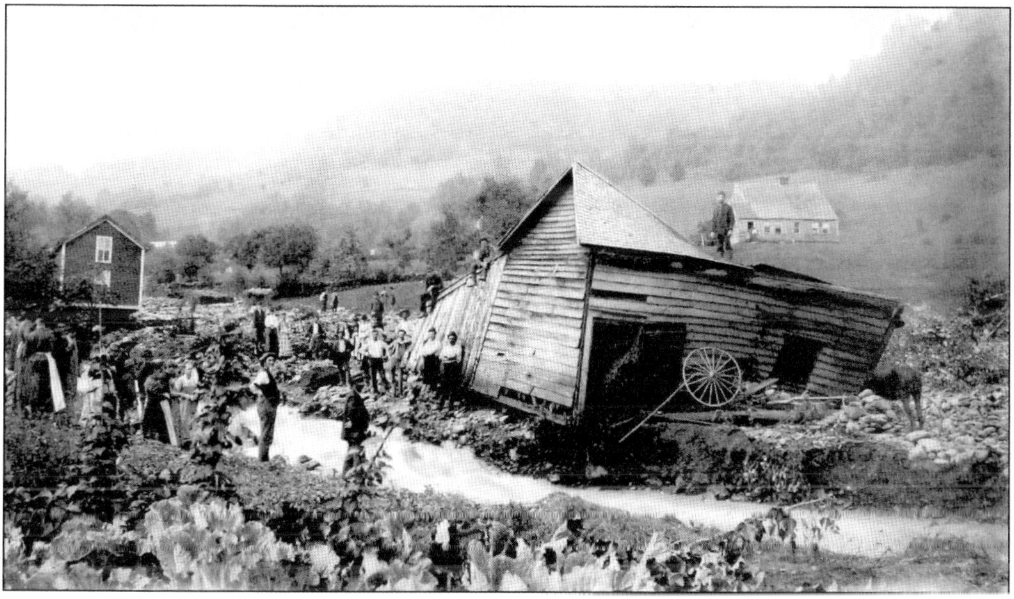

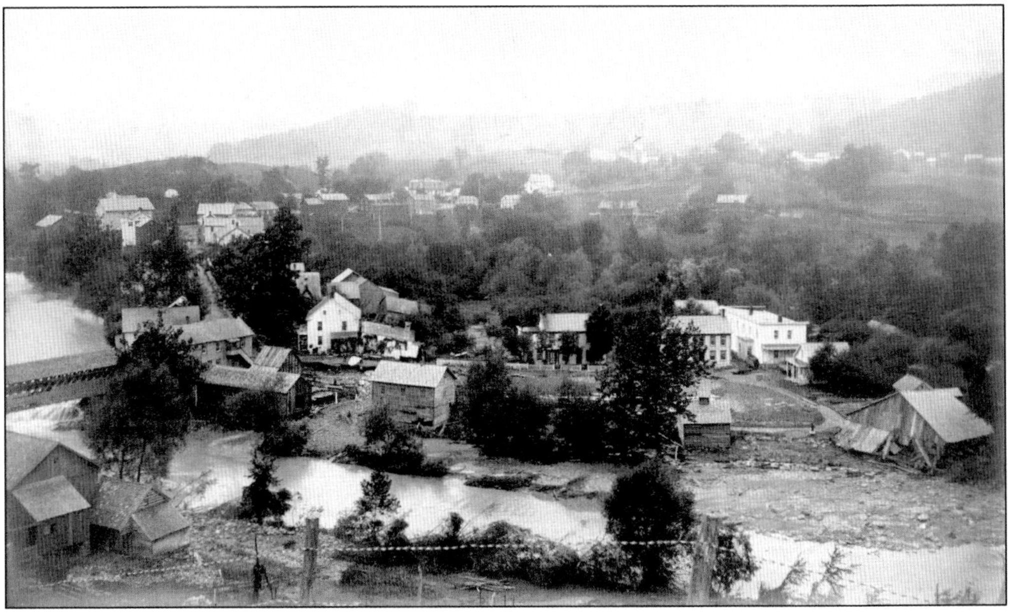

The rain-swollen Little Hoosic River (above) damaged a number of structures in downtown Petersburgh. Access to the lower covered bridge (below) was temporarily blocked, but the bridge was soon repaired.

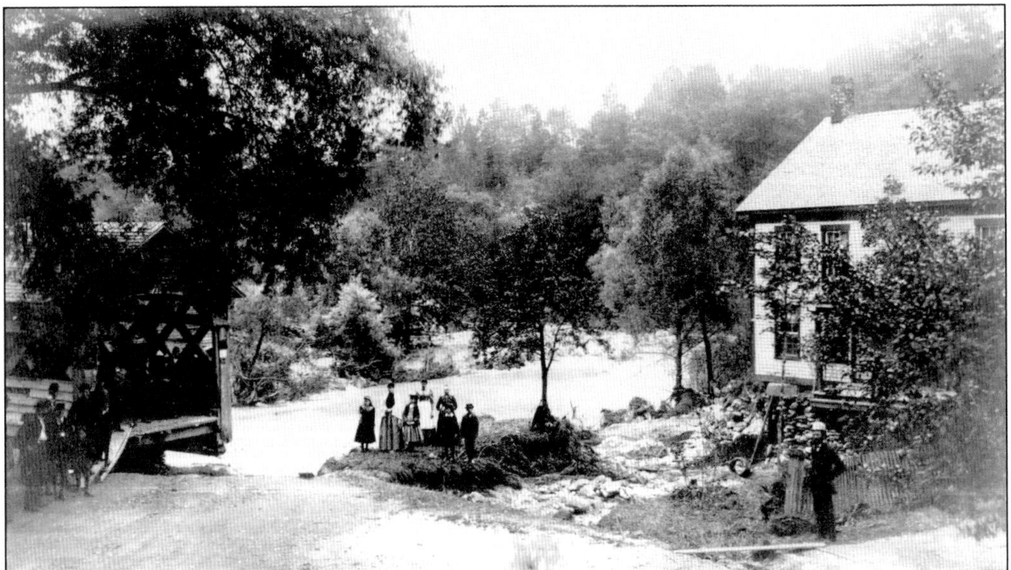

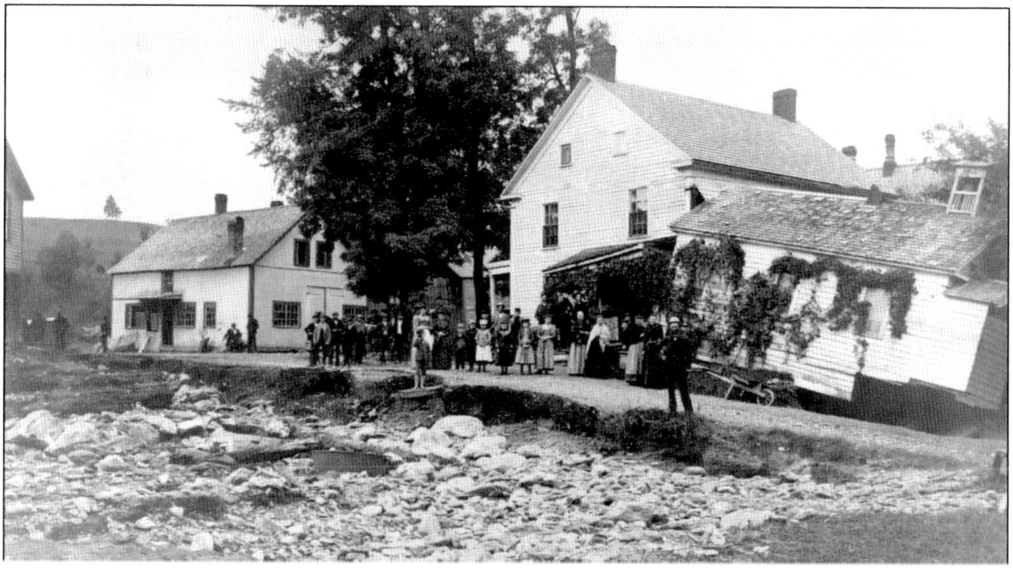

The Wells house in Mill Yard at Petersburgh (above) survived the flood and stands today. Young boys pose for the photographer (below) in a washout in front of the nearby Kellyer and Reynolds shirt factory.

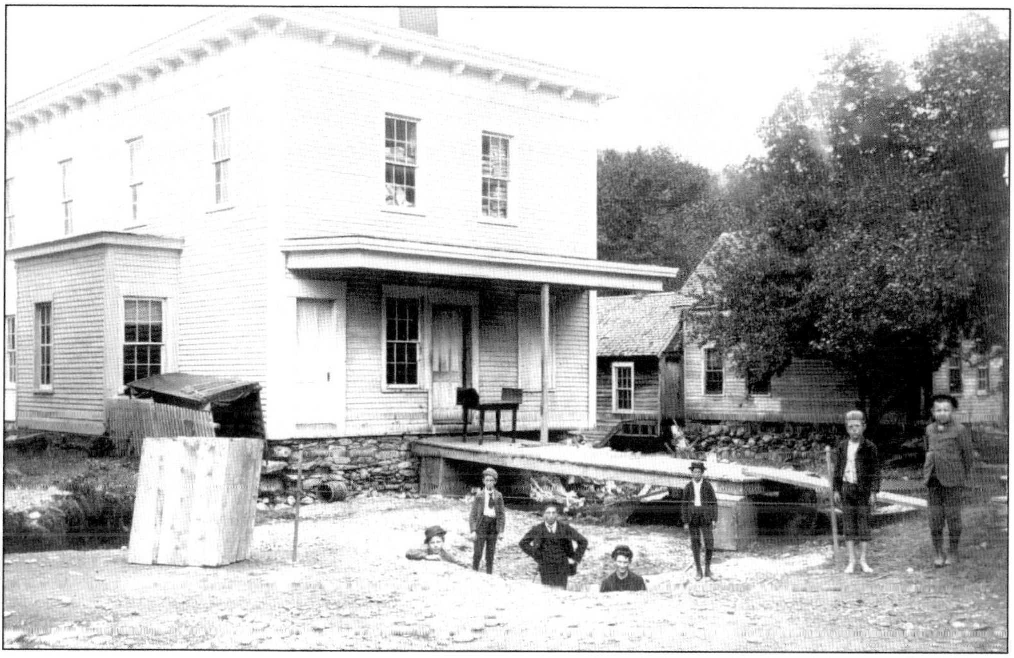

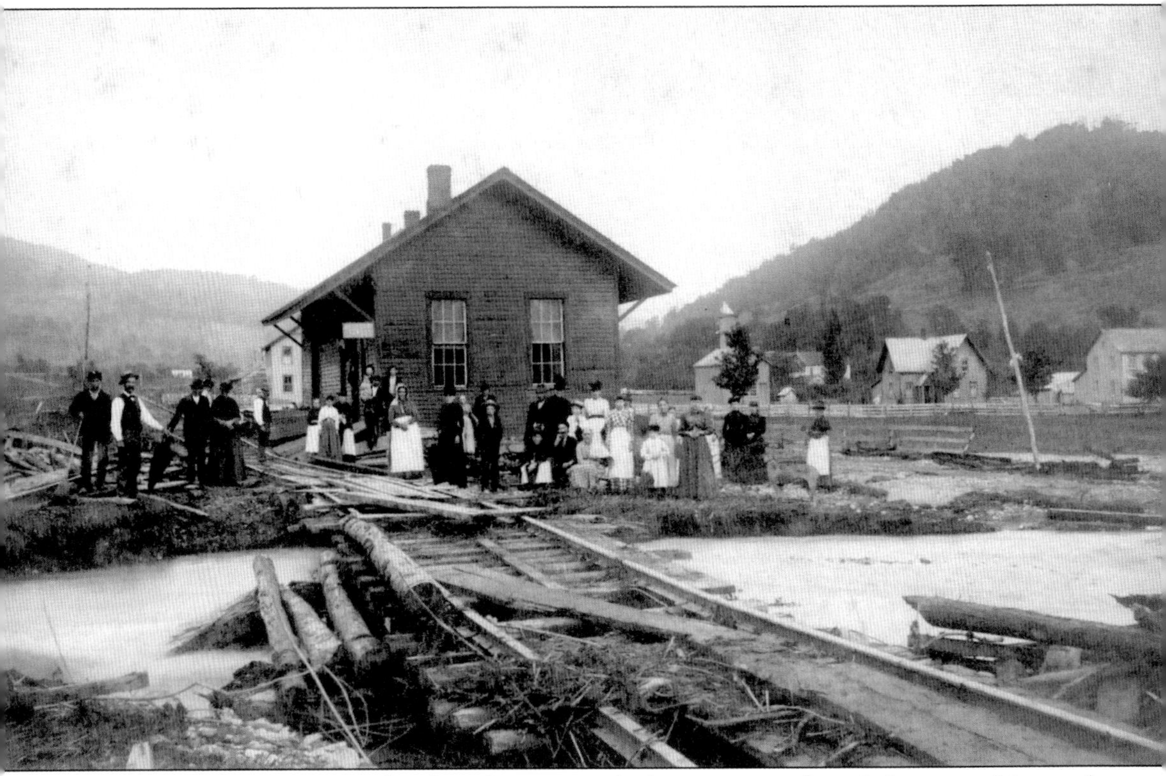

The Lebanon Springs Railroad tracks were washed out in a number of places, in this case by Greene Hollow Brook at the Berlin station. (Courtesy of the Berlin Free Town Library.)

Seven

Stereoscopic Views

Stereoscopic photography flourished between the 1850s and 1930s. Two nearly identical photographs were mounted on an oblong card and when viewed through a special hand-held viewer known as a stereoscope, recreated the illusion of depth by imitating binocular human vision. These views were immensely popular and published sets depicting world landmarks, famous personages, and major events comprised the majority of contemporary collections.

James E. West created stereoscopic views of various local scenes and marketed them to local collectors as well. The views of Berlin and Petersburgh reproduced on the following two pages are not duplicated by any surviving full-size photographs in this collection. By the early 20th century, stereographic views of local scenes became supplanted to great extent by "real photo" postcards, which West also produced and marketed.

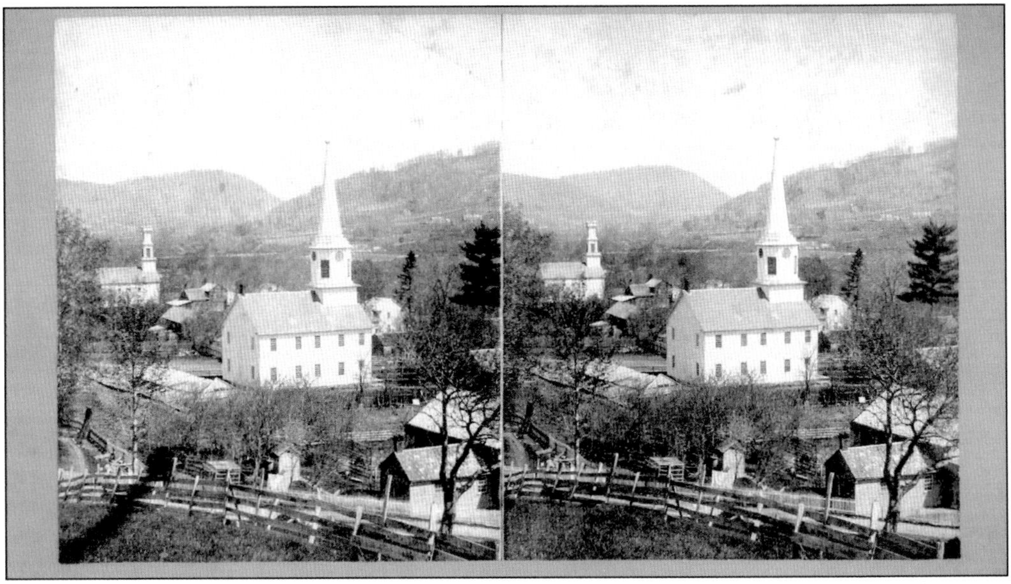

This view of Berlin showing the two Baptist church edifices (above) was taken from the west, a short distance up Plank Road. "Green Gables," an impressive Victorian home (below) that stands today on the east side of Main Street in Berlin, was constructed by Udolpho J. Nichols in 1869.

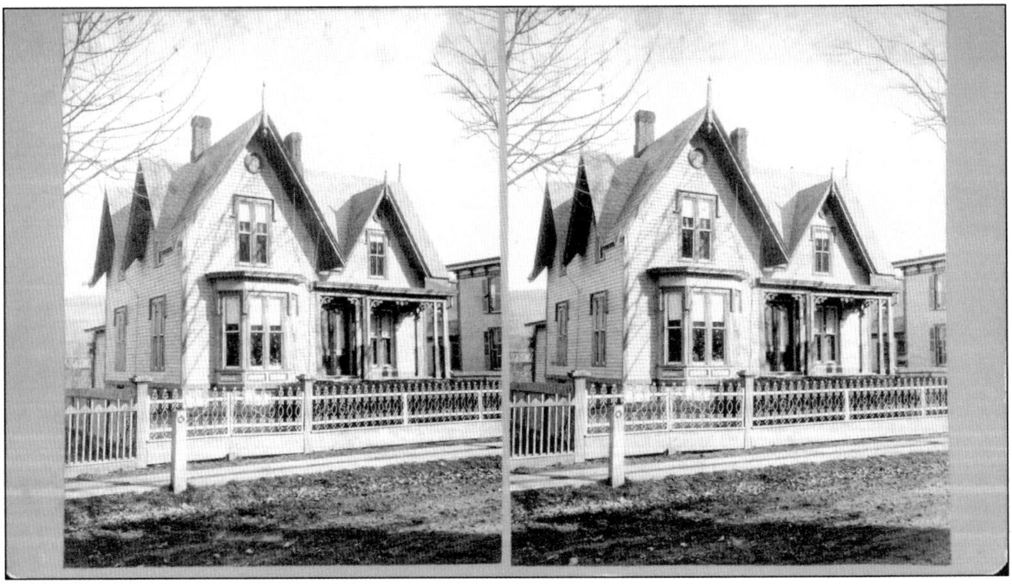

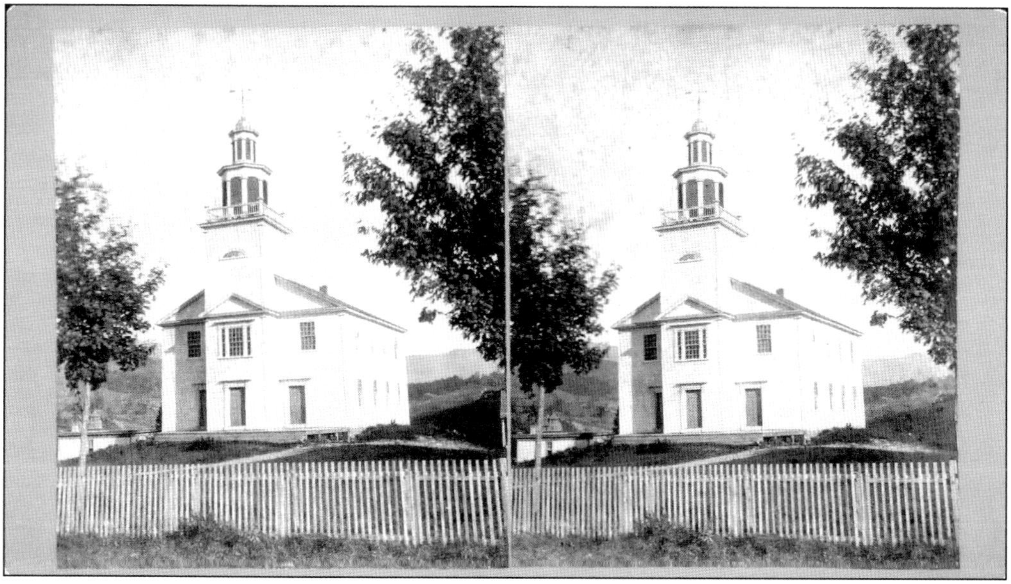

This stereoscopic view of the Petersburgh Baptist Church (above) was taken in the late 1880s, prior to some exterior renovations. This dam and waterfalls on the Little Hoosic River in Petersburgh (below) were located just south of the upper covered bridge; the dam no longer exists.

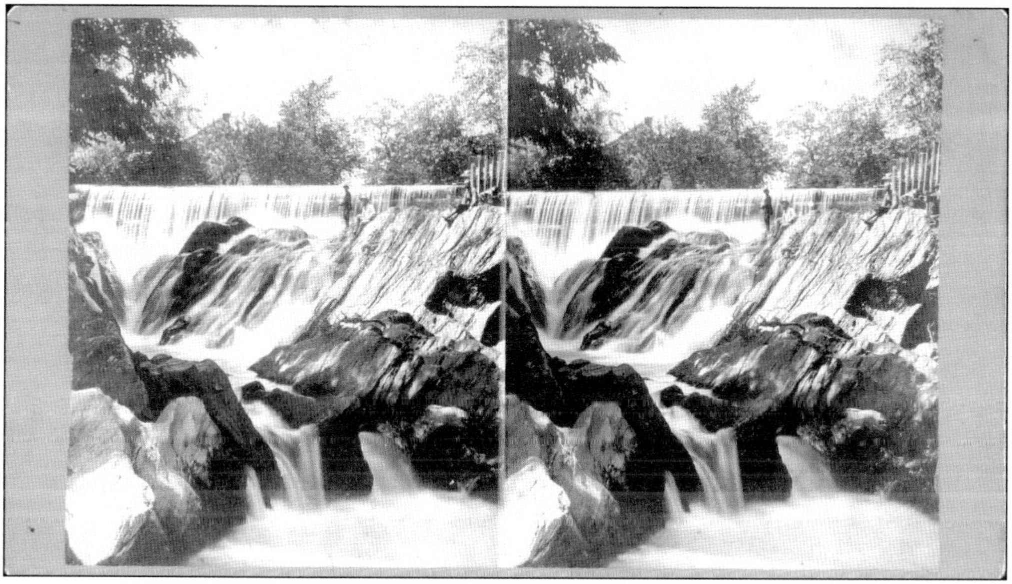